WHO ARE THEY REALLY?

New Approaches to Identifying

UFOs, Abductions, and Extraterrestrials

DANIEL HARRAN PhD

SCHIFFER
PUBLISHING

4880 Lower Valley Road • Atglen, PA 19310

Designed by Molly Shields
Cover design by Brenda McCallum
Type set in DINEngschrift/Cambria

ISBN: 978-0-7643-6190-6
Printed in the United States of America

Published by Schiffer Publishing, Ltd.
4880 Lower Valley Road
Atglen, PA 19310
Phone: (610) 593.1777; Fax: (610) 593.2002
E-mail: Info@schifferbooks.com
Web: www.schifferbooks.com

To my wife,
for her patience and support
throughout the writing of this book

to Ardy Sixkiller Clarke and
all of the Amerindians who shared
their personal accounts
of "close encounters of the third kind"

to Rudolf Steiner, founder
of Anthroposophy, and Selim Aïssel,
founder of Psycho-Anthropology,
for the precious knowledge contained
in their teachings

CONTENTS

9   **Author Note**

10   **Foreword by Sociologist Sylvie Joubert**

14   **Introduction**

14   Beings from Another World Are Knocking at Our Door

16   Two Different Sources of the UFO Phenomenon?

17   Abductions: The Most Disturbing Facet of the UFO Phenomenon

18   Vulnerable Human Beings: Victims of Abductions

19   Important Philosophical and Spiritual Implications

21   **Chapter 1: Abductions of Human Beings into UFOs**

21   Incredible Accounts

23   Case Studies of Abductions

23   The Abduction of Corporal Valdès (Chile, 1977)

26   The Abduction of Jeff (United States, circa 2000)

29   The Abduction of Antonio Villas-Boas (Brazil, 1957)

32   The Abduction of Ed (United States, Case Study by John Mack)

36   The Abduction of Jerry (United States, Case Study by John Mack)

41   The Abduction of Catherine (United States, Case Study by John Mack)

46   Description of a "Typical Abduction"

46   General Considerations

49   The Primary Characteristic of the Abduction Phenomenon

50   The Second Characteristic of the Abduction Phenomenon

52   Return to Normal Life

53   The Implant Issue

53   First Account

55   The Analyses of Dr. Roger Leir

59   Chapter 2: Preoccupation with the Future of the Earth: A Persistent, Common Denominator in UFO Phenomena

59   UFOs Preoccupied by Nuclear Power

59   Official Declassified Documents

60   Deactivated Nuclear Missiles

61   UFOs Intervene at Chernobyl

62   UFOs Concerned about Pollution

63   Another Form of Manifestation

64   An Urgency to Respect the Earth

64   A New Channel for Reaching Humankind

66   Chapter 3: Abductions and Mating: Ancient, Widespread Practices

66   Already in Antiquity

66   Incubi and Succubae of Medieval Times

67   Diverse Testimonies of High-Ranking Ecclesiastical Authorities

68   A Pope Expresses His Apprehension

69   Witch Hunt

70   Tangible Evidence

70   A Study of Incubi and Succubae

71   A Permanent Recurrence in Europe

72   An Incubus Infatuated with a Lady of the Renaissance

73   L. M. Sinistrari's Account

76   Remarkable Elements

77   Reflections of L. M. Sinistrari

78   Mysterious Abductions in Medieval Times

78   Mysterious Abductions in France in the Middle Ages

80   Mysterious Abductions in Celtic Countries

81   Other Accounts from Iceland and Scotland

82   Djinns in the Countries of Maghreb

83   The Work of Gordon Creighton

85   A Modern Account of a Mixed Marriage

88   A Modern Account of the Abduction of a Newborn

89   Abductions in the Amerindian Population

90   The Abductions of Tiffany

93   The Abduction of Russell

98   Jesse's Encounter

100 Abductions: A Modern Form of an Ancient Practice

103   Chapter 4: Two Different Sources of UFO Phenomena

103 The Characteristics of the Kidnappers

104 Several Cases of "Encounters with Star People"

105   Ross's Account

108   Chee's Account

110   Darren's Account

112   Brett's Account

114   Harrison's Account

118   Sam's Account

119 Other Cases of "Close Encounters with Avoidance"

120   The Famous Case of Valensole, France

122   The Case of Cussac, France

124   The Case of Trans-en-Provence, France

125   The Case of Socorro, New Mexico

127   Mysterious Disappearance of Apples

128   Mysterious Beings next to a Crop Circle

129 Two Different Origins of UFO Phenomena

130   Description of the Two Different Categories of UFO Occupants

134   Differences between the Two Categories of UFO Occupants

136   Chapter 5: What Can We Say about These Visitors?

136 What "Close Encounters with Avoidance" Teach Us

139 Where Science Stands Today

141 Discussion

141   Beings Who Are Truly Extraterrestrial

142 Neither Mask nor Spacesuit

143 A "Subtle Physical" Body and a "Dense Material" Body

146 Subtle Physical Body and Interstellar Travel

148 Telepathy

148 Immense Philosophical and Spiritual Implications

149 Extraterrestrials in Our Midst?

155 Conclusion

155 Extraordinary Discoveries

156 The Limits of Modern Science

157 Models of More-Advanced Human Beings

159 Chapter 6: Who Are the Abductors?

159 Flaws in the Extraterrestrial Hypothesis

163 The Hypothesis of Fairies in Celtic Countries of Yesteryear

166 The Hypothesis of Djinns in the Countries of Maghreb

169 Elementals: Forgotten Supernatural Creatures

170 Urgent Ecological Concerns

171 An Ancient Sexual Plan

171 Elementals: Present Everywhere and throughout Time

172 The Elementals' Trademark: Based on Spiritual Knowledge

173 Knowledge from African Traditions

174 Beings from Another World

175 A Powerful Personal Story

176 Excerpts from *The Healing Wisdom of Africa*

178 Highlights from *Encounters with Beings from Another World*

179 The Twelve Reasons We Can Say Elementals Exist

184 A Psychic's Account

186 Two Responses from Spiritual Science

187 The Four Components of a Human Being

188 A General Principle

188 First Response: Wandering Human Souls

189 Basic Notions of Cosmogony

194   Second Response: Elementals

198 Conclusion

198   The Abductors Are Elementals

199   Elementals Are Master Illusionists

201 Conclusions

201 UFOs and Abductions

202 Two Different Sources of UFO Phenomena

204 A Series of Revelations

207 The True Identity of the Kidnappers

210   The Meaning and Final Aim of the Abductions of Human Beings

210 Paradigm Shifts

212 Appendix

212 The Abduction of Barney and Betty Hill (United States, 1961)

216 The Abduction of Travis Walton (near Snowflake, Arizona, 1975)

220 Endnotes

AUTHOR NOTE

The readers of this book, who will be discovering the phenomenon of abductions of human beings into UFOs, are encouraged not to let themselves be put off by the implausibility of the numerous events related here in the testimonies and descriptions of this phenomenon. These accounts are indeed unbelievable from a scientific perspective and may seem more like far-out stories, but they are for real.

The characteristics of these abductions so defy our view of the world that, at first glance, it is very difficult for us to consider them as really taking place. This means that the study of this phenomenon invites us to question the validity of what we currently know and understand to be true, and to come to realize that our current knowledge is largely supported by unconscious belief systems and conditioning. We must reevaluate our vision of the world. It is for this reason that both the phenomenon of abductions into UFOs and the phenomenon of UFOs in general are still mysteries for us today.

This book aims to shed light on these phenomena in a rational way while at the same time trying not to succumb to the influence of the unconscious, limiting belief systems and erroneous patterns of thinking that our so-called modern era has imposed upon us. This means that the analyses and conclusions made in this book can be alarming for those readers who are not ready to reconsider their current worldviews. The reader is therefore encouraged to have an open mind, be well grounded in logical reasoning, and be devoid of preconceived ideas before examining the coherence of all of the reports and conclusions presented herein.

FOREWORD

by Sociologist Sylvie Joubert

If we needed additional proof of the paradigm shift at work in our postmodern era, this book gives it to us. No one can escape the fact that our perception of what is real is undergoing a powerful upheaval, which is both disconcerting and constructive. The laws of physics and causality are no longer enough to explain the functioning of our world, because yesterday's questions are not those of today. It is fruitless to deny or grumble about this new direction that human understanding and awareness is taking, for another adventure is awaiting our collective consciousness, and it has already begun. A highly complex era is knocking on the door of our civilization. It is demanding that our generations consider as priority the relationship between the whole and its parts and recognize the encounters that our human species is making with other dimensions and other space-times.

We can objectively say that the questions we are asking today address this complexity, and that all disciplines are asking them. But the questions of today require novel answers needing venturesome research that deviates from the path taken by the classical sciences, especially when the questions concern the presence of unidentified flying objects in our skies or contact with nonhuman intelligences.

Motivated by convenience and a desire to preserve their supremacy, the exact, classical, and human sciences have placed most UFO phenomena in a compartment labeled as "supernatural" or "paranormal," taking great care to keep the lid firmly on it in order to devote their time to other subjects that they can control and maintain intellectual mastery over. It is thus that entire blocks of information about "strange" manifestations are retained in a sort of underground knowledge vault, not because they are considered as invalid, but because they upset the principles of reality stemming from an academic way of thinking with its established modes of validation, anchored in its certainty and resistant to any epistemic change. At the very most, we can accept that with the help of sophisticated technology, we can search for nonhuman intelligences far, far away in the Universe, and we can fathom that other intelligent life, if it does exist, is hundreds, thousands, millions, and even billions of light-years from us. But is this the case? Daniel Harran's response is an unequivocal no.

To understand the originality of Dr. Harran's working hypothesis, one must look at nature in a new, more subtle way, extending all the way to its nonvisible dimensions. What does this mean exactly? It is a given that nature on Earth is an ecosystem: an ecological unity made up of the environment and the organisms living within it. This definition of ecology is pretty much understood by all and is considered as ordinary; today no one really denies its importance. The question now is to know whether or not this approach to understanding the earth and nature is enough to describe our planetary environment. For Dr. Harran and for all those who, like him, think that reality is more complex than what our senses can perceive, it is not enough. No, the earth cannot simplistically be reduced to this ecological dimension, because it is also a permanent home to nonhuman entities, which Daniel Harran calls "Interdimensional Manifestations" or IDIMs.

Who are these entities? They are those mentioned by ancient religious and spiritual knowledge and referred to in numerous tales and legends throughout history. They appear in stories in the form of supernatural entities who, although diverse, all spring from a common dimension. In our day, we more readily refer to them as elementals or nature spirits. Tradition frequently describes these entities as facetious—somewhat like magicians—who like to occasionally toy with human beings. Is it possible then that these elementals use our obsession with the extraterrestrial to dupe us into thinking that they are responsible for a large part of the experiences that ufologists call "close encounters of the third kind," particularly those that involve abductions? Dr. Harran, in a pleasant manner, responds affirmatively to this question throughout his book. He supports his scholarly analysis with multiple testimonies, either well known or unfamiliar. If his hypothesis is daring, it is also interesting and well defended.

Dr. Harran does not claim that all the reported experiences are interactions with nonhuman, intelligent elementals, but he puts forth the possibility that there are two different sources of UFO phenomena: one that is earthbound and interdimensional, embodied by nature beings with surprising abilities, and the other that is extraterrestrial.

This book distances itself from technical and material analyses of the UFO phenomenon. Since humans are not the only intelligent beings on Earth, and science has proven itself unable to enlighten us about the origins of these phenomena that are beyond our comprehension, it is possible then that the questions that have been asked up to this point have been the wrong ones. Daniel Harran invites us to start asking the right questions.

Examining UFO phenomena from the angle of nonhuman elementals coming into our human plane from a parallel one is thus an additional thesis made available to ufologists and the general public alike. Dr. Harran takes us into this hybrid adventure, which is at the same time rational and magical, intellectual and intuitive. He shows us why it is possible to find an earthly explanation for some of the accounts reported by abduction victims. Yet, he puts limits on his hypothesis, affirming that some close encounters of the third kind do come from visitors outside Earth. The earthly and extraterrestrial hypotheses are therefore not mutually exclusive and can be seen as complementing one another.

This dual path of reflection aimed at all those who are curious about UFOs and extraterrestrials, and for parascientists, will no doubt have its believers and nonbelievers. There is nothing unusual in this, since the role of ideas is either to please or displease, to attract or put off. From my standpoint, juxtaposing "supernatural" and "extraterrestrial" is not at all foreign to the work I am doing concerning those I refer to as "the Others" (intraextraterrestrials, spirit guides, angels, nature spirits, celestial veterinarians or doctors, ghosts, et al.).

I adhere to the idea that strange, nonhuman presences intersect with our plane of existence, and furthermore it has been shown that they can leave behind diverse material evidence (e.g., visual, auditory, tangible). I can only be delighted then at the hypotheses formulated by Dr. Harran, because it is with such perfectly defended initiatives that we can enrich and develop knowledge in general, and ufology in particular.

No one can deny that the field of unidentified flying objects has become extraordinarily prolific in its propositions and perspectives. The mind of the ufologist not only works within the laws of physics but also focuses its intelligence and intuition beyond. This is precisely what is lacking in our academic research, which remains prisoner to its perpetual cycle of mental schemas and refuses to break out of its conventional, convenient epistemology.

But ufology's productivity is also due to the diversity of its active members—researchers and autodidacts—coming from all disciplinary horizons to seek an explanation for these objects seen in the sky and for accounts given by abduction victims. Yes, the field of ufology dares to think outside the box, it dares to envision what classical—and hesitant—science leaves behind, and, above all, it dares to consider itself as a discipline that has no one to answer to but itself and an ever-developing world.

Ufology is no longer hesitant to educate us about its findings, since the vectors of interdimensionality and spirituality allow us now to explain some of the phenomena within its scope of study without having to reject the rigor of the scientific method. Furthermore, the field of ufology understands that the "supernatural" and the "real" are not separate categories. There is therefore nothing illegitimate in using parallel worlds to explain some of the extraordinary occurrences that are either seen, heard, touched, or felt. Finally—and this is a major aspect of the work of Dr. Harran—the strange, extraordinary phenomena witnessed by perplexed humans remind us that the meaning is already within us and around us in the interactions we have here below with nonhuman terrestrial species—who are as omnipresent as they are invisible. In a myriad of ways, these experiences resonate in our collective memory.

Expressed another way, interspecies and interdimensional connections begin here in our planetary environment. We therefore must get used to the idea of the plurality of the earth in its dimensions and its inhabitants, with all the consequences that this can have for our lives, our observations, and our behaviors. We also must grasp that these same connections extend well beyond our earth within the infinite cosmos, through the concrete or telepathic encounters that sometimes occur with those whom humankind considers as aliens, extraterrestrials, et al. It is our obligation to think of these connections holistically, all the while distinguishing between them. The reader will see that Dr. Harran accomplishes this perfectly.

All these connections between species, either overt or subtle, human or nonhuman, earthly or interdimensional, form a loop of information and interdependence at the heart of an enlarged, extended environment, going way beyond the idea we have of our earthly, natural ecological system. We consequently enter into what I termed several years ago as a "meta-ecology," which holds that merely studying physical milieus where living beings live no longer suffices, because now we must understand that the environment that is already home to mineral, vegetal, and animal life is equally a shared space with presumably nonvisible and conscious life forms. We must therefore add another layer to our notion of ecology. If we are living in a situation of compresence in a multidimensional environment, it is not surprising that encounters occasionally occur: encounters that are incomprehensible at first glance.

This meta-ecology is a fundamental building block of reason and rationality and most likely provides the fertile cognitive ground for our civilization yet to come. Nothing there is natural or supernatural, normal or paranormal, because everything that a human being can experience is normal. There are simply things that we understand already and things that we will understand later on, with or without our intellect—which is just a tool of our mind—and never our mind per se. For now, our priority resides in making sure that our theories, methods, postulates, hypotheses, and research can englobe and serve this complex body of knowledge while trying to make it all coherent for us.

Humankind is heading toward an eminently complex thinking, made up of an entanglement of different forms of life and dimensions—and without any exaggeration, the study of UFO phenomena is pushing it in this direction. By shaking up our certainties, these strange phenomena make us creative and imaginative, and conscious that the world in which we live is infinitely more complex than what we had thought.

Daniel Harran is among those authors who does not shy away from plunging into this imbroglio of logics. This professor and doctor of physics, educated in the principles of materiality and reality, is not afraid to say that we are an intricate part of a more subtle physics not subjected to the laws of matter, which says that it is possible to have encounters between intelligences. In this universe of coexistence, both materialization and dematerialization become things we can envision, things that are practically banal, whether we are referring to "elementals" or "extraterrestrial visitors." Each has, however, a different agenda, says Dr. Harran.

By introducing the notions of a "subtle, physical" body and levels of "etheric density" that are not dependent on material laws, Daniel Harran invites all of his readers to join him in the construction of a new science: a spiritual science not validated by the science of today. But, one may ask, "Does he really need the endorsement of modern science?"

INTRODUCTION

Beings from Another World Are Knocking at Our Door

The UFO (unidentified flying object) phenomenon is one of the most mysterious phenomena that humanity is confronted with today, even if it is not accorded the importance in society that it deserves. In no country is it officially taken seriously, and it suffers from a marked concealment of information on the part of political authorities, so much so that a large part of the population is not even convinced of its reality. Yet, all the studies conducted over the past decades have demonstrated that unknown forms of intelligence—which cannot be human—are manifesting themselves through these flying objects with a remarkable insistence.

These past years in France, a number of high-ranking military officials who are responsible for the security of their country have publicly divulged their reports of repeated, affirmed nonhuman presences, clearly showing the extent of their preoccupation with this matter—and this in spite of the silence of public authorities. The COMETA report, published in 1999,[1] was destined to raise awareness among not only political authorities, but the public as well. In Canada, it was the former defense minister Paul Hellyer who took it upon himself to disclose information on the subject of UFOs. In the United States, two large press conferences were held in Washington, DC, before a large number of journalists, with officers who provided their personal eyewitness accounts of UFOs. The first took place in 2001 on the initiative of Steven M. Greer, and the second occurred in 2010, thanks to the tenacity of Robert Hastings.[2] But all these efforts did not succeed in making any changes to the status quo.

One of the reasons is that the UFO phenomenon is characterized by a large number of contradictions that leave all researchers perplexed. These paradoxes are, first of all, linked to its very nature:

These objects can often be captured by photography, all the while being invisible to the naked eye.

In other cases they can be seen directly and can disappear just as quickly, only to sometimes reappear in another place altogether.

They can change form or dimension (or both) as if under the influence of a magic wand.

They manifest themselves sometimes under a material aspect—as solid objects—and yet their behavior defies the laws of physics.

The consequence of all this is that science finds itself ill equipped to study this subject, and researchers are disarmed: so much so that the question is not even explored as to whether UFOs are physical or merely figments of the imagination of eyewitnesses whose brains may have been under some unknown influence.

The resulting situation can itself seem completely paradoxical,

- even though all researchers acknowledge that nonhuman intelligences are behind UFOs and that they are apparently seeking to get our attention and inviting us to communicate with them,
- and even though we consider ourselves to be intelligent and therefore capable of responding to this invitation in spite of its extraordinary nature.

It is as if our society would rather put its head in the sand to avoid seeing this reality, as if we were afraid to enter into contact with other forms of intelligence.

Indeed, public authorities never speak of this phenomenon, and no public research organization shows any interest in it. It is as if our entire society would rather block it all out— implying that we are not ready to deal with the shock to our current beliefs that the consequences of this acknowledgment could have. Yes, it is natural to imagine that through these relatively harmless manifestations that are UFOs, intelligences that exist outside humanity as we know it are intending to intervene in the affairs of humankind.

This denial of reality endorsed by public authorities appears completely outlandish to all those who, either from their own personal observations of UFOs or from other evidence of their existence that they have found in numerous published testimonies, are convinced of the necessity and the urgency to recognize this reality and bid welcome to this other world that is knocking at our door.

For those who have really understood deep down that this door is, in spite of it all, ready to open—and it is the intention of this work to open it even a bit more—we are living in an era that is as exalting as that of the great maritime expeditions of the fifteenth century. During that time, the accepted model of the world was completely turned upside down for Europeans, thanks to the exploits of Christopher Columbus, Vasco de Gama, Magellan . . . and others. Although, before that time, the only known territory was limited to Europe for those living in the West, their vision was enlarged thanks to the discoveries of other continents, and from then on they could see themselves as inhabitants of a "Planet Earth." By the same token, thanks to the understanding of phenomena such as UFOs, which is advancing slowly, humankind is led to a larger vision of the world in which it lives. We will see in this work that we humans are invited to turn our gaze in two different directions. Not only are we asked to open our minds to other worlds similar to the earth *within the Universe*, but at the same time we are asked to open our minds to the existence of other, parallel worlds *right here on Earth.*

Two Different Sources of the UFO Phenomenon?

Another possible cause of the blockage of research in the field of UFOs is the fact that this phenomenon could be coming from two distinctly different sources. This would partly explain its multiple, different facets that are perplexing to researchers. For a very long time, the extraterrestrial hypothesis was put forth as an acknowledgment of these mysterious phenomena manifesting themselves on Earth, which clearly were caused by nonhuman intelligences. This interpretation seems perfectly logical and rational, and it has become all the more popular since it is the only hypothesis considered as being compatible with current scientific knowledge. Indeed, it is recognized by practically all UFO enthusiasts as well as the majority of researchers. We can even consider that today, this extraterrestrial hypothesis has entered into the collective unconscious of humanity—or at least those who are interested in the UFO phenomenon— no longer as just a hypothesis, but as the only valid explanation.

But for the past few years, a number of researchers have shown that this hypothesis is not compatible with several characteristics of the UFO phenomenon. It is worth noting that a large number of documents and ancient drawings did reveal that this phenomenon has existed on Earth for at least several thousand years. Furthermore, the number of reported authentic UFO sightings (excluding errors in observations and optical illusions) is now up in the millions. These two characteristics—and there are others—are not compatible with the idea that all UFO sightings should be attributed to beings from civilizations outside Earth, who are supposedly more evolved than we are, and who, for some reason or another, are visiting us in these flying vessels known as UFOs.

Also, research took another direction as early as 1969, thanks to Jacques Vallée's book *Passport to Magonia*,[3] which has been revisited by several authors,[4] and in which the UFO phenomenon is considered as having an earthly origin. This interpretation is based on the fact that our ancestors formulated descriptions of the UFO phenomenon that are similar to ours, but they attributed the occurrences to fairies or demons— beings whom the large majority of people of our day consider as mythical and not real. But are they really imaginary or are they real? The problem is that they are invisible to ordinary humans because they exist in an etheric plane—a parallel world—which does not easily let us confirm their existence. This is why this interpretation is not shared by the research community as a whole. Yet, more and more individuals who are gifted with sensitive perceptual capacities do recognize the existence of these supernatural beings. Later on, we will read the highly enlightening testimony of one of these people.

It will be shown in this book that this second earthly hypothesis can be validated by several authentic sources of knowledge left behind by science, and consequently unknown to most. Furthermore, we will see that these two hypotheses, linked to two different causes of UFO phenomena—one earthly and multidimensional, and the other extraterrestrial—seem to exist together, and we will also see how we can distinguish between these two sources in the accounts of sightings. This understanding that there are two sources of UFO phenomena will no doubt enable us to make great strides in the study of this phenomenon.

Abductions:
The Most Disturbing Facet
of the UFO Phenomenon

Of the many mysterious phenomena linked to UFO sightings, the phenomenon of human beings abducted into UFOs is no doubt the most perplexing and troubling one and also the most difficult to address due to its completely irrational appearance. This phenomenon cannot be explained using the knowledge base of current science. Let us first of all clarify that the term "abduction" refers to a disappearance that is limited in time; that is, an individual is taken from their environment and transported by a UFO into another world for a length of time ranging, in general, from fifteen minutes to several days.

We can obtain only very little information about abductions of human beings when the victims are transported into another world and have no memory of what they went through. Only some details have been provided by the rare eyewitnesses present when the abductions occurred. After returning to their normal life, some of these victims either did remember or were able to retrieve the memories of what they had experienced, and their memories could be completed sometimes by testimonies of others who were present. But these memories are always incomprehensible through the lens of current science, and it is what makes these phenomena still very mysterious.

What characterizes these abductions above all is that the victims are, according to their accounts, confronted with nonhuman, living beings of humanoid appearance who intrude upon their private lives. They take them against their will into a flying vessel (UFO) and make them undergo a "protocol," which appears completely outlandish and is nearly always experienced as something very painful. The victims are thus treated as living things, without having the strength or the means to resist. It is this aspect that renders this phenomenon so harrowing for each of the victims and very disconcerting for the rest of us. Here we are not referring to simple UFO sightings in the sky; those who are abducted are literally wrenched from their environment and find themselves face to face with their captors. The kidnappers look human but can also take on diverse appearances. The victims are then taken inside a flying vessel to undergo a sort of "protocol," mentioned above, before being sent back to their normal lives. This is what is always reported.

Several terms are used for these mysterious kidnappers. The one most often used is "extraterrestrial," but its usage is debatable because it implies that the origin of these beings is known, although it has never been proven that these abductions are of an extraterrestrial nature. The term "alien" means almost the same thing and poses the same problem, unless one uses it in its true sense; that is, an alien is a being that does not belong to the human race. The abductors are also sometimes referred to as "little gray men," a term related to their physical appearance as seen in many cases, even though they have been described as having other aspects as well. In the current study, we will stick to the words "kidnapper," "abductor," or "captor" as long as their identity remains unknown to us.

This phenomenon of abductions is not well known to the public, first because the victims of these abductions do not always keep their conscious memory of the events they have experienced, and second because the victims do not always talk about what they have gone through. Indeed, the events are quite traumatizing, completely outlandish, and impossible to believe. This is the reason why it is hard to have an accurate idea of the number of abductions that really occur. But studies have shown that this number is in the hundreds of thousands—if not more—and that the largest number, around 80 percent,[5] has happened in the United States. In France, an association has been set up to support the victims of these abductions.(CERO-France).

Vulnerable Human Beings: Victims of Abductions

After undergoing such an ordeal, the large majority of kidnapping victims are traumatized for the rest of their lives, and some of them even more so because they go through it several times. Both men and women alike can be victims of this phenomenon; there is no evidence that it targets a particular category of the population. Even if this phenomenon is not well known throughout the world in general, the singularly high number of victims in the United States demonstrates the vulnerability of human beings. Indeed, they can find themselves—at any time and without warning—at the mercy of nonhuman beings: nonhuman beings whose identity is unknown to us, who demonstrate a certain form of intelligence, but who are indifferent to the physical and psychological suffering they inflict.

The phenomenon of abductions described here is obviously malevolent toward humankind, even if there are rare cases of kind actions such as "spontaneous" healing taking place after an abduction. In most cases, the abduction phenomenon goes against human morality; it is degrading and violates human dignity—even more because those concerned have absolutely no power to stop it.

The truth is that this vulnerability is part of our human condition, because we are helpless in the face of the abduction phenomenon. This realization should lead us to take on a more humble attitude with regard to the mysteries of the Universe, an attitude that opposes the all-powerful image we have of ourselves—a self-image that our modern society, limited by its materialist vision, has ingrained in us.

The fact that human beings have no idea as to the origin of these phenomena renders us even more helpless and vulnerable. We know neither the nature nor the identity of these kidnappers, nor do we know the reason for their acts. Is it possible then to protect ourselves from their aggressions? The first thing to do would be to uncover the veritable identity of these abductors, and, then, if possible, the goal they are pursuing. This is the twofold objective of this book.

Important Philosophical and Spiritual Implications

The vulnerability of human beings in abduction cases is necessarily accompanied by philosophical and spiritual implications. This phenomenon gives us new evidence that we are not the only intelligent beings on Earth—as if we still needed proof of this. Although the very existence of this phenomenon is unfathomable by using the knowledge base of today's science, the fact that it exists implies that the place of human beings within the Universe needs to be reexamined by those who unwaveringly adhere to this science. We come to realize that the image of the human being as conveyed by today's science and linked to a materialist vision of the world—the image of the human being as master of the earth and conqueror of the Universe—needs to be abandoned completely. We must replace this image with the notion of interdependence between human beings and these other entities who are still unknown but who regularly manifest their presence among us. Such an awareness could help humankind develop a form of humility, which in these times is sorely lacking—particularly in the Western world.

This observation was made by the psychiatrist John Mack, who extensively studied the phenomenon of abductions after having seen a large number of victims in his psychiatric practice.[6] He wrote: "It would seem that an intelligence is trying to establish a connection, that it is trying to get through to us." "It is impossible to start seriously envisioning something as absurd as 'extraterrestrial kidnappings,' without accepting at the very least to examine the possibility that our vision of the Universe is incomplete and perhaps erroneous." It is this very vision of the Universe that the UFO phenomenon and the abduction phenomenon in particular are inciting us to reconsider.

These excerpts illustrate perfectly how difficult it is to address and study the phenomenon of abduction into UFOs, as well as all other types of mysterious phenomena that remain unexplained by science. Indeed, each one of us is certainly affected and limited by the materialist vision of the world, and it is very hard to rid ourselves of this vision because it is deeply ingrained in our collective unconscious mind. It is this materialist representation of our Universe, limited to what our senses can perceive, that keeps us from correctly addressing these mysterious phenomena and in particular the phenomenon of abduction into UFOs.

CHAPTER ONE

ABDUCTIONS OF HUMAN BEINGS INTO UFOS

Incredible Accounts

At the beginning of the 1990s, John Mack, a professor of psychiatry at Harvard Medical School, recognized by his peers for his significant experience, was confronted with completely incredible personal stories. More and more people suffering from profound psychological disturbances were coming to see him, claiming to have been abducted by extraterrestrials. This all seemed like total craziness, impossible, unreal. But he gradually discovered that this phenomenon was being reported by people of all origins and age groups, people who had no connections between them and who were all recounting a similar phenomenon.

John Mack had the intellectual courage to undertake a rigorous clinical study of this phenomenon and to put his reputation on the line, because at first glance, none of it seemed very legitimate. He realized that the people he was seeing in his practice were not at all like the diverse population of psychiatric patients that he had been treating for thirty years. After seeing dozens of people claiming to have been victims of abduction, he had to admit it: this was not about mental illness. These patients were sane and spoke in good faith of occurrences that for them were very real and had totally turned their lives upside down. These people were conscious of the fact that they sounded completely crazy, and they themselves were asking many questions that had no answers.

John Mack published the results of his clinical research in 1994, after having worked for two years on a hundred or so cases, thirteen of which are detailed extensively in this book. The title of one of his books is very explicit: *Abduction: Human Encounters with Aliens.*[1] One can read in the introduction:

The experiences reported herein have all of the characteristics of real events.

- The accounts are extremely detailed, logical, and coherent down to the minutest detail.
- There is intense emotional and physical trauma.
- The physical trauma is sometimes accompanied by visible lesions on the bodies of the victims.

He states, "The energy and emotions flowing through these people when they are talking about their ordeal have an intensity equal to none that I have seen throughout my years of practice as a therapist." When telling their story, these patients were actually reliving their abduction and, therefore, were suffering greatly.

As one might expect, the publication of his first book attracted a lot of criticism from those who accused him of "turning rationality and objective truth on its head," considering that "extraterrestrial kidnappings are antirational and antiscientific" and that the so-called "victims" of these abductions are simply crazy. In his second book, John Mack retorts: "What is hiding behind such revelations is a vision of the world that requires that we ignore a great amount of data for the one and only reason that it is in conflict with this same vision. This, I fear, is more irrational and comes out of a rather dangerous approach to knowledge."[2]

This exchange of viewpoints perfectly illustrates how difficult it is to address and study the abduction phenomenon. According to John Mack, there was nothing that indicated that those reporting such experiences were mentally ill. "None of the patients showed any symptoms that were characteristic of mental illness. Nothing led me to classify their accounts under the category of hallucinations, oneiric interpretations or figments of the imagination."[3] And he then asked the following question: "What the victims describe is not supposed to be possible. Should we not then recognize that the definition of what is possible is really a question of how we see the world? . . . I consider that the world vision we have is an arbitrary one[,] and my experience in medicine incites me to believe my patients much more than I believe in this world vision."

We therefore give John Mack immense credit for having raised awareness of the reality of nonhuman creatures abducting human beings. His psychiatrist's approach provided a valuable addition to the first research carried out by those such as Budd Hopkins,[4] Dr. David M. Jacobs,[5] Aimé Michel,[6] Jean Sider,[7] Gildas Bourdais,[8] and many others. But if the victims had experienced something "real," then the question becomes: What reality? And who are these beings responsible for these kidnappings? Where do they come from?

These are questions that are fascinating but mind-boggling, because for the past fifty years or so, we are talking about tens of thousands and perhaps even hundreds of thousands of men, women, and even children throughout the world who are concerned. But we don't talk about it because it goes beyond our comprehension and is completely opposed to the world vision that is dominant today. According to Marie-Thérèse de Brosses,[9] it would seem that one out of fifty Americans (2%) meets all of the criteria of being an abduction victim. If we were to extrapolate this to the entire US population, this percentage would give us the stupefying number of three million potential victims.

Case Studies of Abductions

The primary challenge for those interested in UFO abductions is understanding that this phenomenon is indeed real and that the victims really experience what looks like a kidnapping; they leave this world and are taken into another world. Here we will provide some excerpts taken from the most-significant cases and then analyze them. Other case studies have been done, notably on the most famous UFO abductions of Barney and Betty Hill (New Hampshire, United States, 1961) and of Travis Walton (Arizona, United States, 1975), because these cases were both the first and the most mediatized ones in the 1950s and '60s and continue to be today. But so as not to weigh down this chapter, these have been included in the appendix.

Below we present two examples of abductions that took place in the presence of eyewitnesses who in turn were able to provide their proper observations. We shall try to make a rational analysis without letting ourselves be influenced by the limited schemas of thinking that are deep inside every one of us—schemas that are linked to the materialist vision that dominates today's world.

The Abduction of Corporal Valdès (Chile, 1977)

This abduction is one of the best-known and best-documented cases. Its authenticity is therefore incontestable. Corporal Valdès recounts:[10]

On April 25, 1977, I was commanding a patrol in the Andes, in the northern part of Chile. My mission was to watch over a thousand horses and llamas. Suddenly, in the middle of the night we observed a large light which descended rapidly on the hillside, just facing us. After several seconds, it got bigger, only to disappear behind the hill. Another light then appeared, facing in our direction. It was oval in shape, about 20 meters in diameter and even brighter in the center.

From that moment, my men and I started feeling strange sensations. The animals regrouped around their oldest members, as they normally did when they were roaming freely. They all were looking at the light, which proved to me that they saw it just as we did. On top of that, the dog that was with us hid behind us and shivered as it looked toward the light.

Then it was as if a force pushed me to walk toward this light. From this point on, I remember nothing more. The next day, my men told me what had happened next. They told me that I disappeared out of sight, only to reappear fifteen minutes later in the same exact spot. I was behaving oddly and speaking incoherently along with having bouts of hysteria. When I came to my senses, I felt a great fatigue and a strong pain in my lower back as if I had strained it somehow. I was on the verge of a nervous breakdown. On top of that, my beard looked like it was several days old, even though I had shaved the night before. What is strange is that none of my men showed any of these same signs. They had been only a bit traumatized by the whole thing and were more than anything else worried about me. But they did notice to their surprise that my watch had stopped at precisely 4:30 a.m., the exact time of my reappearance, and, in particular, that the date on the watch was reading April 30; that is, five days in the future.

ANALYSIS

1. Lights and strange sensations:

The abduction was preceded by the sighting of a "large light" that moved and increased in size, followed by another large light (roughly 20 meters). Such intense, unidentified lights that are seen moving in an uninhabited mountainous region and that change size cannot be of human origin. This is one of the forms in which UFOs often appear: simple luminous objects that move in the sky and that can easily change their size and their intensity. The strange sensations felt by the men and the animals, as well as the behavior of the dog, are clearly linked to the presence of these unidentified luminous objects.

2. The influence of some outside force:

The corporal reported being pushed to walk toward the UFO by a mysterious force. He therefore did not go on his own initiative. He then disappeared out of the sight of his men. The fact that he was alone in walking toward the UFO before being abducted means that he was under the control of some outside will coming from some invisible intelligence, which would logically be linked to the UFO. The corporal was the only one who went through this unheard-of experience, although his men were just several feet away.

3. A dimensional shift:

The most remarkable aspect of this account is that Corporal Valdès had temporarily disappeared completely out of sight, and that his men were able to recount everything that happened before he reappeared instants later. Even if all of this goes against scientific principles, everything happened as if the corporal had "dematerialized" in order to disappear from the material world of human beings before "rematerializing" fifteen minutes later back in his world—in the exact same spot. Even if his physical body had become invisible, he did not die nor had his body been destroyed, since this very same man reappeared a bit later with the exact same physical body, albeit quite affected by what it had been through.

An objective analysis of this account brings us to the conclusion that Corporal Valdès had undergone a "dimensional shift." Under the influence of invisible forces, he left the material world of humans to go into another dimension, and then through an inverse dimensional shift, he was brought back to the material world. The existence of this dimensional shift reveals that an intelligent force was at work, a mysterious force that has the ability to impose such a dimensional shift. Obviously, this intelligence is linked to the UFO and therefore associated with the presence of nonhuman, invisible beings in this UFO.

We can say that this dimensional shift, this "dematerialization," which occurred without any damage to the body of Corporal Valdès, consisted of a transformation of his physical body, clothes and all, such that he became invisible, and that this process of transformation could be reversed. Everything happened as if his body had gone into a subtle, invisible state of matter—a state unknown by science—before coming back into its initial, dense, solid, and visible state, with the exact same structure intact. This simple but logical reasoning that is well beyond the limits fixed by science seems to show that:

- the UFO, or the intelligence associated with it, has the ability to modify the density of a material body, whether it be living or not, and
- matter has levels of density that are invisible.

4. Transported into another space-time:

Another very important part of this account is the discrepancy between the length of the disappearance as interpreted in the material world of Corporal Valdès's men—fifteen minutes—and what reads on the corporal's watch after his return from the "other world"—five full days. The extreme fatigue felt by the corporal shows that he had undergone hardships that he did not remember. His several-day-old beard also confirms the longer duration of his absence, even if this seems unbelievable.

This very large difference between the two interpretations of the duration of the event is coherent with the idea that the corporal had been taken into another world. This signifies that the passage of time in the world of humans and in this other world was very different. We realize here that time is not an objective concept as we are used to thinking, but, rather, a relative one that depends on the world in which one is perceiving it. The most appropriate way to describe this dimensional shift is to say that Corporal Valdès had truly been transported into another space-time in which the concepts of space and time do not have the same meaning as they do in our material world.

5. No to hypnosis:

Corporal Valdès always refused to undergo hypnosis, since this would have brought memories to the surface of what he had gone through: painful memories of what happened while he was in the hands of his kidnappers.

6. Analysis summary:

Simple and logical reasoning gives us the following description of this kidnapping case: Corporal Valdès was taken for a time into a parallel world where time passes differently. In this different space-time, matter is in a more subtle state that is invisible to us, and this transformation is reversible. This dimensional shift was controlled by nonhuman intelligences linked to the UFO—intelligences who, through this experience, wanted to make themselves known to humans. The question then becomes this: What is the nature of these nonhuman intelligences?

The Abduction of Jeff
(United States, circa 2000)

Abductions taking place in the presence of lucid eyewitnesses are rare and, therefore, all the more priceless. The following is an account taken from a book specifically devoted to accounts of abductions of Amerindians in North America. Unlike those living in the modern Western world, these people are very familiar with the phenomenon of abductions into UFOs, or, as they put it, encounters with "star people." This is the term that the Amerindians use, a term in line with their beliefs. Their accounts of these encounters easily circulate among their population. Ardy Sixkiller Clarke, an Amerindian whose heritage allowed her to easily meet with those who had had such experiences, was able to gather a large number of these incredible stories and publish them.[11]

Jennifer recounts:

It was a lovely fall afternoon in the month of August, when my two cousins, a friend, and I all decided to go camping. At around eight o'clock in the evening, we started to go down the canyon on horseback—we knew the path very well. After a mile or so, we saw a huge space machine sitting at the bottom of the canyon. It was an immense circular object with white and red blinking lights at its base, and it lit up the canyon walls with a reddish glow. We were petrified. The horses got scared and started bucking, so we dismounted. We were afraid that someone would see us. Terrence wanted us all to get out of there, but Jeff moved forward in order to get a direct view of the vessel. I was also curious and started following him . . . and this is when it all started: he disappeared. In a second, Jeff was no longer there. At the time I was about ten feet behind him.

We were terrified and didn't know what to do. We didn't want to call out from fear that whatever was on board the vessel would take us too, but we were also afraid to leave without our friend. We decided to wait and observe, hidden in the shadows of the canyon walls. Jeff reappeared in what must have been two hours. He emerged from the intense light as if nothing had happened.

Several seconds later, the vessel slowly rose straight up, illuminating the canyon walls before disappearing into the night sky. We hadn't seen any creature around the vessel, and yet something or someone had taken Jeff and held him captive for two hours. When Jeff came back, we all left on horseback. Jeff remembered nothing of what had happened. The next day his body was all red as if he had a sunburn. That evening he became so ill that he had to go to the clinic. The doctors there said that he was suffering from a severe sunburn, and kept him in observation for several days.

ANALYSIS

1. A fortuitous abduction?

The vessel was already on the ground and perfectly visible when the four friends found themselves, by surprise, face to face with it. The circumstances seem to suggest that this abduction was a spontaneous one and took place only because the vessel encountered the four friends. It was not the result of an intentional plan previously thought out by the captors, as it most often is. The captors took advantage of the opportunity to abduct a human being, as they sometimes do.

2. The reaction of the horses:

It is very common that animals feel the energy emitted by flying vessels as being hostile, and they consequently either react aggressively or with fear.

3. A dimensional shift:

Jeff disappeared suddenly, as did Corporal Valdès. We can therefore make the same analysis. This sudden disappearance leads us to think that he was "dematerialized" in order to enter another world, and then he reentered the material world two hours later by a process of "rematerialization." His body bore no apparent traces of this incident, except for a severe "sunburn."

We can say that Jeff was the victim of a "dimensional shift" caused by unknown forces. Because what occurred was not at all natural—all the more because he was the only one to experience it—we can attribute the event to invisible beings with a certain intelligence, beings who logically must have been passengers on the vessel that had landed at the bottom of the canyon.

4. No information about what was experienced in the other world:

In this account, Jeff never talked about what he had been through nor what he had felt after returning among his friends. We don't know if he went toward the vessel out of his own volition, motivated by his own curiosity, or if he advanced toward it under the control of some outside force. Two hours had gone by when he came back "from the other world." He had no memory of what had happened, as if his memory had been taken from him.

This two-hour lapse of time is an average duration of "missing time" in the schedules of abduction victims, who more often than not have no memory of what happened. Because this length of time is rather substantial, we could reasonably think that "something happened" in the vessel, but we have no information. Jeff did not see a therapist after this incident and did not take advantage of hypnosis sessions that would have allowed him to fill in the gaps in his recollection of the event.

We can suppose that the severe sunburn Jeff suffered from after his return was connected to him being close to the vessel's powerful luminosity in the material plane, right before and right after his return.

5. The connection between the kidnappers and the vessel:

The vessel left immediately after returning Jeff to the material world right in front of the eyes of the three witnesses. It also seems that the vessel remained visible in the material plane for the two hours that the three friends waited and observed from their hiding place in the shadows. This allows us to clearly link the abduction of Jeff to the presence of the vessel, although in the case of Corporal Valdès, the UFO simply manifested itself in the form of intense, large lights before the abduction and was no longer visible afterward.

The two preceding accounts are obviously incomplete since the victims did not keep what they experienced in memory. Their memories of what happened to them would provide us with the full meaning of their abduction. The work of the psychiatrist John Mack was first of all meant to help his patients retrieve their memories in order to free them of their trauma and thus continue on to lead normal lives. But his work also sought to understand what happened in this other world and to study the phenomenon of abduction into UFOs.

The Abduction of Antonio Villas-Boas (Brazil, 1957)

This abduction is the first one ever to be reported in our era and is known throughout the ufologist world. It was the object of an excellent investigation conducted by Dr. Olavo Fontes, of the Medical School of Rio de Janeiro, who examined and questioned the victim.

On the night of October 15, 1957, twenty-three-year-old Brazilian farmer Antonio Villa Boas was busy working one of his fields. Alone on his tractor, he worked at night in order to avoid exposure to the hot temperatures during the day. At one o'clock in the morning, he looked up at the starry sky and saw something that looked like a red star. It got bigger and bigger until it became a brilliant object in the form of an egg. It hovered over him and then landed gently on the ground. Antonio first tried to get away on his tractor, but its motor stopped and its headlights went out. He continued to try to escape, but he was grabbed by a short humanoid (about 5 feet tall) wearing a gray outfit and a helmet. After a brief struggle, four other like beings took him inside the vessel.

In spite of his resistance, he was undressed and his body was washed with something resembling a wet sponge. He was then taken through a strange door marked with symbols, and he found himself in another room. Antonio remained alone in the room for what seemed to be a very long time. When he heard a noise at the door, he turned around and was "extremely startled" by what he saw: the door opened and a woman entered, just as nude as he. Her hair was blond, and she had blue, slanted eyes; a straight nose; high cheekbones; and a very large face with a pointy chin. Her lips were very thin, nearly invisible; her ears were very dainty, but otherwise ordinary. She was much shorter than he was, her head reaching only to his shoulders.

She very quickly makes it clear as to the reason for her visit, and they have sexual intercourse. Shortly after, another man enters and gestures to the woman, who, in turn, points to her abdomen, smiles, points to the sky, and then follows the man out of the room.

The men came back with Antonio's clothing and then took him into a room where other members of the "crew" were seated. They seemed to be communicating with each other using growling noises. Antonio, now reassured and certain that no one would be doing him any harm, examined his surroundings carefully. Among other things, he noticed something that looked somewhat like an alarm clock: a little box with a glass lid on it. The "clock" had a needle and several symbols on it, which seemed to correspond to the numbers 3, 6, 9, and 12 of an ordinary alarm clock. Antonio noticed, however, that the needle was not moving even though time was passing.

Antonio strongly felt that he had to bring back proof of this extraordinary experience and, therefore, tried to take the "alarm clock." No sooner did he attempt this than one of the men furiously pushed him away from it. Finally, another man gestured to Antonio to follow him to a circular platform. Antonio was walked completely around the vessel before he was taken to a metallic ladder and motioned to go down it. From there he was able to observe all the details of preparing for departure, and he watched the vessel take off and disappear into space in just several seconds. He noticed the time was 5:30 a.m., indicating he had stayed four hours inside the strange vessel.

For a month after the incident, Antonio needed a lot of sleep. It was also worth noting that he volunteered to provide information after spotting a newspaper ad asking for reports of UFOs. But he became extremely reluctant when he had to provide more-intimate details of his experience inside the vessel and did so only under the insistent questioning of Dr. Fontes, the doctor who was treating him. Dr. Fontes recorded his testimony and conducted a thorough investigation into his experience. Antonio Villas-Boas went on to become a lawyer, marry, and have four children. Until the end of his life, he never wavered from the story of his abduction.

The details of the event reported by Villas-Boas were divulged by O. Fontes and G. Creighton, and, later by Mr. and Mrs. Lorenzen, who in their book *Flying Saucer Occupants*[12] provided a complete account of the experience, including the professional opinion of Dr. Fontes based on his medical examination of Antonio.

It is also worth noting that in the days leading up to his abduction, Antonio and his brother had seen strange lights several times near their house and in the field where they were working.

ANALYSIS

1. Change of appearance:

The flying vessel into which Antonio was taken was first perceived in the form of a red star. This change in appearance leads us to think that it was not made up of ordinary matter as we know it, even if it subsequently landed on the ground like a material machine would. Consequently, it had to have come from a parallel world that is different from our material world.

2. Lights that go out:

Antonio's escape attempt was thwarted when the motor of his tractor suddenly stopped and the lights went out. Indeed, all eyewitness accounts of UFOs demonstrate that when a UFO is nearby, motors and electrical devices stop functioning. This is exactly the same scenario as the one experienced by Barney and Betty Hill (see the appendix).

3. The objective of the abduction seems clear:

Antonio naturally stored what happened that night in his memory. According to his account, the only thing that gives any meaning to the kidnapping is that he was abducted in order to mate with a female humanoid creature, who, according to his description, was not "human."

He had clearly been chosen by his captors, and most likely so because he was a young man alone, isolated in his fields. Without any explanation, he was taken by force on board a vessel, and then, once the sexual act consummated, he was let go. The gesture that the "woman" made to him clearly confirms that the goal of this abduction was for her to become pregnant by a man. She needed the semen of a man, and Antonio played the role of the unwitting donor. There was therefore no regard for his human dignity.

Antonio was then given permission to walk around the vessel before leaving it. This can be interpreted as a small gesture of thanks. He was not forced to watch film images about Earth's ecology, as is the case in most abductions—which we will see in the following accounts. It is important to reiterate that this abduction case is the first known case of our modern era and took place in 1957.

4. A physical makeup comparable to that of human beings:

If the goal of this kidnapping was evidently to make a female humanoid-type creature mate with a male human being in order to give birth to a hybrid child, this implies that the two types of genitalia were compatible. This therefore signifies that the physical constitution of the female was akin to that of human beings. This is very important and shows that there is a surprising similarity between human beings and these nonhuman entities.

5. A different space-time:

The incident of the alarm clock could mean that time does not pass in the same way in the world of the vessel as it does in the earthly world. Also, upon consulting his watch after the vessel had disappeared, Antonio was surprised by how long his abduction had lasted (four hours).

6. A crazy story:

This account appears totally outlandish and absurd because it is completely contrary to our way of thinking and challenges our innermost beliefs about our place as human beings within the Universe. Furthermore, being based only on the account of one man, it can easily be disregarded.

And yet, this account was recorded and communicated by a reputed doctor who in so doing accepted to put his reputation on the line. Furthermore, the victim never derived any benefit from his testimony and never tried to enhance the story. He went on to lead a healthy life with a privileged profession. Finally, this account was only one of a long series of similar accounts.

The Abduction of Ed
(United States, Case Study by John Mack[13])

One summer day in 1989, Ed started to remember an event that he had experienced back in 1961, when he was in middle school. In the months that followed, many details started coming back to him little by little. He started becoming interested in UFOs and attended a conference held by MUFON (Mutual UFO Network, a private American organization that investigates UFO sightings), and it was then that he contacted John Mack in 1992.

His adventure took place in the summer of 1961 during a trip to the seaside with a friend and his friends' parents. He was about to go to sleep in the car with his friend while the adults slept in a cabin close by. Thinking he was already asleep, he recalls, he found himself naked in a "glass bubble" inside a small compartment with curved, translucent walls that was above a precipice. Inside the bubble was a petite feminine creature with long, silver-blond hair. She had a tiny little mouth and a dainty little nose, large dark eyes, and a triangular head with a high forehead. She seemed to be able to read his mind without Ed having to say a single word, and took great care to reassure him. Ed felt sexually excited, and they then engaged in sexual intercourse.

After the sexual encounter, the female entity started to convey information about the way that humanity was behaving concerning ecology and the management of the earth's resources. She explained that humans were committing nothing but errors, that they were headed in the wrong direction, and that this was going to lead to a world disaster that also threatened "the humanoid planet." It was as if the information passed directly from the entity's mind to Ed's. And, reading that Ed was worried that he would not remember, she added that it would all come back to him when necessary.

At this point in the story, the reader can certainly wonder if Ed had not simply had a dream that particular night. But his behavior changed after this encounter. He surprised himself in intuitively making declarations about social, political, and scientific issues. He found that he was feeling very close to nature and conducted conferences on these subjects for the youth at his middle school.

ADDITIONAL INFORMATION
OBTAINED THROUGH HYPNOSIS

Numerous critiques have been made concerning the reliability of information obtained under hypnosis—for example, that it is influenced by the therapist and therefore is neither objective nor truthful. It is clear that precautions must be taken in order to avoid this. During the period when John Mack carried out his work on abduction victims, he had already had an extensive professional experience (he was born in 1929 and published his first book in 1994) and was the head of the department of psychiatry at Harvard Medical School. His renown was such that, even if the originality of his work had triggered protest on the part of some of his colleagues, he was never criticized for his work methods.

During his consultation with John Mack, Ed expressed the desire to talk about his memories under hypnosis. After the preparation phase, he found himself transported back to the time when his adventure began, the night in 1961 when he spent the night in the car. It all began when he saw one or two silhouettes through the car window, silhouettes with large eyes, small mouths, and small ears. He felt the fear rising in him, and then he realized that he was being taken out of the car and that his body was flying. He was perplexed when he flew above the ocean as fast as an automobile without any apparent momentum or force. He could see the houses and streetlights below him. Then he saw that he was moving toward a luminous capsule in the form of a dome that was hanging in the air. He did not know how he got inside.

He then found himself in what looked like an operating room with white lights all around. There were at least a half-dozen beings there. One of them had the appearance of a female, with long silver hair and large black eyes—but with neither pupils nor irises. Ed noticed her large chest. She seemed to introduce herself as the "head doctor" and looked at him intensely while emanating a pronounced sensuality. Ed tried to speak but was unable to. He felt as if under her spell, without any will of his own, and realized that she was reading his mind. Then he remembered that his mind started receiving all sorts of erotic images that plunged him into a state of intense excitement. The female-like being then explained to him that they needed his sperm "to create different babies." A sort of tube was placed on his penis, triggering a feeling of such pleasure that he ended up ejaculating.

After the female being expressed her satisfaction to Ed, the decor started to change, as if Ed was in another place altogether. He found himself again in the capsule with translucent walls, not knowing how he had changed environments. A solemn atmosphere permeated the room. Using telepathy and allegory, the entity communicated a message about the ecological, spiritual, and emotional instability of our planet. She spoke of enormous waves as well as a tidal wave provoked by humankind's stupidity that would throw everything off balance and destabilize the earth. And in speaking directly to Ed: "You are very lucky, Ed. You have an inner sensitivity." She pointed out that he had a certain responsibility due to his special gifts and individual powers. "Listen to the earth, Ed, and you can perceive the anguish of its spirits. When you talk about this you must do so with wisdom."

Ed's mission was thus to teach anyone willing to listen. Humans must learn how to work on this planet while respecting the laws of nature and not pillaging the earth. At the end of the hypnosis session, Ed went on to say: "Love is the key, love and compassion for the earth or the beings on the earth, be they corporeal or incorporeal—not love in the mush and gush sense, but there is a deeper sense of love." But at the time when he contacted John Mack, which was thirty years after the abduction, he continued to wonder how he could make himself useful, how people could come to believe him. It is interesting to note that this abduction took place when Ed was a teenager, and he was able to retrieve his memories only when he was around forty.

Unlike others who experience abductions into UFOs, Ed wasn't too badly traumatized by his encounter with these "beings from another world." John Mack did notice, however, that before Ed's descent into the hypnotic state, his conscious memory tended to simplify certain details of his experience (in particular, the sexual encounter). The version of the story issuing from Ed's unconscious mind while in the hypnotic state was more typical of what happens during the abduction of human men and therefore was more credible.

ANALYSIS

1. Weightless in another world:

Ed was pulled from the car without his friend noticing. He doesn't know how he left the car, nor how he entered the "capsule." Then he found himself flying through the air in the middle of the night without any motorized propulsion. This is clearly not possible in our material world, where all material objects necessarily obey the universal law of attraction: the law of gravitational pull that pulls an object toward the ground. If one accepts the truth of Ed's account and thus the validity of John Mack's work, this ability to be free of one's weight and to "fly" like this in space means that Ed's body, like the bodies of his captors, was not a material one in the ordinary sense of the word and was not composed of ordinary matter. He had undergone a transformation that had rendered this matter more subtle, with a density that was either nonexistent or so slight that it was not subject to the law of gravity.

This state where matter finds itself at a level of subtle density is unknown to science; it does not exist in our world. Ed had been transported into another world, a world in another dimension or another plane of existence.

And yet, Ed clearly saw lights coming from the houses and the streetlights. This observation indicates that he was in a world that was close to the material one that makes up our normal environment. But it is a different world that nonetheless allows us to see what is going on in our material world.

2. A parallel world:

The information conveyed by the female entity stating that the behavior of human beings was leading us to a worldwide disaster that also threatened the "planet of humanoids" is full of meaning. It signifies that the planet of men and women and the planet of humanoids are interdependent and, therefore, near one another. It is difficult for us to fathom that the widespread pollution of nature here on Earth can have a direct consequence on another planet in our solar system, and even more so on a planet that is outside the solar system. It would seem more correct to see this message as an indirect way of saying that the humanoids in question live in a parallel plane connected to our same planet Earth.

We can see confirmation of this idea in the words of Ed when he tries to sum up what he had retained from his adventure: "Love is the key, love and compassion for the earth or the beings on the earth, be they corporeal or incorporeal." His kidnappers are beings that are normally invisible and quite preoccupied by the many destructive acts that man inflicts on the earth. They therefore live in a parallel plane, and it can be understood that it is a parallel plane that is *connected to the earth.*

3. Humanoid beings:

Ed focused his attention mainly on the feminine entity, who seemed to be the one in charge and was the one who took care of him. He described her as being a humanoid being, but with features that were quite different from those of humans. This appearance is similar to what we usually attribute to so-called "extraterrestrials."

4. Communication using telepathy:

There was no verbal communication, only communication via thoughts. Furthermore, Ed was aware that this entity was reading directly into his mind, without him having to say anything. She therefore had highly developed telepathic abilities. Ed himself received her thoughts, which had a calming, reassuring effect on him.

5. Two phases during the stay in the capsule:

At the time of the event (in 1961), the UFO phenomenon was still not well publicized by the media, and this no doubt explains Ed's use of the word "capsule" to designate the vessel in space where he found himself.

This account clearly defines two parts or phases of what happened in the capsule. The first phase was the forced collection of sperm for some sort of fertilization project that was not really specified ("different" babies). The second phase consisted of the entity communicating a certain amount of information about an imminent ecological disaster on Earth that would be triggered by mankind's irresponsible behavior. The goal of this second phase seemed to be to incite Ed to take on the responsibility to teach others in order to make them aware of ecological issues.

The Abduction of Jerry
(United States, Case Study by John Mack[14])

Jerry had just turned thirty when she called John Mack in 1992. She had already been storing in her conscious memory a lot of dreams about UFOs and abductions that went back all the way to when she was seven. She had even started to keep a journal in which she recorded the details of these abduction experiences.

In spite of an affectionate relationship with her husband, Jerry couldn't bring herself to have normal sexual relations with him: "When it came time to make love, I was seized by panic every time; the same feelings swept over me as when I was being kidnapped. I would then feel terrorized and revolted to have to be subjected to this, and I was completely a prisoner to these feelings." Those around her were incapable of understanding her; she felt more and more isolated and left on her own to deal with her problems—until she met John Mack.

Jerry's three very young children seemed to have also been involved in abduction phenomena. They often had nightmares about seeing UFOs and little creatures and were also terrorized by television ads showing UFOs.

Jerry had the feeling that these abductions and all the related consequences were pursuing her throughout her life. The sudden, unexpected appearance of diverse wounds, marks, scars, and other small lesions on her body after the kidnappings helped her appreciate the realness of what she had gone through.

During a regression session, Jerry chose to explore with John Mack the episode when she was terrorized at the age of thirteen. Under hypnosis, she again saw an intense bright light shining throughout her room. She felt a presence there. She noticed two beings who told her to follow them, all the while completely ignoring her protests. "They picked me up by the arms and carried me through the air, after passing through the window of my bedroom as if there was nothing there." She all of a sudden felt a sense of paralysis as they forced her onto an enormous vessel.

Jerry felt an extreme embarrassment when the entities took off her pajamas. One of them put his hands over her eyes while pressing a sort of tube above her belly in order to penetrate deeply into it. Then she noticed that one of the beings was holding a shiny object in the form of a horseshoe with a handle, while the others lifted and spread her knees apart. Fear came over her again when she felt a pressure inside her vagina. Jerry had the impression that something had been placed inside her body, perhaps in her uterus.

When she saw them remove the horseshoe-shaped instrument from her, she exclaimed, "Oh no, I can't believe this is happening! I am only thirteen!" What Jerry saw was an extremely thin, emaciated infant about twelve inches long. The infant was placed in a plastic cylinder, where it floated in a liquid. The beings seemed very satisfied with the result, and they wanted Jerry to feel proud of having helped in making this creature. But what she felt was intense anger and a feeling of betrayal. The beings then helped her get dressed and they took her back home. After her regression session, she realized she had had no control over the whole process. She saw the selfishness and arrogance of these beings; to them she was merely a pawn to achieve their ends.

In 1990, now an adult and a mother, Jerry underwent the most traumatizing experience of all the ones involving abductions. While in a conscious state, she was able to remember many significant details. She could not say how things began, other than that she felt a presence in her bedroom and that she was taken into a room inside a circular, shiny vessel. The room was equipped with diverse objects. While undergoing an examination there, she remembered that her necklace had fallen on the floor and it was picked up and put inside of a sort of "plastic bag." Through telepathy she was told that it was "contaminated" and that it would be given back to her another time. Several months later, Jerry's mother found a necklace similar to the one Jerry had lost; it was in a box in her house.

During this traumatic episode, the abductors applied a procedure involving the back of her skull, causing the most excruciating pain she had ever experienced. "I really believed that they were killing me," she said, remembering that she was screaming at the top of her lungs, even while incontrollable spasms racked her entire body. She felt hatred and rage. She lost consciousness and woke up later in her bed. Still in a state of shock, she tried to shake her husband awake, but to no avail.

In November 1991, Jerry again awoke to the feeling of a presence in her bedroom. The room was illuminated by a red-orange glow that diminished very softly. The next day, she was flooded with thoughts and information of a universal nature, which was not like her at all. It is after this that she started to write voraciously. She wrote around a hundred poems in a month and a half, even though she had never written a poem in her life. She even commented on great philosophical ideas, sometimes using words that she did not know. Having discontinued her education when she was still very young, she wondered where she possibly could have acquired such knowledge and this sudden ability to write. It did not take her long to understand that many of the thoughts did not come from her, but from another source. She also had dreams of our world being destroyed—and therefore her role as a procreator took on its full significance. One of her dreams was about the future destruction of planet Earth due to a nuclear war.

During another incident in September 1992, she saw a golden light illuminating her entire room; it was so bright that it hurt her eyes. The beings entered her room through the closed door. She again felt all the fear that was humanly possible as she was led through her bedroom window to the vessel and to the place she had come to know so well. She saw herself nude on a table. In the room there was a cabinet with hundreds of drawers, each containing a fetus. Jerry recognized one of them as being hers. Jerry estimated that the number of procedures carried out on her since the age of thirteen, including implants or extractions through her vagina, numbered close to fifty. She remembers being taken many times to a place where she was shown what seemed to be sickly, hybrid beings.

Thanks to the help of John Mack, Jerry came to understand that her inability to have a healthy sexual relationship with her husband was because she had always associated sex with pain. The abuse she had undergone throughout twenty years of abductions is what ruined her sex life with her husband.

ANALYSIS

1. Transported into another dimension:

In each of her experiences, Jerry was abducted from her bedroom by beings who entered through a closed door. She was then taken into a flying vessel after passing through a glass window "as if there was nothing there." This signifies that there was no mechanical interaction between the bodies—of neither the beings nor Jerry—and the ordinary matter that makes up our environment (doors and windows). This observation is inexplicable by using the current knowledge base of science, and it implies that Jerry's body had been transformed ahead of time before leaving her bedroom, in order to go from the level of density corresponding to the solid state that we know, to a level of subtle density unknown to our science.

This is confirmed by Jerry's observation, like that of Ed's in the preceding example, of "floating in the air" upon leaving her bedroom. She was not subject to the law of gravity, meaning her body was no longer made up of ordinary dense matter, but, rather, a matter that was subtle.

Here it can be said that she was transported into another world, another dimension or a parallel plane.

2. A more subtle physical body:

This, however, does not mean that this incident was an "out of body" experience. Such an experience is what happens at the beginning of an astral journey: where the astral body, or consciousness, leaves the physical body and moves freely in space. Indeed, the fact that Jerry would find diverse wounds, marks, scars, and other small lesions on her body after the abductions is the proof that her physical body had been touched.

We can deduce from all of this that each time Jerry was abducted, she was abducted with her physical body. But this physical body (along with her clothes) had undergone a transformation, allowing it to easily pass through a solid object such as a door or a window without any resistance. As has been already mentioned, this transformation's effect was to change matter (which comprised her body and clothes) into a very subtle level of density. This transformation is reversible because Jerry found herself back in her normal state after the incident.

Furthermore, she recounted that while lying on the table in the vessel, someone inserted an instrument deep into her stomach, above her navel, and also well into her vagina without hurting her, even though she did physically sense these intrusions. This all seems to indicate that the interactions between her physical body and the instruments used were more subtle than in our material world, and as a result, these experiences took place in another world that is more subtle than the one we know.

Meanwhile, the procedure that Jerry underwent in 1990 took place in her head, causing her a lot of pain (it seems that they inserted an object into the back of her skull), which indicates that there was a strong interaction between the object and the physical body. Yet, there was no apparent lesion left behind since Jerry did not note any particular aftereffect. We can imagine from this that there had been contact with an area of high nerve density.

3. Victims as early as childhood:

Jerry's example shows that the UFO abduction phenomenon is not reserved only for adults, but that young children can also be victims. It seems that these children are then "followed" and subjected to other kidnappings throughout their lives. Jerry related that this was what happened to her and also to her younger brother. She remembered that he had already been abducted along with her when she was only seven years old, and that as an adult he too had problems in his relationships.

Jerry's three children were victims of kidnapping, and it has been recorded in UFO abduction accounts that several members of the same family can be victims of this phenomenon.

4. Another source of knowledge:

Starting in 1991 and for a certain length of time, Jerry was inspired, as if by force, to write things down that went clearly beyond her personal abilities—whether it be content or vocabulary related or with respect to form (poetry). This means that she was a conduit for information coming from another world, information that was conveyed by beings living in a spiritual plane. It is logical to think that there was a link to the kidnappings and that these were the very same beings who were manifesting themselves to her in this way.

5. Very real phenomena:

The very large number of kidnappings that Jerry claimed to have undergone and the intensity of the trauma she experienced can lead one to believe that it was all way too far out to be credible, that it could not have possibly happened, that it could not be for real. As a matter of fact, this was the opinion of those around her and of her family in particular. Yet, the "diverse wounds, marks, scars, and other small lesions on her body" were proof that something very real occurred during these abductions. The question then becomes this: In what world do these realities exist? The necklace incident is another proof of the authenticity of these events and that other forces or beings were involved (the necklace was found in her mother's house). We will see (this is the subject of the work of John Mack and other researchers) that Jerry's case was far from being exceptional. Many people have been traumatized for life by recurring experiences such as these: experiences that are no less than rapes and therefore not always stored in conscious memory.

The Abduction of Catherine
(United States, Case Study by John Mack[15])

Catherine was twenty-two years old when she experienced upsetting events inciting her to consult Dr. John Mack in March 1991.

The first abduction experience that she recalled took place when she was three. One day when she was watching *The Invaders*—a science fiction television series about a spaceship with extraterrestrials landing on Earth—memories started coming back to her. In one scene, a woman who is kidnapped sees a dog barking at her window. Upon seeing this, it came back to Catherine that one night when she was three years old, she was awakened in the middle of the night and saw someone at her window while a blue light flooded her bedroom. The entity had enormous black eyes, a pointy chin, a slit instead of a mouth, and a small bump for a nose. He entered through her bedroom window. Completely terrorized, Catherine cried out to her mother for help, but she couldn't utter a sound. She then saw five or six more beings who looked like the first one, and remembered that they did something to calm her fear. She started to float in the air like them. She saw that her living room was all lit up, even though all the lights were turned off, and she was surprised when she passed through the front door, headfirst. A disc-shaped vessel was parked on the ground near her house.

After this first meeting with John Mack, other memories came back to her naturally over the following weeks. Inside the vessel, she was taken into a round room where there were other children. A being with a female appearance, taller than the others, entered and suggested that they play with an odd sort of ball. But Catherine could not remember the rest of her story and was unable to continue with her account.

Catherine experienced several abductions during her childhood and on into her adult years, and she was able to retrieve fragments of some of these memories. The following is an episode that took place at Christmastime in 1990, when she was an adult. The day after Christmas, as she was waking up, she remembered having dreamt about something as she saw an image in her mind: she was in a room on board a vessel. Later, she underwent a hypnotic regression session with John Mack in order to retrieve her memory of what had happened. As the session commenced, she saw rays of light filling her room. Two beings made her leave her bed and had her "enter a bright ray of light." She was seized with an intense fear, but the beings' control over her kept her from overtly showing any resistance. They all passed through the window and then rose up into the sky. She saw her house becoming farther and farther away below her and her town becoming smaller. She surmised that the bright light was helping her stay warm because she was wearing only light undergarments. She then felt herself passing through an entrance in the platform of a vessel before finding herself inside it.

She was then taken into a room where she saw another being who looked like a doctor: taller than the others but shorter than she was. There were all sorts of instruments everywhere on the walls. She felt a growing anxiety as she was made to lie down on a table. One of the beings opened her legs, and the doctor looked closely at her genitals. She realized then that she was wearing no clothes and that she was totally incapable of resisting. The doctor inserted an instrument inside her, which she felt go up farther than her vagina. This did not hurt even though it was a bit uncomfortable. Catherine had the sense that tissue samples were being taken from her uterine lining, or perhaps from even farther inside.

When Catherine asked the doctor why he was doing this, he replied: "It is for scientific research. I am doing research on your planet; we are trying to stop the massacre caused by pollution."

While the scenes of this abduction were coming back up into her conscious mind, John Mack asked her if she had been asleep or completely awake. She replied: "Neither one nor the other. I was in a sort of intermediary state of consciousness." And prompted by another question, Catherine noticed that she could very clearly see everything that was around her, as if she were wearing her contact lenses, even though she didn't remember having put them in and didn't think she had them on her. This was noteworthy because usually without her contact lenses, "everything was one vast fog."

After this, several of the beings helped her off the table, and they took her into another room, where she saw something horrible: containers stacked on top of one another from floor to ceiling—containers holding small, deformed creatures who were floating straight up in a sort of liquid. They all had large heads, like miniature versions of the beings she had encountered. "These must be baby extraterrestrials," she thought to herself.

Then Catherine was brought into another room, which was huge and much bigger than all the others she had seen. She found herself in a forest within the room, complete with trees, rocks, and soil. "This is crazy! I don't get it," she said to herself. Then she was taken into another room that looked like a conference room with an immense screen.

While she analyzed these memories with John Mack, she remembered that when she was in this room on the UFO, "the more she thought of this conference room, the more it looked like one," and she then realized as she went through analysis that it all had been a huge stage setting—a simulation of a conference room. She remembered that the images of this room had grown fainter to give way to the images of the room as she had seen it when she first walked in.

In the "conference room," she was made to watch beautiful scenes of nature projected onto the screen, including majestic scenes of the Grand Canyon, but she suspected that the emotions she was feeling were also the result of manipulation. During subsequent abductions, she received a lot of information about the pollution of the earth's natural environment and the imbalance of the earth's ecosystems, and how they were interdependent. In spite of the methods used by her kidnappers, Catherine did feel that she shared with them the same objective of saving the planet. Later on, her life was transformed and she felt it important to help other abduction victims become aware that the destiny of the entire planet is linked to environmental issues. Finally, she was given back her clothes and then accompanied back to her house. She climbed back into her bed and quickly fell asleep.

The incident that motivated Catherine to consult Dr. John Mack happened on one February night in 1991. As she was getting ready to return home after work, the idea suddenly came to her to take a drive. When she got back home a bit later, she realized that there had been a time lapse of forty-five minutes during which she was unable to explain what she had done. The next day she saw a television news broadcast reporting a UFO sighting that previous night in her vicinity, and a journalist was tracing the path taken by the object on a map. Catherine understood that she had also gone in this same direction. Furthermore, she noted that in the days following the incident, she had unexplained nosebleeds, although she had never had this type of problem before.

As she relived this incident later during a regression session, Catherine expressed that she had been inspired to take roads she was unfamiliar with that led her to a forest. She remembered that all along the way she was looking at the sky and thinking about UFOs. After a short while, the car started slowing down even though she had her foot on the gas pedal. She ended up at a standstill while she felt her body becoming more and more lethargic. She noticed that "It was much lighter out than it should have been." Someone opened her car door, and a hand reached out to take her arm—a hand with three fingers. Catherine was terrified but understood that she had no choice in the matter. The being had enormous, black, almond-shaped eyes. He took her up into the sky and they flew away together. She saw the ground growing smaller beneath her as she arrived at an enormous vessel. She was made to go inside, and they removed her clothing before taking her into an immense room resembling an airplane hangar. There were hundreds of tables with hundreds of human beings lying on them. (Catherine estimates that there were between 100 and 200 humans in the entire room).

She was forced to sit down and the examination began. While a tall being looked deep into her eyes, it seemed to her that he knew everything about her, that he was reading her mind and answering her questions without her having to ask anything. After several moments, he announced that "I am going to remove it from you." "Remove what?" she asked. "He lifted up my feet and spread my legs." He placed an instrument in her vagina and thrust it up inside her. She felt that he was trying to reach something inside her body in order to cut it. He then removed something from her that looked like a fetus; it was the size of a fist and perhaps about three months old. The "doctor" appeared to be proud and said to Catherine: "You should be proud of yourself." Even though she was enraged at being used in such a way and reprimanded the being for having ruined her life, he replied, "You will not remember anything," and laid his hand on her forehead to calm her down. She realized that she had lost all ability to fight. She added, "How many human beings have you done this to?" And he replied, "A large number."

Then the "doctor" left the room, and other beings helped Catherine up off the table and gave her back her clothes. One of them flew back with her to her car and helped her settle back into the driver's seat. She noticed then that the car door had remained open and that the car keys were on the dashboard. As she drove out of the forest, feeling quite groggy, she noted that it was 2:45 a.m.; forty-five minutes had passed. She arrived back at her house. The following morning as she watched the news broadcast on TV, she saw that it was about the very same UFO whose path coincided perfectly with the itinerary she had been guided to take.

Thanks to a friend, she contacted Dr. John Mack. At the end of his work with her, Dr. Mack understood that "For a long time Catherine had been thinking of her abduction experiences as dreams—abductions that she later came to understand as being real, even though she was in a state of consciousness different from ours."

ANALYSIS

1. Transported into another dimension:

As in the previous testimony given by Jerry, the abductions of Catherine took place through a closed door or window. Then, just like Jerry, she "flew off" with her kidnapper and "floated through the sky." This means that the body in which she found herself being taken away did not interact with ordinary matter and was not subject to the law of gravity. She was not in her habitual body made up of dense matter, but rather she was in a body made up of matter that was more subtle. As in the previous accounts, one can interpret these observations by putting forth the idea that the beings involved transformed her physical body by "dematerializing" it, or rather by transforming it—in order to modify its level of density to bring it to a more subtle level of density of matter.

This all seems to be confirmed by the fact that during this incident, Catherine was able to see perfectly without her contact lenses. She was therefore not in her habitual physical body. She found herself in a more subtle, etheric world and was able to see with her subtle body, which was not affected by the limitations of her ordinary physical body.

The fact that the procedures performed by the entities—procedures consisting of deeply inserting instruments inside the body without causing physical pain—seems to confirm this even further. It can in effect be understood that the absence of pain meant that there was no (or very little) mechanical interaction because the matter involved was much less dense—but still dense enough so as to produce the desired effect (in this case, the removal of a fetus from the uterus.

2. Telepathic communication:

As did Ed and Jerry in their previous accounts, Catherine said that the creature perfectly read her mind and did it so well that she didn't even need to ask it questions. The communication thus took place by telepathy, in particular when the being looked deep into her eyes.

3. An influence that took on different forms:

We have seen that Catherine had been under the influence of her captors in several ways both before and during the abduction:

She had been incited to take roads that she was totally unfamiliar with in order to enter a forest. This was perhaps so she would be outside the city in an isolated spot where the abduction could take place without any witnesses.

We notice also that she followed the same path as the UFO reported by the journalist. This can mean that the UFO was in contact with her as early as when she started driving her car, even though she was not aware of it.

The UFO (or the entity connected with it) was capable of progressively stopping the engine of her car.

The intense light that Catherine saw in the dead of night can also be attributed to the UFO.

The entity directly read Catherine's mind.

Catherine's body was used against her will for reproductive purposes.

The presence of the fetus in her uterus, which she was totally unaware of up until she was kidnapped, implies that there had been an insemination process several weeks prior that had occurred during another abduction, again unbeknown to her.

We realize from the above facts that Catherine had virtually no will of her own during this abduction. She was completely under the control of the entity connected to the UFO. She also understood that she had experienced other kidnappings throughout her life that she had often mistaken for dreams. She was completely vulnerable.

3. Total control over matter and space:

Catherine's observation of the dimensions of the room that had turned into a sort of amphitheater is very interesting. As incredible as it may seem, she noticed that the size of the room varied with her thoughts and that her thoughts were creating her very environment: to such an extent that it was capable of making a forest appear inside the room. Let us remember that matter created in this way is a subtle one, as is the entire UFO environment and the beings present with them. This signifies that the kidnappers have the ability to modify matter—either to render it more subtle or more dense—but also to modify space, which totally goes against the knowledge base of science as we know it.

Description of a "Typical Abduction"

The several examples cited prior show some of the characteristics of the abduction phenomenon. An analysis of these cases, conducted as objectively as possible and without being influenced by the limitations of our present scientific knowledge, leads us to conclude unequivocally that the victims had undergone a dimensional change, linked to the presence of the flying vessel (either visible or invisible). They found themselves in a parallel world. But each case is different. Let us now group together all the characteristics of the UFO abduction phenomenon.

General Considerations

Taking place at night—people who are "targeted" and "isolated":

From these several excerpts, as well as upon examination of a large number of known experiences of abductions, it appears that in a large majority of cases, the future victims are surprised during the night while in their beds. It is rare that abductions occur during the day. We can thus describe the general characteristics of these events in this way: a person of any age (even though most often this happens to young adults) is at home in bed, when their attention is drawn to an intense light of unexplained origin, and they feel a presence. They then see one or several short humanoid beings approach, and they suddenly feel paralyzed. Incapable of reacting, defending themselves, or even calling out for help, they are then consumed by a terrible anxiety.

There is also another rather frequent scenario: a person, either alone or in the presence of others, is driving on a deserted road when they see a bright light in the sky coming toward them. The light then becomes a flying vessel that stops and hovers above the car. The car motor suddenly stops and the person finds themselves incapable of reacting.

Taken through the air:

These people report being taken up into the air by small beings of humanoid appearance, and they pass unobstructed through walls, closed doors, or windows. In the case of a person kidnapped from their car, this could very well take place through the roof, but in Catherine's example, she went out through her open car door. While traveling through the air, they see their house or car from above before arriving at the aircraft and going inside. This vessel is described in general as being like a saucer or a disc that emits colored lights and whose shape and dimension can vary. Generally, the abduction victims encounter other strange beings performing different tasks inside the vessel.

The cases where a witness actually consciously observed a kidnapping without being kidnapped themselves are quite rare. It has nonetheless happened that certain witnesses noticed the physical absence of a victim during the time of the kidnapping.[16] This was the case in the kidnappings of Corporal Valdès and Jeff. More often, when a couple is visited while sleeping at night, the husband, for example, becomes as if "tuned out" and plunged into a deep sleep while his wife next to him is kidnapped— and quite frustrated at not managing to wake up her husband for help. But it has not been proven that the victim's material physical body actually leaves the bed. It is the same thing when a person is kidnapped from their car even though they are with someone.

Entirely unclothed and lying on a table:

Abducted people are brought into a room lit most often with white light. In the room there are shelves full of instruments and devices, and the atmosphere is cold and emotionless. They are then, without any explanation, entirely disrobed and made to lie down on an examination table. They are then subjected to a variety of exams of a medical or surgical nature, using instruments that seem very rudimentary. Samples are then taken of skin, blood, hair, and other bodily tissues.

A "doctor" oversees the procedures:

The creatures inside the vessels have a variety of appearances and can be either short or tall. The physique most often described is that of "gray" humanoids, measuring between 3' 4" and 4' tall. They have very thin chests, spindly limbs, and disproportionately large heads with respect to the rest of their bodies. The openings of the mouth, nose, and ears are barely perceptible, whereas their almond-shaped eyes are quite prominent. They correspond to the description of "extraterrestrials" found in popular culture. Sometimes there is one who is taller than the others and seems to be the one in charge, similar to a doctor surrounded by their nurses. Some accounts have reported that this "doctor" looks completely human, which can have somewhat of a reassuring effect on the victims.

The examinations are for the most part quite traumatizing because the victims are abducted against their will without being able to resist. Without any explanation, they are made to undergo procedures that have total disregard for their human dignity, and they are totally in the dark about why this is happening to them. The intensity of these traumas can vary based on the type of procedures carried out and the personal experience of the person abducted (some go through this several times).

Physical marks:

After their return to normal life, some abduction victims notice the presence of unexplained small marks, scars, or lesions on their bodies. They can also sometimes find that a small object had been inserted underneath the skin on any part of the body from head to toe. Several of these "implants" have been removed surgically and then rigorously analyzed, but these analyses remain inconclusive as to the composition of the implants (this will be explored later on in more detail).

Telepathy:

Communication does not always take place between abduction victims and their kidnappers, but when it does, it is through telepathy. The captors rarely give their victims any explanations, and when they do communicate, it is to let their victims know that they have nothing to fear and that no harm will be done to them.

The Primary Characteristic of the Abduction Phenomenon

Fulfillment of a procreative plan:

The essential characteristic of these abductions is that the procedures performed on the victims seem to fulfill a procreative goal between abducted humans—either men or women—and the humanoid kidnappers. As outlandish as it may seem, the accounts report that sperm specimens are often collected from men while they are lying on the examination table and that artificial inseminations are done on women, who in turn are abducted again several months later to have their embryo removed. During this phase of kidnapping, there is virtually no communication or explanation given, other than either to calm the victims or to praise them for their contribution. Examples show that these procedures can be carried out on teenagers, either male or female, as soon as they reach puberty, as was the case with Ed and Jerry. This type of reproductive act is a recurring theme in the abduction phenomenon. As inconceivable as it may seem, the purpose appears to be to create a hybrid species from humans and those who kidnap them.

The following observation of John Mack perfectly confirms this: "Sometimes obstetricians and gynecologists have observed that their patients manifest symptoms of pregnancy with positive test results only to discover that there is no fetus and that the symptoms have ceased." This is very significant because what has been reported seems so incredible that one can justifiably question their veracity.

Rows of glass jars:

Furthermore, during their time in the vessel, it is very common that embryos of humanoid appearance, lined up in glass jars—like incubators—are shown to abduction victims, and that small creatures similar to baby humanoids are placed in the arms of women. The women always find this quite difficult, because on the one hand they sense that these creatures—who on the outside look like real human babies and could be the result of cross-breeding between these nonhuman entities and humans—need their love and their maternal instinct inside a vessel where the atmosphere is devoid of "human warmth," and on the other hand the women realize that they have no control over when they will be able to see this "baby" or this hybrid "child" again, nor whether they will ever see them again at all. They can thus feel exploited as simple "brood mares."

Sometimes abducted children are encouraged to play with other "children" who could be hybrid creatures. These creatures always have a sickly, frail appearance and are lacking in vitality—somewhat "dull witted" as if mentally retarded. For example, when Catherine retrieved the memories of the abduction she had undergone when she was three, she remembered that she had been invited to play in the vessel with other children older than she was, and who seemed to be five or six years old. The game was to guide a metallic-looking ball using a stick with an antenna. In spite of her young age, she was much more able than the other, bigger children—which made them furious.[17]

Extremely traumatizing experiences:

These experiences are extremely traumatizing for the victims, both during the abduction and later on when they remember or retrieve their memories. Indeed, John Mack often had to emotionally support his patients with his presence and reassuring words while they relived the terrifying scenes of their abduction experiences.

But these experiences can have extremely powerful emotional repercussions even for those who learn of this reality without having lived through it themselves. These practices, resembling a sexual/reproductive plan with unknown entities, violently oppose human dignity as well as the deep-rooted belief that human beings are superior to all other living beings on Earth. As a result, the idea that men or women can be subjected to such treatments is inconceivable, and it is very difficult to accept that this is all for real. This is why victims of these abductions have such a hard time accepting the truth of their own experiences, and even more of a hard time sharing them with their loved ones without being taken for crazy or mentally ill. Furthermore, the majority of those who hear or read such accounts, despite their large number, are unable to believe them. The result is that very few people know about this phenomenon.

The Second Characteristic of the Abduction Phenomenon

Ecological preoccupations:

The second recurring theme of kidnappings into UFOs is that when the victims leave the examination table, they are often brought into another room where they are made to watch scenes of apocalyptic destruction juxtaposed with images of sublime beauty. Without it being said explicitly, the victims understand that this is information concerning the state of the earth and the relationship that humanity has with it. They are bombarded with information about the alarming state of the earth's ecology.

This phase of the abduction thus consists of a transfer of information from the kidnappers to their victims. The communication takes place either by

- the transmission of images projected on a screen,
- direct communication through the large mesmerizing eyes of the kidnappers (telepathy), or
- the kidnappers "taking" their victims to places on Earth that are either very beautiful or very polluted.

There can also be an encounter with one of the kidnappers who explains the responsibility of humankind for destroying the earth's ecosystems. At first the abductees feel a great chagrin, but they become more and more aware that they have been chosen to play an active part in the preservation of the earth. They understand how urgent it is to exact change in human society and that they themselves have a part of responsibility in this process.

Once back to normal life, some of these people are profoundly transformed by their experiences and become much more committed to ecology. Their mindset can shift and become more tolerant toward human behaviors. The victims then radically change their way of life and choose to work for environmental causes and organizations. They consider themselves as having been endowed with a mission, thus leading them to develop a positive outlook about their abduction.

A striking paradox:

One realizes that the paradoxical nature of the abduction phenomenon, emphasized in the introduction of this book, also appears in the contrast between its two characteristics.

- The first characteristic—a sexual/procreative plan—consists of a violation of human dignity and is profoundly disrespectful of its victims.
- The second characteristic has a pedagogical, even benevolent objective: to raise awareness of the necessity of respecting the earth's ecology and to participate in the protection of all its forms of life through consciousness of their interdependence. This appears to be motivated by kindness.

Such a paradox would suggest that the intelligence of the beings who commit the abductions, or at least their way of going about it, is quite different from human intelligence and the human way of life.

But it is possible to interpret this all differently by suggesting that since in the first characteristic we see that the kidnappers seem to have little respect for human beings and act out of their own interest, this could be the case in the second characteristic as well. In this hypothesis, it is also in the kidnappers' own interest that they incite their victims to better take care of the earth's ecological balances and better protect nature. This would signify that these beings are themselves dependent on nature, giving credence to the idea that they need this nature to live, meaning that they live in a parallel world—but attached to planet Earth—and like us humans, they too are terrien.

Return to Normal Life

When the procedures are finished, the kidnapping victims are quickly returned to their beds or their cars "as if nothing happened." But sometimes there are errors. Exceptionally, it has happened that certain victims have found themselves back in their beds nude, even though they had been wearing a pajama top or nightgown—and the missing piece of clothing is no longer found in the home. Or, the pajama was put back on the wrong way—the top put on as a bottom or vice versa—or they find themselves wearing something that is not theirs.[18] It has also happened that people abducted while on a road have found themselves back again at the wheel of their car, but on the other side of the road, or even dozens of miles farther away (this was the case of Barney and Betty Hill, noted in the appendix). These concrete elements show that "there was definitely something that happened," even though the victims' memories of the events had been erased.

After their return to normal life, the majority of abduction victims do not remember their abduction, or if they do, it is as if it all were a dream. They can, however, notice a period of time that was unaccounted for in their schedule—of one, two, or three hours in general—which makes them think that something unusual did happen. Also, they feel unusually tired upon awakening.

They are psychologically perturbed, with troubled sleep, recurring dreams, and sometimes excruciating headaches. They may then feel the need to consult a psychotherapist or psychiatrist, and their memories may come back up into their conscious mind through hypnosis or deep relaxation.

But 20 to 30 percent of kidnapping victims (according to Marie-Thérèse de Brosses[9]) recall their abduction scene perfectly. These people are quick to realize that they had been treated with no respect at all: abducted by force by strange creatures and taken to an unknown place where they are made to undergo invasive, humiliating procedures akin to rape. They then live in constant fear of having to go through the same nightmare again. Furthermore, it is difficult for them to share their experiences—experiences so unbelievable that they themselves are not sure that they really happened. They suffer from solitude and isolation, thus finding themselves excluded from society.

John Mack found that those who reported having abduction experiences were suffering from posttraumatic stress disorder similar to those who have come back from war or who have been raped. This indicated that they had experienced something very real, since dreams or hallucinations cannot cause this type of pathology.

Victims who had either kept or retrieved the memory of their kidnappings frequently express that they had been brought into another dimension or another plane of reality that has different properties. They generally know that even though their abduction experiences are as real as the world they perceive with their ordinary state of consciousness, these experiences nonetheless are happening in a totally different reality. One of the characteristics of this reality—when one is in it *or* forced into it—is the different perception of time, space, and dimensions.

The Implant Issue

After abductions, some victims discover the presence of small, solid objects inside their bodies that had been placed under the skin without them knowing it. The location of these implants can vary greatly. They have been found in an ear lobe, a nose, a jaw, a thumb, a leg, a foot, and even in a penis. The nature of these implants and their function remains a mystery to us. In some cases, they have been surgically removed and analyzed.

First Account

Whitley Strieber had many close encounters with nonhuman beings through the abductions he experienced, and he wrote about them in a book. In May 1994, he discovered that there was an object embedded in the auricle of his left ear. He recounts that "Sometimes it would emit a strange sound that was both intense and raspy. At the same time my ear would get hot and become beet red. I became more than ever before sensitive to electrical activity. Often traffic lights would go out when I went past them, either by car or on foot, or electrical equipment would either come on or go out when I entered a room."[19]

"I couldn't stop worrying about my implant. Sometimes while I was plunged in meditation, it would go off with its unpleasant screeching, ruining my ability to concentrate. I felt my ear getting hotter and hotter."

"Finally, in May 1998, I decided that I could no longer put up with having this implant in my ear. This is when I met Dr. John Lerma, who agreed to operate on me." Whitley Strieber goes on to tell about the operation: "First, Dr. Lerma situated the implant in the upper part of the auricle of my left ear. He found that it had been firmly fixed in place. . . . He was able to remove some of the object that he described as being a 'white disc.' When he touched this white disc with his scalpel, something strange and unexpected happened. He noticed that it ceased being solidly attached to the cartilage of my ear[,] as it had been before he made the incision. He said that the object moved—as if it was trying to avoid contact with the scalpel. When he touched it again, this time by grabbing it, he got a stronger reaction. The object moved twenty-five mm away from the incision site.

"After all of this, the surgeon concluded that it would be imprudent to try to remove this implant and he closed up the incision. One week after the operation attempt, the implant moved back to its original location."

Whitley Strieber makes the following comment: "Someone made these implants. Someone wanted to insert them and dared enter defenseless peoples' rooms in order to do so. Mine had been put underneath the skin without even the slightest visible remnant of a scar. Many other cases are similar: there is no trace of incision. In other cases, there are small scars which are evidence of extreme concentration during the operation. Implants are for real."[20]

COMMENTARY

Implants controlled by an outside intelligence:

According to the surgeon, even though the implant had been "solidly attached to the cartilage" before the operation, it moved—a relatively large distance of twenty-five mm—"as if it was trying to avoid contact with the scalpel." Several days after the operation was abandoned, the implant went back to its original spot. Such movement can seem stupefying.

When an object reacts this way to the gestures of the surgeon, it does not behave like an ordinary object, which would have remained inert. Furthermore, its movement is not haphazard; it is obviously a reaction to what the surgeon is doing, and manages to trouble the surgeon so much that he abandons the operation. The object seems to be imbued with an independent intelligence. One can easily fathom that such behavior would appear outlandish and impossible in the eyes of a surgeon, as it would to any rational mind.

The Analyses of Dr. Roger Leir

Doctor and surgeon Roger K. Leir is known for his surgical removal of a dozen or so implants of unknown origin. He published his accounts in a book titled *Alien Implants*.[21] Whitley Strieber fittingly wrote the preface. In the book, Roger K. Leir admits putting his finger on one of the most mind-boggling discoveries in the area of applied UFO research.

Strange physical changes:

Before performing implant extractions, Dr. Leir very carefully studied all the literature available on the subject but found very little information. He read that the rare cases where implants were successfully removed involved strange ulterior transformations, making it impossible to analyze the objects after their removal. There were testimonies describing how these objects, after being extracted by surgeons, transformed themselves into powder, liquid, or gas.

These testimonies confirmed that the implants were not inert, as would be expected of ordinary material objects. The physical changes that were observed of these implants—solid objects becoming powder, liquid, or gas—were spontaneously impossible according to science. These transformations conveyed the fact that the objects were subject to other laws than those of science. Even if this was not expressed by Dr. Leir or his colleagues, everything happened as if an exterior, invisible intelligence acted on the implants in order to surprise and baffle the researchers.

The absence of inflammatory reactions:

Another cause of Dr. Leir's stupefaction was that when he performed his first analyses of extracted implants, he noticed that the samples of soft tissue surrounding the foreign objects showed no signs of inflammation. Medical science holds that it is impossible to introduce a foreign substance into the body without the body reacting to it. Indeed, our system is such that it naturally defends itself against any foreign substance by producing inflammation. An example of this is when organ transplants are performed; the only way this is possible is to administer drugs that prevent the body from rejecting the donor's organ by stopping the natural reaction of the immune system.

The analyses that Dr. Leir performed afterward allowed him to explain what appeared to be an aberration: the analyses revealed that the implants were surrounded by a membrane made up of other materials, including skin. But we know that the human body is not capable of generating skin anywhere else than on its external surface. Yet, this tissue around the implant was found internally, and it is thanks to its presence that there was no foreign-body reaction. This "explanation" leads us to another question, about the human body's intelligence being incapable of creating skin inside the body: What was the other intelligence that made this possible?

Analyses of implants:

The analyses performed on implants by Dr. Leir after their removal to determine their chemical makeup rendered mixed results. He noted that one of them "contained mostly iron" (except for one sample), calcium (except for another sample), and copper (again, except for another sample). In other words, the diversely colored areas and different textures of the same implant contained elements in different concentrations. A sample of this implant also contained aluminum, and another sample of it contained barium.[22]

"Another sample that consisted of a combination of fragments coming from three other samples contained metals and rare soils such as europium, ruthenium, and samarium. These simple chemical elements cannot be found in their natural state and can be obtained only in laboratories, reinforcing our conviction that these objects had definitely been manufactured."[23]

Even though there were only five elements present in large concentrations in the implants of three different people—copper, calcium, iron, barium, and aluminum—they were not all present in every single sample. There were also other elements present in smaller concentrations. This was the case with magnesium, manganese, lead, nickel, silicon, sodium, and zinc.

Commentary

We immediately see the complexity of these results and how impossible it is to arrive at a clear conclusion. The presence of rare chemical elements, nonexistent in their natural state, reinforces the idea that an outside intelligence was indeed at work, an intelligence outside nature and human beings.

We can justifiably ask ourselves if the large diversity of samples and the large differences between one sample and another are not the result of a determination on the part of this outside intelligence to throw off researchers and create confusion in their findings. We have indeed seen that this intelligence had the ability to modify the physical state of the samples. It acted on matter in such a way that is totally beyond human comprehension.

Other analyses of implants:

Dr. Leir also noted: "The metallurgical analyses have for now provided us with the following information: the object in the form of a T is composed of two small metallic rods. The horizontal part of the T contains a form of iron that is harder than the hardest of carbon steel." This fact about the level of hardness again confirms the extent of mastery over matter that the entities who manufactured these implants possess.

Analysis of another implant:

"I suggested that we examine the magnetic properties of the object[,] and I placed a small magnet about four inches away from it. I was surprised to see that the metallic object started to quiver. As I moved the magnet closer to the object, it started to move. At around two inches away from it, I could, by using only the magnet, make the object trace a complete 360° circle without any physical contact. We all agreed that it had to be strongly magnetized and most certainly contained iron.

"Then the metallic object was delivered to a laboratory in San Antonio to be analyzed. When Whitley called me with the first results, he informed me that the conclusions were stupefying. He explained that the analysis was performed using X-Ray [*sic*] diffraction. The procedure was as follows: the sample is wrapped in a radiation-sensitive film and then exposed to a controlled beam of X-rays. The images obtained after exposure to the X-rays are visible circles on the film after being developed. This data is then entered into a computerized database and the computer algorithm identifies the chemical elements found. This allows us to discover the nature of the material contained in the sample.

"But in this case, the computer could not interpret the data. The researchers were so surprised that they doubted the accuracy of their measurements and decided to do the analysis over again—not only once, but fourteen times. They also did tests on the computer to make sure that it was functioning properly. Each time they tried to analyze the implant they got the same result: the substance it was made up of could not be determined. What did all of this mean? Logically, this could signify that the sample's atomic structure was not well organized, indicating that it was made of a simple amorphous mass. But how could we admit this when it exhibited all of the properties of magnetic iron?"[24]

COMMENTARY

These tests conducted using x-ray diffraction led to absurd conclusions because they contradicted the preliminary tests done using a simple magnet. Once again, we realize that this implant did not obey the known laws of science, since the analyses performed using x-ray diffraction did not allow us to form a conclusion about the implant's chemical makeup.

This all needs to be considered in light of the preceding results, which showed that this chemical composition varied from one sample to another and from one piece of a sample to another. The results even seemed to reveal the presence of chemical elements that do not exist in their natural state. In such conditions, Dr. Roger Leir was unable to come to a clear conclusion, and it seems that no other researcher has been able to do better. Everything really happened as if an outside intelligence came into play every time to interrupt the flow of the research and to confuse and disorient the researchers.

At the end of this first chapter, where we have put forth the issue of abductions of human beings into UFOs with their principal characteristics, several questions persist:

- Who are these kidnappers who allow themselves to treat human beings in such a way? What is their nature and where do they come from?
- What are their motives and what are their goals, even though at the outset all of this seems inconceivable?
- But in order to broaden our knowledge of this mind-boggling phenomenon and thus answer these questions more easily, we need to ask another question: Are these abductions uniquely related to our time or did they also exist in the past?

CHAPTER TWO

PREOCCUPATION WITH THE FUTURE OF THE EARTH: A PERSISTENT, COMMON DENOMINATOR IN UFO PHENOMENA

We have seen that the phenomenon of abductions into UFOs as it has been known since 1960 possesses two very specific characteristics. As mentioned before,

1. a sexual/reproductive plan whose objective is to create a hybrid species, and
2. awareness-raising about the serious threats to the earth, with apocalyptic images of a devastated planet as if after a nuclear war.

Let us first examine this second characteristic. The information received by the abduction victims includes images of apocalyptic landscapes where they see the earth devastated by planetary ecological disasters that bring to mind nuclear war. The kidnappers are visibly quite preoccupied by the serious problems of pollution and destruction of nature. But such preoccupations have also been present in UFO appearances since the middle of the twentieth century, even in the absence of abductions.

UFOs Preoccupied by Nuclear Power

Official Declassified Documents

The UFO phenomenon is very old; images of flying saucers abound in drawings, sculptures, and texts going as far back as ancient times. But it has been observed that UFO appearances have been on the rise since the end of the Second World War, and this increase is clearly associated with the development of nuclear technology.[1] Indeed, several statistical studies have revealed that as soon as the first nuclear research was being performed in the 1940s, UFOs started to appear more often near nuclear installations than in any other area. They appeared mostly near research laboratories or manufacturing plants, but also near silos stocking nuclear arms and nuclear energy plants. In spite of the little information that has been communicated on this subject by political and military authorities, who enforced secrecy, as well as the heads of the companies concerned, the large number of known sightings has led us to understand that these appearances signified that the intelligences linked to the UFOs were greatly concerned about the dangers of nuclear energy.

Most of this information comes from the United States, thanks to officers or technicians who upon leaving the army had the courage to reveal to the public the events they had witnessed directly throughout their active duty, and for which they were held to secrecy. It is also thanks to a law that allowed for a large number of formerly *top secret* documents from the US Air Force, the FBI, and the CIA to be declassified. Because of their official nature, these documents are undeniable evidence of the reality of UFOs and the appearances of these objects near nuclear installations. They also reveal that political, military, and civil authorities alike were extremely concerned about the repeated appearances of objects whose nature and origin were unknown to them.

Thus, according to these numerous eyewitness accounts and documents, not only were UFO appearances quite persistent above nuclear installations, but they were visibly trying to attract the attention of people by their often-quite-spectacular maneuvers. Even if these objects were still completely a mystery, one could see in their presence and behavior a meaning: to warn us and alarm us about the use of nuclear power. Yet, political and military authorities have always refused to take these warnings into account. They have done everything in their power to cover up the reality of UFOs and keep it from the public; they have done nothing to change their plans for the development of nuclear arms. Whether it be Soviets or Americans, they continued on with the manufacturing of nuclear arsenals, and even the end of the Cold War did not bring about any change in this situation.

Deactivated Nuclear Missiles

This provoked a reaction. In the 1960s, UFO activity went to a higher level: several times nuclear missiles were deactivated while in their silos, right under the noses of the military personnel who were constantly watching over them in order to ensure their functionality at any moment, but never were they destroyed. This seems to reveal that the UFOs' objective is to clearly show that they (or the intelligences linked to them) are opposed to the use of nuclear technology and that they have the capacity to materially intervene by using means that are largely beyond those of humans. But the UFOs nonetheless have always respected the free will of humans and have never forcibly intervened to destroy the nuclear weapons or the nuclear plants.

In spite of their spectacular demonstrations of superior capabilities, the UFOs didn't seem to intend to do anything to thwart the activities of the engineers and military personnel. The leaders of the nuclear powers therefore continued with their plans for the development and manufacture of more and more powerful and sophisticated nuclear arms—fueled by a clear determination not to let themselves be dominated or influenced by unknown, nonhuman intelligences.

UFOs Intervene at Chernobyl

But at the Chernobyl nuclear power plant on April 26, 1986, it was proven that nuclear technology is really a technology of death and potentially devastating for the entire planet. Following a series of maneuvers where engineers had lost control of the nuclear reactor and where the reaction of nuclear fission went out of control, it was established that the necessary physical conditions were all in place to produce what would have been a real nuclear explosion creating a gigantic atomic mushroom cloud.[2] It was also established from several convergent pieces of evidence that if this explosion did not happen, it was thanks to the immediate action of one or several UFOs that arrived on the scene. The UFOs took their own measures, measures well beyond human capabilities, to prevent such a cataclysm. There was an initial explosion in the machine room, followed by a series of explosions and fires over the next ten days until the site was completely ravaged, but there had not been a nuclear explosion strictly speaking . . . with an atomic mushroom cloud.

The Chernobyl disaster was nonetheless the biggest industrial tragedy of all time. It would have been even more disastrous—beyond measure— if the UFOs had not intervened. All of Europe and a large part of Asia would have been devastated and rendered uninhabitable for thousands of years. The consequences of an excessive level of radioactivity would have been horrendous in terms of the number of deaths on these continents but would have also affected the other forms of life there and would have destroyed the ecological balances for thousands of years to come. But hardly anyone knows of these facts; they have remained hidden by the authorities, even though their authenticity has been confirmed by several independent, irrefutable pieces of evidence. For more details, one can refer to a study found in another book.[3]

One can see here in the connection between UFO appearances and nuclear power plants the extreme preoccupation these intelligences have concerning ecological issues, which is also recurrent in the abduction phenomena. This shows that the preoccupation with ecological problems is not limited to the intelligences behind these abductions but is a concern that is also shared by the intelligences connected to UFO appearances in general.

This observation leads us to suspect that there is a link between the intelligences behind the abductions of human beings into UFOs, and the intelligences connected with UFO phenomena in general. This would seem natural at first glance, but it is worth noting that the abductions take place on board flying vessels, described as flying saucers, although the majority of sightings of unidentified flying object involve luminous objects, some of which appear as material objects that change form.

UFOs Concerned about Pollution

A statistical study published in 2015 by three French university professors and using French documents showed that UFOs appear most often not only near nuclear installations, as we have just seen as being the case in the United States, but also above areas where nature has been severely damaged by pollution.[4]

To contribute to the existing data related to UFO appearances, these researchers used the database of GEIPAN—an organization devoted to the study of unidentified aerospace phenomena—which collected all the "type D" unidentified aerospace phenomena from the last sixty years in France. Type Ds are those phenomena that could not be accounted for by any rational explanation and can truly be referred to as "unidentified phenomena": another label used for UFOs.

The data concerning nuclear activity was taken from the site of the association Sortir du Nucléare (Abandon Nuclear Power). Two hundred nuclear plants were counted, essentially nuclear energy plants, plants for the exploitation of uranium, and plants devoted to the treatment and storage of nuclear waste.

The study led to the following conclusions:

Conclusion 1: "The connection between the nuclear activities and the type D phenomena—which had been suspected for a long time—has now been measured and it appears to be surprisingly high."[5] The researchers measured the statistical significance of this connection as having a p value (calculated probability) of 0.00013 (a p value is never greater than one, and the smaller the number, the higher the correlation).

Conclusion 2: "We also discovered that there was a strong correlation between type D phenomena and contaminated sites." The p value of 0.00542 was not as small as it was for the nuclear sites, but it was still quite significant. The data concerning this variable was taken from the website of the French government's Ministry of Ecology. At the end of 2007, this ministry counted 3,985 sites that were contaminated by industrial pollution. These sites represented risks both for health and the environment to such an extent that the French government took corrective action.

The other variables that were used in this statistical study—such as the density of the population, the number of airports, the percentage of swampland (which influences the amount of humidity), the percentage of forests, and the amount of sunshine—turned out to be insignificant, with a higher p value between 0.07 and 0.30.

This statistical study shows irrefutably that the frequency of UFO appearances is not only greater near nuclear plants, but also above sites that—more so than other areas of the country—have been severely polluted by diverse industrial activity. UFO flights over these sites are sometimes deliberately conspicuous: we can remember a wave of UFO appearances above practically all the nuclear plants in France during the months between the end of 2014 and the beginning of 2015. At that time, the UFO reality was not being officially recognized, and the flights over the nuclear plants—something forbidden—were attributed to drones. But the uncontrolled "drones" had never been shot down or captured, and no photographs were ever published.

Through their insistence in hovering over polluted sites, the intelligences connected with UFOs have clearly shown us their preoccupation with all forms of pollution generated by human activity. This preoccupation is therefore not unique to the entities who kidnap human beings into UFOs, but seems to be shared by the intelligences connected to UFOs in general.

Another Form of Manifestation

The nature of UFOs is still a mystery to us today. The extraterrestrial hypothesis is a very popular one, but it has never been proven, and a number of researchers have pointed out its incoherencies. A study was published in 2016 by the author of this current work in which he put forth the interpretation that these unidentified flying objects are not necessarily of extraterrestrial origin but rather are interdimensional manifestations.[6] This study drew upon several sources of knowledge left behind by science.

According to the conclusions of this study, the UFOs are manifested by beings who live on Earth with humans, but in another dimension: they are called nature beings or elementals. These beings are attached to the elements that compose nature, and according to ancient and spiritual knowledge, nature would not exist were it not for them. This is why they suffer from the extensive pollution that humans inflict on nature. One can therefore understand that they feel compelled to show themselves in order to remind humans that they exist—humans who have not only forgotten their existence but who are destroying their environment. This analysis and this interpretation will be developed further in chapter 6.

An Urgency to Respect the Earth

In light of this interpretation, one can understand that these nature beings (attached to the earth as we humans are) are trying through all possible means to communicate to humans to help them become aware of the multiple degradations they are inflicting on nature and the necessity to respect nature.

We have seen that the abductions of humans seem to be a way to make us aware of this fact, and deliberately conspicuous UFO flights over polluted sites are another.

But the reality today is that humans are not taking these manifestations seriously, since the reports are kept from the public, and pollution and degradation of all kinds are continuing and even intensifying.

It is in these conditions that a new "channel" seems to have been set up by these nature beings in recent years to try to get through to humans in another way.

A New Channel for Reaching Humankind

It so happens that the author of this book was recently contacted by a person named Christiane, who, since 2014, has been receiving messages that come through in the form of automatic writing. She noticed that these writings seemed to be teachings aimed at saving the earth, and she has been encouraged by the messengers to make them known by publishing them. It is likely that others are also receiving similar messages, but they have not come forth.

Automatic writing is considered to be a spirit technique, meaning that the person who does it has psychic-medium abilities and comes in contact with a spirit who dictates a text to them. In the case of Christiane, she points out that it is always the spirits who come to her and not the other way around. Once in a while, she finds herself suddenly in a hypnotic state, nearly asleep. During these moments, she no longer controls her thoughts and can say and do things that she has absolutely no recollection of. She communicates with these spirits by telepathy and writes what they dictate; her hand is "guided" although her consciousness is as if "disconnected." When she comes to and discovers the content of what she has written, she strongly feels the need to share it.

It can be said that the spirits who manifest themselves during these writing sessions live in another world, a nonmaterial parallel world. Automatic writing is therefore also an interdimensional manifestation. The objective is the same for these spirits who are manifesting themselves to Christiane through automatic writing as it is for those behind the kidnappings into UFOs; that is, to raise human awareness about the necessity to "save" the earth. We can then think that the spirits belong to the same world and are perhaps of the same nature. The fact that this new "channel" has been opened in recent years seems to emphasize the urgency to convey to humans the idea of respect for nature and for the earth.

Concerning the nature and identity of the beings behind abductions into UFOs, the comparison with this spirit technique leads us to think that they are spirits: supernatural beings connected to the earth. They are naturally present in a parallel, invisible world but have the ability to act in the material world of humans. This description relates to elemental beings. We will come back to this in chapter 6.

CHAPTER THREE

ABDUCTIONS AND MATING: ANCIENT, WIDESPREAD PRACTICES

Let us turn now to the first characteristic of the phenomenon of kidnapping into UFOs as it has been known since the 1960s; that is, the implementation of a sexual/reproductive plan whose apparent objective is to create a hybrid species.

Already in Antiquity

Even though little is known about this in our day, it seems that the practice of mating men and women with nonhuman entities has existed throughout human history. These practices were already present in the Greek and Roman myths of pre-Christian days, myths describing the actions of supernatural beings known as satyrs, fauns, lamias, et al. And we know that myths, like legends—even if they have undergone change over the course of time—are based on reality.

The satyrs of Greek mythology are described as being half-man, half-goat hybrid creatures with a human body, horns, and ram hooves. They are often represented nude in a state of sexual arousal. The reputation of their lustful behavior explains that in modern language, the term "satyr" refers to a man obsessed with sex who brutally abuses women. The fauns of Roman mythology are also licentious, libidinous beings.

Incubi and Succubae of Medieval Times

After the rise of Christianity, numerous texts refer to sexual relations between women and entities called incubi, and between men and entities called succubae. The Catholic Church considered these entities as demons, or supernatural beings. These entities were nonhuman but nevertheless had the ability to mate with humans and incite them to engage in intercourse with them by arousing their sexual tendencies. One must of course examine these texts by laying aside, for the time being, scientific considerations, which hold that sexual union between humans and nonhumans is impossible. The church naturally condemned these sexual acts.

Diverse Testimonies of High-Ranking Ecclesiastical Authorities

In the fifth century, Saint Augustine, bishop of Hippon, (a city in Algeria known today as Annaba) wrote in his book *The City of God*: "It is a widely held opinion, confirmed by direct or indirect testimonies of people of good faith, that sylphs and fauns, ordinarily called incubi, have often tormented women, soliciting them and obtaining relations with them. There are even demons called *dusii* (meaning "elves") by the Gauls, who have frequently engaged in such impure practices. This is supported by authorities so numerous and high-ranking that it would be imprudent to deny it."[1] It is interesting to note that Saint Augustine made an explicit connection between sylphs and fauns—nature spirits—and incubi, in keeping with the terminology used at the time. Many other accounts are similar.

In the seventh century, Saint Isadore, archbishop of Seville, in his work titled *Origins*, where he quotes Pope Gregory I, explains, "Incubus comes from the expression 'lie down on,' meaning 'to rape.' Indeed, often incubi are attracted to women and lie on them. The entity known commonly as incubus, the Romans refer to as 'faun with figs.'"[2] Thus, incubi are described as mysterious beings who abuse women and who are related to the fauns of Roman mythology. These two excerpts suggest there is an analogy and a continuity between the practices of satyrs and fauns of the Greek and Roman civilizations and the practices of the incubi and succubae of the Middle Ages.

In the eighth century, Saint John of Damascus wrote, "Some, who are more ignorant, recount that witches, also called 'geloudes,' are women who travel through the air. Barred by neither locks nor barriers, they penetrate into homes through closed doors, and kill children there by sucking their blood. Others affirm that these women entered houses through closed doors, either in both body and soul, or in spirit only."[3]

A comparison is warranted here between these "witches" and the entities of our day who, before abducting their victims into a UFO, also penetrate into their rooms at night through closed doors or windows. In the above text, these entities are called witches. They are thus considered as women who have taken on supernatural powers. For the reader of today, this ability to fly through the air and penetrate into houses through closed doors suggests that these are not women but, rather, supernatural beings.

Stories of incubi and succubae: Jean Sider has gathered together several references of little-known ancient works that recount stories of incubi and succubae. He wrote: "Before the bloody repression of witchcraft practices began as early as the fourteenth century, all of the countries of Western Europe had integrated incubi and succubae into their respective folklores for a long time. But popular traditions, not yet influenced by the excessive fanaticism of inquisitors obsessed with the very active pagan cults in their lands, spoke only of fairies and malicious, playful country spirits. The mentalities of illiterate populations had not yet been permeated by the demons that were being chased by theologians."[4]

Jean Sider therefore explicitly makes the connection between the entities referred to as incubi and succubae by the Catholic Church and the entities of popular traditions known before as fairies or country spirits. The ufologist Jacques Vallée also wrote that "the study of folklore is full of accounts of abductions by objects from the sky, of mixed marriages with light beings, and theories about the genetic and racial motivations of these beings."[5]

We will see later on that several sociological studies have indeed established that among the rural populations of the Celtic regions in particular, it was well known that mysterious abductions of human beings were carried out by fairies. Depending on the countries and the regions, a large number of different names were given to these fairies. In France, we can cite the names of lutins, follets, and lamignacs (from the Basque country), all of which had the reputation of kidnapping pretty girls.

A Pope Expresses His Apprehension

All of these little beings from country folklore were very early on considered as demonic by Catholic authorities, who referred to them as incubi and succubae. The papal bull *Summis Desiderantes Affectibus*, issued in 1484 by Pope Innocent VIII, warns against witchcraft. In one of its paragraphs it states: "We have recently learned for certain, and not without extreme chagrin, that in certain parts of northern Germany, as well as in the provinces, cities, territories, localities, and dioceses of Mainz, Cologne, Trier, Salzburg, and Bremen, that a certain number of people of either sex, forgetting their own salvation and straying from the Catholic faith, are giving themselves to the demons incubi and succubae, who, through their incantations, subsequently destroy the fruit inside of the women."[6]

This way of expressing things seems to mean that the sexual relations between incubi and women resulted in pregnancies that were then terminated, where the women would lose their fetuses. This resembles the current accounts of women who, during an abduction incident into a UFO, realized they had been pregnant when their pregnancies were terminated inside a UFO.

The fact that a pope and other ecclesiastical high dignitaries would publicly denounce manifestations of incubi and succubae numerous times over the course of the centuries clearly indicates that these sexual practices were relatively common in Europe and posed a problem in medieval society. Many great thinkers, jurists, and theologians focused on this serious issue in the fifteenth and sixteenth centuries, and their works are full of information.

Witch Hunt

In 1486, the first edition of the book *Malleus Maleficum* or *The Witches' Hammer*[7] was printed. This book was to become the reference for witch hunters in all of Europe, in spite of it being banned in 1490 by the Catholic Church. The first part of this book deals with the nature of witchcraft. Women, because of their weakness and "inferior" intelligence, are, by their very nature, predisposed to succumbing to the temptations of Satan. The authors of the book emphasized the licentious nature of the sexual relations that witches had with demons.

This witch hunt swept Europe for over two centuries, up until the 1680s, leaving a considerable number of victims in its wake. The only way to understand the belief in witchcraft is to delve deep into ancient mentalities. In this cultural context of the Middle Ages, nature was considered to be filled with supernatural forces, and a human being could, through invocations or rituals, make these forces do their bidding, either for good or for evil. In the latter case (evil), the witch or warlock was considered a criminal and thus arrested and sentenced as such. But the nature of these supernatural forces remained a mystery.

Witchcraft is associated with the ceremony of the Sabbath, where witches and warlocks would gather at night in an isolated place after traveling through the air (according to ancient beliefs, on a broomstick). The ceremony consisted of a banquet and supposedly was topped off by a so-called general orgy where the warlocks would have intercourse with the succubae and the witches would have intercourse with the incubi. Witchcraft, which had haunted mentalities for a long period in Europe, was therefore closely linked to the idea that men or women could have and maintain sexual relations with entities that were not well identified: entities known as incubi or succubae.

DEBATE ABOUT THE EXISTENCE OF INCUBI

In 1489, Ulrich Molitor, in his *De Lamiis et Pythonicis Mulieribus*[8] ("Witches and visionary women"), denied the existence of incubi and succubae: "It does not seem possible that the devil, acting as a succubae with a man, can gather seeds and then transmit them, acting as an incubus, to a woman." He thought that the woman was impregnated by the man and that there were no other entities who could mate with them. For him, the witchcraft phenomenon was a figment of the imagination. Judging from this, one can see that the debate around the existence or not of sexual relations between human beings and nonhuman beings—whether they be called demons, incubi, or succubae—is hardly a recent one.

Tangible Evidence

EVEN IN CONVENTS, WITH TANGIBLE TRACES

The following significant information dates from the time of the Inquisition: Alphonse de Spina, in his *Fortalicum Fidei* (1467), wrote that "Nuns are particularly vulnerable to these demon incubi. When they wake up in the morning, they find themselves soiled as if they had been with a man."[9] The existence of this text seems to affirm that these observations of material traces were common and that sexual relations with mysterious entities were quite real.

ANOTHER TESTIMONY

Johannes Klein, in his work titled *Meditation Academica Exhibens Juridicum Judicialis* (1731), expounds extensively on the possibility of offspring born of mating between humans and demons: "A woman had two children spawned by a demon. After the birth of the first child, she was put in prison. During her incarceration, she claimed that the demon came back to rape her and she again found herself pregnant. But the demon took her second child from her when it was still inside her. Moist traces of uterine debris as if following a birth were found both on her clothes and on the prison cell floor, but the baby had disappeared."[10]

Here again, this testimony is very similar to the testimonies of women of our time who have been abducted into UFOs. In the text above, not only is it stated that this woman found herself pregnant while isolated in a prison cell, but that her pregnancy had been terminated and material traces of a birth had been found, which supports the veracity of this story.

During a trial in 1698, this same author pointed out that a woman had been impregnated by an incubus looking like her husband, who had been dead for a long time. This is not an isolated case. Other incidents of this kind can be seen in specialized literature.

A Study of Incubi and Succubae

A study titled "Incubi and succubae" was published in 1897 by Jules Delassus.[11] Here one can read: "Boethius, in his history of Scotland, reports that a young man was tempted by a ravishingly beautiful succubus. It penetrated into his home through the doors and walls and did everything it could to possess him. But the young, virtuous man sought out his bishop[,] whose spiritual remedies delivered him. Quite often, the demon would take on the form of a beloved in order to reach its prey more easily." This point is very important; it seems to show that the succubus can take on the form of any human being (including that of a person who is deceased).

This account equally shows that it is sometimes possible to resist the assaults of incubi and succubae. "In order to chase away impure spirits, the most[-]effective weapons are blessings, exorcisms, the sacraments, and especially the sign of the cross and the Hail Mary."

The same author wrote: "Among the northern peoples of Iceland and Norway and in Scotland, we find similar traditions. Trolls and elves very often mate with the sons and daughters of men. Elves live in the elements: clouds, rocks, caves, streams, or the sea. Their daughters, in spite of their blue skin, are incredibly beautiful." Thus, according to Jules Delassus, the peoples of the North explicitly attribute the mysterious unions of men and women to nature spirits—these supernatural beings who live in nature. The "incredible beauty" of their daughters implies that these nature beings can take on a human appearance.

He continues: "In the nineteenth century, the characteristics of incubi and succubae have changed very little, and the cases involving them seem less frequent or, rather, are not as well known. Science, which disdains the occult, sees these things observed by doctors as only sexual diseases and does not look for the causes behind them. It is nearly only the priests who know of these particular examples. But they hide behind their confessional secret and refuse to speak, fearing the scandal that such revelations could cause."

Concerning the interpretation of this phenomenon: "Cabalists see only the work of elemental spirits. Theologians with their devils and cabalists with their elementals agreed with each other in theory, but as early as the Middle Ages and the Renaissance, the learned had cast doubt on the objective reality of these phenomena.

"Modern theologians claim that an active apparition has no objective reality. It is purely subjective; the sexual arousal comes from the nerve centers and not from outside the body."[12]

A Permanent Recurrence in Europe

The researcher Jean Sider wrote: "In the past, the European country fairies would abduct young women in order, it was believed, to serve as spouses or concubines for male entities. Others, who were wet nurses, were captured so that they could feed and coddle the babies of the fairies who apparently had a galaxy. These accounts from popular traditions, abounding in specialized literature, indicate a permanent recurrence of the theme of abductions throughout Europe—from the Middle Ages up to the dawn of the Industrial Revolution. Folklorists had always judged that these stories came straight out of the fertile imagination of rural populations to spice up their long winter evenings around the fire. Yet one can find again the thread of these so-called 'wives' tales in the work of Dr. Jacobs and many other specialists on the subject of abductions taking place in our time."[13] This is what we have also seen in the several examples of case studies in chapter 1.

These supernatural forces or beings have thus been manifesting themselves throughout history. But their names have changed over time. They have been successively called satyrs or fauns; incubi or succubae; demons, sylphs, and elves; nature spirits or elementals. Are these the extraterrestrials of today—to whom we attribute abductions into UFOs? We will come back to this in chapters 5 and 6.

An Incubus Infatuated with a Lady of the Renaissance

The following is a very detailed account of acts attributed to an incubus and was the object of an in-depth study done by a high-ranking ecclesiastical authority in the second half of the seventeenth century, Ludovicus Maria Sinistrari. He reported it in his manuscript titled *De Daemonialitate, et Incubis, et Succubis.*[14] Ludovicus Maria Sinistrari was an illustrious scholar who entered the Franciscan order in 1647. He dedicated his life to teaching philosophy and theology in Pavia, Italy. He also served as advisor for the Council of the Supreme Inquisition and as theologian under the archbishop of Milan. In 1688, he presided over the revision of all the statutes of the Franciscan order. L. M. Sinistrari was therefore one of the highest authorities on human psychology and religious law at the service of the seventeenth-century Catholic Church. His testimony is priceless, and this is why he is widely quoted by ufologist Jacques Vallée in his work *Passport to Magonia.*[15]

It is perhaps useful to mention beforehand the warning found at the beginning of this current work: *The readers of this book are encouraged not to let themselves be put off by the implausibility of the numerous events recounted here in the testimonies and descriptions of these phenomena. These accounts are indeed unbelievable from a scientific perspective and may seem more like far-out stories, and yet, the large number of testimonies coming from a great diversity of sources renders it very difficult for anyone to seriously doubt them. They are for real. The study of these phenomena invites us to question the validity of what we currently know and understand to be true, and to come to the realization that our current knowledge is largely supported by unconscious belief systems and conditioning. We must reevaluate our vision of the world.*

L. M. Sinistrari's Account

Around twenty-five years ago, when I was a professor of holy theology at Holy Cross Convent in Pavia, there lived in this city a young married woman of excellent morals. All who knew her, and the clergy in particular, had nothing but the highest praises for her. Her name was Hiéronima and she belonged to the parish of Saint Michael.

One day, Hiéronima prepared some bread dough and brought it to the local baker to bake it for her. When he brought it back to her, he also gave her a large crepe in a strange shape with some butter and Venice pasta, as the inhabitants of this city had the habit of making. She refused to accept the crepe, saying that she hadn't prepared such a thing.

"But," said the baker, "I didn't have any other bread than yours to bake today. The crepe came from your home; you probably just don't remember." The good woman let herself be convinced, and she took the crepe and shared it with her husband, her little three-year-old daughter, and the servant.

The following night, when she was in bed with her husband and the two of them were asleep, she was awakened by the sound of an extremely soft voice, resembling somewhat of a high whistling sound. Very softly, the voice murmured clearly into her ear: "How did you like the crepe?" Seized with fear, the good woman began to make the sign of the cross and invoke over and over again the names of Jesus and Mary. "Do not fear," said the voice. "I wish you no harm. On the contrary, I will stop at nothing to make you happy. I fell in love with your beauty and my greatest desire is to enjoy your embraces."

At the same time, she felt a kiss on the cheek that was so soft and gentle that she could have believed it was simply the cotton quilt rubbing against her. She resisted without saying anything, repeating over and over again the names of Jesus and Mary and making the sign of the cross. The temptation lasted around a half an hour, after which the tempter went away.

When morning came, the lady sought out her confessor, a wise man full of experience, who strengthened her in the practice of the Faith and encouraged her to keep up her strong resistance and to make use of holy relics. The following nights came with the same temptations, with words and kisses of the same kind, and the same resistance by the lady. However, as she was tired out from the latest ordeals, she sought advice from her confessor and other learned men and asked to be examined by professional exorcists who would know whether or not she was possessed.

The exorcists found nothing in her that indicated the presence of the spirit of evil. They blessed the house, the bedroom, and the bed and ordered the incubus to cease his evil doings. All of this was in vain; he continued to tempt her, pretending that he was dying from love, crying, and shivering with the desire to reach the lady. With the grace of God, she remained unmoved. The incubus then used a different means: he appeared to her in the form of a young boy or small man, with golden curly hair and a blond beard. He shone bright as gold and had eyes as green as the sea. To add to his power of seduction, he also appeared elegantly dressed in a Spanish costume. He started appearing to her even when she was not alone; he lamented as lovers do, while blowing her kisses. In short, he used every means of seduction in order to obtain her favors. She was the only one who saw him; the others saw nothing.

This excellent woman had been relentlessly defending herself for several months when the incubus resorted to a new form of abuse. First, he stole from her a silver cross full of holy relics and a blessed lamb made of wax—a papal lamb of Pope Pius V—that she always wore. Then rings and other jewelry made of gold and silver followed. He stole them without touching the locks of the jewelry case in which they were kept. He then started cruelly beating her, and after each series of blows, one could see on her face, her arms, and other parts of her body the bruises or marks that would last one or two days, then disappear all of a sudden—unlike the gradual way that ordinary bruises would go away.

Sometimes, when she was feeding her little girl, he would take the child from her lap and carry her to the roof, setting her down near the gutter. Or he would hide her, but never doing her any harm. He would also create disorder in the house, sometimes breaking dishes into pieces, or breaking earthenware. But in the wink of an eye, he would make them like new again.

One night when she was in bed next to her husband, the incubus appeared to her in his usual form and insisted that she give herself to him. She refused, as was her wont. Furious, the incubus left but soon returned with an enormous pile of flat stones that the inhabitants of Genoa and Liguria in general used to cover their houses. With these stones, he built a wall so high all around the bed that it practically touched the roof, and the couple had to send for a ladder in order to get out. This wall was built without cement. The wall was then demolished and the stones were put in a corner for all to see, but two days later they disappeared.

On Saint Steven's feast day, the lady's husband invited several of his military friends over for dinner. To honor his friends, he prepared a good meal. While they were washing their hands according to custom, the table suddenly disappeared with its dishes, its pots, its plates, and all of the kitchen's pottery: jugs, bottles, and glasses as well. You can imagine the surprise of the guests. There were eight of them, one of whom was a Spanish infantry captain who said: "Have no fear, it is only a joke; there was a table here and it must still be here. I will find it." This being said, he walked around the room, extending his arms and hands, trying to grab the table. But after going around many times, seeing that he was touching only air, the others started laughing. And as the dining hour had come and gone, everyone took their coats with the intention to leave. They were already at the door, politely accompanied by the husband, when they heard a huge ruckus in the dining room. They stopped to find out what was going on, and the servant came running out and told them that the kitchen was filled with new plates full of food, and that the table had been put back in the dining room.

The table was now covered with place settings, dishes, glasses, and silver that did not come from the household, and there was an assortment of precious cups filled with rare wines. In the kitchen also, there were new pots and utensils that had never been seen before. The guests, meanwhile, were hungry and ate this strange meal that they found completely to their liking. After the dinner, while they talked around the chimney, everything disappeared and the old table reappeared, complete with the dishes that they had not touched. But—and this is rather strange—no one was hungry anymore; no one could touch any of the supper after having eaten a dinner so magnificent, which proved that the dishes that had replaced the original ones were real and not imaginary.

After several months of torment, the lady went to seek inspiration from Blessed Bernardino de Felter, whose body is venerated in Saint James church, located some distance from the city walls. At the same time, she made the vow to wear, for an entire year, the gray robe of a monk with a rope belt, as were worn by the friars of the order to which Bernardino belonged. She was hoping that through his intercession, she would be delivered from the torment of the incubus.

Indeed, on September 28, which is the eve of the dedication of Saint Michael the Archangel and the feast of Blessed Bernardino, she wore votive attire. The next morning was the Feast of Saint Michael. Our tormented lady went to the church of this saint, which, as I have already mentioned, was in her own parish. It was around ten o'clock and a large crowd was there to hear mass. The poor lady had hardly set foot inside the church when all of a sudden her clothing and her adornments fell on the ground and were blown away by the wind—leaving her stark naked. Quite fortunately, in the crowd there were two knights, mature in age, who, upon seeing what happened, hastened to remove their coats in order to hide the nudity of the woman as best they could. And placing her in a carriage, they took her back home. As for the clothing and jewelry stolen by the incubus, he gave them back six months later.

To finish with this story, even though this incubus played a number of tricks on her, some of which were quite surprising, suffice it to say that he continued tempting the lady for many years to come. But in the end, realizing that his efforts were in vain, he put an end to his incessant annoyances and vexations.

COMMENTARY

After reading this story, the reader may think that it was more of a fairy tale and that L. M. Sinistrari had a fertile imagination, but it is real. This document is authentic and coherent with the preceding testimonies as well as with many other documents.

Remarkable Elements

This account, thanks to its numerous details, is very instructive because it allows us to take inventory of the panoply of supernatural resources used by the incubus to act on matter:

- The incubus orchestrates a way to offer a crepe to Hiéronima and have it delivered by the baker.
- It is capable of manifesting itself through words—or what are perceived as words—by kisses and by taking on the appearance of a very attractive young man.
- It can appear to Hiéronima without being seen by others present.
- It can steal objects enclosed in a jewelry case without touching the lock.
- It beats her to the extent that she has visible bruises on her body, and then it suddenly makes all traces disappear.
- It is capable of taking her little girl and setting her in another spot without hurting her. (It is worth noting here that this act is like an abduction.)
- It breaks porcelain and just as quickly makes it like new again.
- It builds a wall without cement, but solid nevertheless, with stones similar to those of the local land, and makes them disappear in the wink of an eye.
- It makes a dressed banquet table disappear, then replaces it with another that has a whole assortment of silverware, cups, cooked dishes, and fine wines. It then makes it all disappear after the food on the dishes had been eaten, to put the first dressed banquet table back in its place.
- It is capable of undressing Hiéronima in public and making her clothing disappear without anyone noticing.

We can thus sum up this long list by saying that the incubus, who is an intelligent being and normally invisible, lives in a parallel world and has the ability to manifest itself in the material world and is capable of (1) materializing and dematerializing matter and (2) controlling its visibility.

1. **Materializing and dematerializing objects in the wink of an eye.** This ability can be used in order to remove objects locked in a jewelry case. The objects are first "dematerialized" in order to remove them,

then "rematerialized" elsewhere. This ability can even be used on human beings. Two examples were given in L. M. Sinistrari's account: the first recounts the bruises inflicted on the body of Hiéronima—bruises that were erased two days later; the second explains how Hiéronima's little girl was dematerialized when she was sitting on her mother's lap, and then "rematerialized" on the roof of the house without being harmed.

2. **The incubus can control its visibility.** It can make itself visible with the complete appearance of a human being and express itself through gestures and words, and this visibility can be limited to a chosen person, even when the person is with other people.

These aspects will prove quite valuable later on when we discuss the real nature of entities such as incubi.

Reflections of L. M. Sinistrari

L. M. Sinistrari wondered how he was to judge the case of this woman in light of religious law. A large part of his manuscript is devoted to a detailed study of this question. In the above account, Hiéronima did not allow the incubi to have relations with her. But the church's document archives (particularly those used in trials) contain many documents mentioning many cases where relations did take place. L. M. Sinistrari asked himself a first question: "How are such relations physically possible?" This very same question is asked today.

He adds: "There are few people, prideful in the little knowledge they have, who dare deny what the greatest scholars have written and what daily experience has shown: the demon, whether it be incubus or succubus, unites carnally not only with men and women, but also with animals."

L. M. Sinistrari is therefore perfectly convinced of the reality of these sexual relations, but he does not deny that young women often have visions and imagine that they have attended a witches' Sabbath. Indeed, for the Church, ordinary erotic dreams are placed in another category. Sinistrari differentiates these psychological phenomena from cases of demonology and authentic physical relations, such as those mentioned in texts on witchcraft. Indeed, Father Francesco Maria Guazzo, Italian priest in Milan in the seventeenth century, in his book *Compendium Maleficarum*,[16] dealt with the subject of witches and described in detail the sexual relations taking place between men and succubae as well as between women and incubi.

Concerning the possibility that children are born of these unions, Sinistrari's opinion was: "For theologians and philosophers, it is a fact that human beings are sometimes born of sexual relations between humans and the demon."

Mysterious Abductions in Medieval Times

Several studies exist from very different eras, which speak of abductions of human beings without any details about what happened during the abductions, but where human beings really did momentarily disappear.

Mysterious Abductions in France in the Middle Ages

We credit the archbishop of Lyon, Agobard (779–840), for investigating the case of an abduction and reappearance of four people. It is important, while reading this account, to place it in the cultural context of its time. He spoke of this case in a short treatise titled *Hail and Thunder* (written in Latin). The account was reported in an eighteenth-century book devoted to the "secret sciences."[17] This story has also been told by several ufologist researchers of our day, in particular Jacques Vallée in his famous work *Passport to Magonia.*[18] He further examined this case of abduction in his later work *Dimensions—a Case Book of Alien Contact.*[19]

The testimony of Agobard is extremely important for the study of abductions, and Jacques Vallée was able to locate the original text, written in Latin, and in 1841 printed a translation of it at the municipal library of Lyon. The archbishop Agobard was an enlightened, intelligent man who played an active role in the affairs of his day. He was ordained into the priesthood in 804 and became archbishop in 814. An early "rationalist," says Jacques Vallée—Saint Agobard left behind no fewer than twenty-two books, several of which are treatises against heretical superstitions and beliefs. The translator of the 1841 edition noted: "All writings whose style is always correct and often elegant deserve the honor of being translated because they teach us about the usages and customs of the first half of the ninth century better than any other writer of this time period."

Jacques Vallée wrote that the main objective of Agobard's book was to remove certain superstitions from people's minds concerning weather. In particular, he fought against the idea that wind and storms were due to the influence of witches (known by the people as *tempestarii*). It is within this context that in his book *Hail and Thunder* he raised his voice against those who were crazy enough to believe that there are vessels (*naves* in Latin) that fly through the clouds.

THE ACCOUNT

The 1841 translation of the work of Agobard tells us: "We have seen and heard many people crazy and inane enough to believe and affirm that there is a certain region called Magonia, a land where vessels flying among the clouds come from. These vessels (so they say) bring fruit to the region—fruit that is destroyed by storms and that falls because of hail. Aerian navigators pay the 'tempestarii' for this wheat and fruit. We have even seen how one day, some of these crazy people, who, believing in the truth of things so absurd, dragged three men and one woman in chains before a crowd. They claimed that these four people had fallen from such flying vessels. After keeping them in captivity for several days, they brought these men and woman before me, followed by the crowd, so that they could be stoned. After long deliberation, the truth triumphed, and those who had exhibited them to the people found themselves, as said the prophet, in the same state of confusion as a captured thief."

The following excerpt from the account of Agobard was published by Jacques Vallée in his book *Passport to Magonia*; the translation is from the book *Entretiens sur les sciences secrètes*, published in 1715 by Nicolas P. Henri de Montfaucon.[20] "It so happened that one day in Lyon, three men and a woman were seen descending from flying vessels. The entire city gathered around them, crying out that they were magicians sent by Grimoald, Duke of Bennevent, the enemy of Charlemagne, to destroy the French people's harvests. In vain, the four innocent people defended themselves by saying that they were of the people and had been abducted a short time before by extraordinary men who had shown them marvels that they had never heard of before, and they wanted to tell the story of what they had seen themselves.

"The unruly crowd took no heed of the four people's defense and were just about to throw them into the fire when the valorous Agobard, bishop of Lyon, having been a monk in this city, and having gained a considerable reputation, ran to them. After hearing the accusations of the people and the defense of the accused, he declared solemnly that everyone was wrong, and that it was not true that these people had fallen from the sky and that what they said to have seen was impossible. The people believed more in the wise words of their good father Agobard than in what they saw with their own eyes—they calmed down, freed the four ambassadors of the Sylphs, and received, in awe, the book that Agobard wrote to confirm the sentence that he had pronounced."

REMARKABLE ELEMENTS WORTH NOTING

The archbishop Agobard reported that many people of his time believed in the existence of "vessels that fly among the clouds," which, oddly, remind us of the UFOs of our days. This testimony is part of the long list of reports that show how extremely old the UFO phenomenon is.

One also finds here the idea that men and women could be transported by "flying vessels" since "they were seen descending from these vessels," but these people were considered as "magicians" by the populace. The phenomenon of abduction of humans into unidentified flying objects is therefore a very old one, but we have no information as to how the four people were treated inside the vessel.

Agobard, eminent representative of the Church, and "an early rationalist" in the words of Jacques Vallée, did not believe in the existence of these "flying vessels" and therefore did not believe that human beings could descend from them. It is pleasant to compare this attitude with the position of many rationalists of today. They are prisoners of their materialist vision of the world, and for them, UFOs do not exist. As a result, the so-called abductions into UFOs cannot be for real either.

This account, translated and reported by Nicolas P. Henri de Montfaucon, author of *Entretiens sur les sciences secrètes*, presents the four people as being "ambassadors of the Sylphs," which clearly expresses that, according to him, the occupants of the "flying vessels" were Sylphs: nature spirits connected to the element of air.

Mysterious Abductions in Celtic Countries

Walter Yeeling Evans-Wentz (1878–1965) was an ethnologist at the University of Los Angeles. Over a period of two years, starting in 1907, he met with dozens of witnesses—often elderly people—to collect their last living testimonies about the little people (this is what they call gnomes, fairies, and other creatures) throughout Ireland, Wales, Scotland, and Brittany. He gathered all of these accounts together in a book about the folklore of Celtic countries called *The Fairy-Faith in Celtic Countries.*[21] This ethnological study is a very priceless contribution to the subject at hand and has been cited by many authors, including Jacques Vallée.[22]

In the historical information presented by Walter Evans-Wentz, we find this: "The Celtic people, whether they be cultivated or not, affirm that the land of the fairies exists. It is an invisible world in which our environment is immersed, like an island in the middle of an unexplored ocean, peopled by countless species." And, to come back to the subject at hand: "This sort of belief, which holds that fairies are capable of kidnapping people, was very popular and still exists in a large part of the west of Ireland." To affirm this, Walter Evans-Wentz himself met with people who knew or knew of victims of such abductions, which were attributed to fairies. He added that a person who came back from the land of the fairies generally did not remember what they had seen or what they had done, and this is why he was unable to go any further with his study. It is worth noting that this amnesia concerning what happens during an abduction is also what we find in our day with a large number of people who are victims of abduction into a UFO.

But "the general belief deep in Brittany's countryside is that fairies did exist, but they disappeared when the province became transformed by the conditions of modern life. In the department of Ille and Vilaine, it is said that fairies have not existed for more than a century, and on the coast where it was firmly believed that the fairies dwelled in the caves of cliffs, the opinion is that they disappeared at the beginning of the nineteenth century. The oldest of the Bretons say that their parents or grandparents would often speak of the sightings of fairies that they had heard about; but very rarely did they say that they saw them themselves."[23] We realize here that along with the development of industrial society and modern technology came the loss of contact between the populations and the little people, the fairies. Popular belief sees in this the proof that the fairies disappeared and are no longer. But we can also envision the idea that this loss of contact is a consequence of human evolution; we have lost the ability to perceive subtle planes of existence as we have become more and more rational and our material vision of the world has taken a firm hold.

According to the study by Walter Evans-Wentz, fairies remind us of anthropomorphic beings. Accounts describe them as leading a life similar to that of humans. The "little people," the fairies, live in the wild and form a society that mimics that of humans, with women, men, and children, even if their supernatural powers set them apart from us. "Fairies can be either good or evil. They can enter a house without opening the door." This way of getting into people's homes is similar to that of the kidnappers, who, in our time, intrude into the bedrooms of their victims in order to take them into a flying vessel.

The following comes from the stories collected by Walter Evans-Wentz: "My grandmother, Catherine Mac Innis, used to tell us about a man she knew named Laughlin who was in love with a fairy. The fairy had decided to visit Laughlin every evening, and he grew tired of her and started to fear the consequences. Things got so bad that he decided to leave for America in order to get away from the fairy. It was thus that he emigrated [sic] to Cap-Breton and landed at Pictou in Nova Scotia. In his first letter to his friends back home, he confided that the same fairy was haunting him there in America."

Walter Evans-Wentz added his own commentary: "It is extremely interesting to discover a tale that is so rare and so intriguing. It proves that fairies in our day, who, through love, seduce mortals—are pretty much the same, if not exactly the same—as the demons of Medieval times."

Other Accounts from Iceland and Scotland

Concerning sexual relations between elves (in other countries known as fairies or sylphs) and humans: "Torfeus, a Danish historian who lived in the seventeenth century, included in the preface to his *Saga of Hrolf* the opinion of a venerable Icelandic priest named Einard Gusmond, concerning elves: 'I am convinced that they really exist and that they are creatures of God; they marry as we do and have children of both genders. We have proof of this from what we know about the love between some of their women and simple mortals.'"[24]

It is amusing to note that according to this Icelandic priest, the reality of sexual relations between elves and humans was well established, because he used this fact to demonstrate that elves were for real.

William Grant Stewart, in his *Popular Superstitions and Festive Amusements of the Highlanders of Scotland*, in a chapter titled "Passions and Preferences of Fairies," says the following about the sexual activity of these beings: "Fairies are remarkable through their amorous qualities and they don't take very long to become attached to people who are not of their own species."[25] Jacques Vallée, in citing this excerpt, noticed this "roundabout way" of evoking sexual relations between humans and fairies.

William Grant Stewart continues: "We must, in all fairness to both the human community and that of the fairies, say that today, the relations that we have described as taking place between the two are extremely rare."

Djinns in the Countries of Maghreb

The Christian Bible speaks little about beings that it calls genies or demons and is not at all explicit as to their characteristics. But the Koran recognizes the existence of three distinct species of intelligent beings in the Universe: angels, humans, and djinns. Angels are superior light beings, and the bodies of humans are made up of the rustic elements of the earth. The bodies of the djinns, however, are composed of subtle matter, often translated by "fire without smoke," and according to the Koran they were created before humans.

In North Africa, the djinns were particularly present in the past but are still quite present today in the lives of Muslims. They are creatures who live on Earth or underground. They are normally invisible to humans but can become visible or take on diverse forms, including animals or humans. It is worth noting that the word "djinn," in Arabic, comes from the verb *janna*, which means to hide or to dissimulate. They, however, can see us. Their way of life is very similar to humans': they eat and drink, they are born, they grow up, they marry, they have children, and they die. Their life span, however, is much longer than ours in human years.

Like humans, the djinns are organized into kingdoms and peoples, or tribes. They have laws and religions—they espouse different religious beliefs or are atheists—and they have either a masculine or feminine gender. It is also said that some humans are possessed by an amorous male djinn known as an *achîq* or a female djinn known as an *achîqah*. Marriage can take place with humans, and such unions can give humans certain tangible powers and the gift of clairvoyance. The Koran asserts that among the numerous djinn species, some are well intentioned toward humans, while a large majority of them are demons. It is also said that they are present next to psychics and oracles and are behind the conducting of séances. Mediums live constantly in their presence.

The Work of Gordon Creighton

Gordon Creighton (1908–2003) was an English diplomat. He was greatly affected by his first UFO sighting in 1941 while on assignment in China. For several years, he was also an intelligence officer and worked closely with the British Aerospace Ministry and the Royal Air Force. He therefore had direct access to the US Army's reports about UFO sightings, and it seems that it was during this very period that he became more interested in the UFO phenomenon. He was a regular contributor to the British magazine *Flying Saucer Review* for many years before becoming an editor himself in 1982.

Gordon Creighton compiled a remarkable selection of Islamic texts concerning djinns. He realized that these texts provided a lot of precise and surprising information about the nature of djinns, their role, and their activities—information that is unknown to the Western world. Most Koranic specialists agree that the "best way to represent the djinns is to see them as beings who are very close to and yet very far from humans. In other words, they live in another dimension than humans do, a parallel world, or another space-time."[26]

The result of this compilation is an article titled "A Brief Account of the True Nature of the 'UFO Entities,'" published in the *Flying Saucer Review* in 1983.[27] In our day, when diverse forms of UFO appearances remain totally mysterious while being the object of more and more documented reports, Islamic religious and traditional knowledge collected in this article provides some elements of response that are exceptionally valuable. It is regrettable that this work has not been recognized by the ufologist community, but it is true that its conclusions are quite far from the materialist vision of the world held by most people of today.

It is clear that there is a parallel between djinns and nature spirits (elves, fairies, sylphs, et al.). We can consider that djinns, well known by Muslims, represent one species among many varieties of nature beings. Gordon Creighton's work completes the research started by Jacques Vallée, who was the first to show the close analogy between the mysterious phenomena in the Middle Ages attributed to fairies, elves, and other nature spirits, and the UFO phenomena of our time attributed to extraterrestrials.

According to Gordon Creighton, "There is a close relationship or a sort of link between the destiny of djinns and the destiny of humankind." The main characteristics of djinns, enumerated below, are the summary of this compilation from religious Muslim texts and diverse Islamic traditional sources. As the author points out several times, the parallel with what we know of the characteristics of UFOs is self-evident. Here we use the classification as it was proposed by Gordon Creighton.[28]

THE PRINCIPAL CHARACTERISTICS OF DJINNS

Dj1: In their normal state, they are invisible to the ordinary human.

Dj2: They are nonetheless capable of materializing and appearing in the physical world. They can thus make themselves visible or invisible at will.

Dj3: They can change form and take on any aspect, whether it be large or small.

Dj4: They also have the ability to appear in animal form.

Dj5: Incorrigible liars, they take impish pleasure in disorienting and confusing humans in all sorts of absurd ways.

Dj6: They love to abduct humans.

Dj7: They love to incite humans to have sexual relations and liaisons with them, and Arab literature abounds with reports of this kind of contact between humanity and "good" as well as "bad" djinns. There is even a considerable number of reports of encounters between "good" djinns and well-known holy Muslims. In official Islam, the existence of djinns has always been completely accepted, even legally, and is so even to this day in Islamic jurisprudence.

Dj8: Djinns have the habit of grabbing humans, transporting them, and leaving them, if they so choose, miles away, in the wink of an eye.

Dj9: Arab tradition reports that throughout known history, several human beings, thanks to a strange favor, "allied themselves with djinns" or had an "arrangement with djinns" to such an extent that the djinns bestowed on them supernatural gifts, or psychic powers. These humans subsequently gained reputations as psychics, seers, or magicians (either white or black) depending on the type of djinn they were allied with.

Dj10: They also possess immense telepathic abilities and the power to easily seduce their human victims.

Three of the above characteristics are still well known by Muslims today:

1. their ability to make themselves visible or invisible at will
2. their ability to take on different forms
3. their inclination toward playing with humans and deceiving them

But Gordon Creighton also points out two other characteristics of djinns that, although not generally well known to Muslims today, are quite relevant to the subject of abductions into UFOs:

1. their tendency to abduct humans and have sexual relations with them
2. their telepathic abilities

Indeed, these are the very attitudes that define the phenomenon of abduction into UFOs, which is the subject of this book. Thus, not only is this phenomenon very old and well known in the Islamic world of yesteryear, but the Islamic traditions and religious knowledge found in the Koran offer us a highly detailed interpretation of this phenomenon. This has never been taken seriously in the Western world, even if Gordon Creighton published his article a second time in 1988 in the same magazine. It is regrettable that he contented himself with writing this one article, which is a summary of his work. He could have, for example, developed his subject further and cited more of his sources. We will come back to this interpretation later on when we analyze the possible origins of the abduction phenomenon.

A Modern Account of a Mixed Marriage

The story recounted below took place in mid-twentieth-century Morocco. It is an unpublished account, and all the more valuable due to its rarity. In these modern times, it seems that the manifestations of djinns have become less frequent than in times past, as much in Morocco as in other North African countries. Furthermore, in Moroccan society, which is quite Westernized, stories of experiences with djinns are not easily shared, since they are completely out of touch with modern society. This is even more the case when they are about mixed marriages between djinns and humans.

This story is about a man named Mohamed, who was born in 1930 and is still alive at the time of this writing. The author of this book received this testimony directly from Khadija, who employed Mohamed for fifteen years as groundskeeper for her property at Beni Mellal and thus knew Mohamed well. This account is guaranteed authentic in spite of its implausibility for us Westerners who have all been educated in "modern" society.

THE STORY

Mohamed used to own several successful businesses in the city of Demnate (at the foot of the high Atlas Mountains, to the east of Marrakech). Life became even more easy for him starting one fateful day when, every morning thereafter, he would find a sum of money in banknotes mysteriously placed under his pillow. Mohamed probably had to know that these miraculous, very tangible gifts could have come only from a djinn, but at the time he was young and carefree and gave it no more thought. Mohamed serenely took advantage of this generous "manna."

Then one day, a female djinn appeared to him and asked him to marry her, most likely with the intention of having his children. But Mohamed, already married, refused. The female djinn, however, no doubt considering that she had already paid for him and that he had accepted, would not hear of this and complained in court. The case therefore was brought before a djinn court, which functions like human courts.

According to Mohamed's wife, during this period Mohamed became a wanderer with unkempt hair and beard, refusing to wash and to eat. She had to take great pains to try to get him to come home. Mohamed could not believe it when his wife told him this, because, in his memory, they lived in a beautiful home and had a wonderful life. This shows that he was extremely perturbed by what he was experiencing, and was not in his right frame of mind.

The trial was very long, but, remarkably, Mohamed was allowed to attend the trial, and even more extraordinarily, he was able to personally defend himself. He defended himself so well that after having put forth all of his arguments, he ended up winning his case. Greatly relieved, he was able to return home—and finally wash and shave. He regained his dignity and related everything that had happened to him.

But as early as the following day, he saw that all of his businesses had burned down and all of his possessions had been destroyed; he suddenly found himself without a cent. Ashamed of himself in the eyes of others, he had to leave the village with his family. He started by going to Agadir and offering his services as laborer on a farm close to the city of Taroudant. The farm belonged to Khadija's father. Shaken by his sudden ruin and the change in lifestyle that came with it, Mohamed was difficult to work with. He did not tolerate the orders coming from the manager of the farm and ended up quitting. He then had to go seek work as a laborer elsewhere in order to earn a living and support his family, which was very difficult for him.

Several years later, Mohamed came to live in the city of Beni Mellal, where Khadija lived. She had bought land to build a house and wanted to dig a well. But the rock was too hard and it was impossible to cut through it. She was told that there was someone who knew how to dig into this hard rock. This person was none other than Mohamed, who from then on became her employee. This is how she learned of his story.

It is understandable that if Mohamed had found a way to dig through very hard rock in order to make a well, although other well diggers were unsuccessful, it was because he was capable of using other means. It can therefore be surmised that he was helped by djinns, whose mastery of matter is superior to that of humans. This hypothesis is validated by the fact that Mohamed later confided in Khadija that he saw djinns at her home in Beni Mellal and that from time to time he even attended their evening religious ceremonies.

Khadija ended her story by saying that Mohamed was an honest, conscientious, and loyal man. He now has a good life, and his children are successful as well. After his retirement, he went back to live in his city of Demnate, where he built his own house and regained his place in the community. Khadija saw him again several times over the past few years, but due to his age and declining health, he can no longer travel, and she remains in contact with his children.

ANALYSIS

1. Mastery over matter:

Every morning Mohamed would find banknotes under his pillow. This can sound crazy, but if we accept the reality of this story, it shows that supernatural beings really do have the ability to create any object and do what they want with it. The fact that a female djinn came into Mohamed's life leads us to think that she was the one behind the banknotes, and perhaps behind the burning and destruction of Mohamed's businesses right after the trial.

2. Psychic abilities:

What is remarkable is that Mohamed was able to attend his own trial—a real trial in djinn society—and that he was able to personally defend his cause. This means that he could directly see the djinns and really communicate with them. He thus had psychic abilities allowing him to directly see into the subtle, etheric plane where djinns live. It is probable that the communication took place by telepathy, something that the djinns master perfectly, and Mohamed therefore mastered it as well.

Mohamed himself recognized that he had these psychic abilities when he later admitted to Khadija that he saw djinns on her property and that he even sometimes attended their religious ceremonies.

It is also his close connection with the djinns that allowed Mohamed to dig through hard rock, making use of this ability of the djinns to control matter.

We therefore realize that this exceptional story can indeed be real because Mohamed himself was an exceptional man; he had psychic capacities and had the rare ability to see and really communicate with the etheric plane and the entities living there.

3. Living like humans:

Among the strange things in this story, one can also see how the djinns live in a society that is similar to that of humans—with its marriages and trials with accusation and defense. They also had religious ceremonies, which implies that they had religions.

Geoffrey Hodson (1886–1983), an English Theosophist also with psychic abilities, devoted his life to observing fairies and nature spirits. He was able to see them clearly thanks to his etheric vision and was thus able to describe them in detail. It was through observing gnomes in their daily life that he was able to attest that they do indeed behave in all respects like humans—inside their homes, for example. In their subtle world, they mimic the way of life of humans, mirroring their habits and their physical needs down to the minutest detail. This reveals a great closeness between these beings and humans, even though we are completely oblivious to them.[29]

4. Like a fairy tale:

One can find similar stories in fairy tales where a fairy offers a man or a woman a bag filled with gold pieces— and later if she considers that the man or woman has not behaved as they should, the gold is suddenly changed into a rustic material. Here we have the same scenario: after the fairy gave a large sum of money with the intention of marrying Mohamed, the marriage contract was not respected, and all of Mohamed's businesses and sources of revenue were destroyed. Perhaps the fairy tales of yesteryear should be taken more seriously?

A Modern Account of the Abduction of a Newborn

The following story took place in the early 1970s and was reported to this author by one of the parents of a woman named Souad, who lived in the city of Rabat. Souad was married and living a normal life with her husband, up until the day when she found herself possessed by a djinn. From then on, her husband could not get near her because she could no longer stand being touched by him, and they therefore had no more sexual relations.

Then Souad found herself pregnant. Her pregnancy progressed normally, and for the birth she withdrew into her bedroom, asking to be left alone without a midwife or anyone else. Her husband was kept from entering the room, as if by an invisible force that physically opposed him. The birth went well, and those present in the house distinctly heard the first cry of the newborn; it was therefore very much alive. But when they were finally able to get into the room, the mother was alone. The baby had disappeared. For everyone present, it was clear that the baby had been taken back by the djinn into its world. Afterward, Souad was freed from the presence of the djinn and was able to again have a normal life with her husband.

ANALYSIS

1. Pregnant without human intervention:

Souad found herself pregnant even though she wouldn't let her husband come near her, and her pregnancy progressed normally. In any other Western country, those around her would have concluded that she had been unfaithful to her husband, but in the Moroccan society where she lived, her family was open to the existence of djinns. Her husband had to accept that forces beyond human control had been at work.

2. The baby disappeared as soon as it was born:

The story becomes disconcerting when we look at its paradox:

- Everyone in the family could tell that Souad was really pregnant; she could not hide the signs of her physical condition.

- Everyone heard the cry of the newborn baby, which serves as evidence that the birth did take place and that the baby was very much alive.

- Yet, no one was able to actually see the baby. It disappeared as soon as it was born, never to be seen again.

We can conclude that the baby was abducted from the earthly material world and transported into an invisible world by an invisible force. Kidnapping by djinns would therefore appear to be a natural explanation— an explanation that, in any case, was accepted by Souad's family.

Abductions in the Amerindian Population

The book titled *Encounters with Star People*,[30] written by the Indian Ardy Sixkiller Clarke and cited at the beginning of chapter 1, is very interesting for our current study in several ways:

- It first of all shows that the same phenomenon of abduction is occurring even among the Amerindian peoples of North America: a population that stands out as having been on the fringe of Western civilization for a very long time, and having remained in contact with nature. This population is continuing to experience the phenomenon of abductions in this twenty-first century.

- Sixkiller Clarke pointed out that all the accounts reported in her book were experienced in a conscious state and were remembered without having to resort to hypnosis. None of these accounts were reported as dreams. Because hypnosis and its methods are still controversial, this frees us of any doubts we may have as to the validity of these accounts.

- The Amerindians have another way of looking at this phenomenon that is different from other cultures. They think that it is "star people" who manifest themselves during these encounters, and many think that these "star people" represent their ancestors. This interpretation is, however, not shared by everyone, in particular when the abduction victims are raped.

- Certain accounts from her book cited below provide us with new information allowing us to deepen our knowledge of the beings responsible for abductions, and this will help us better identify who they really are.

- Finally, it is significant to note the great diversity of the reported accounts, which allow for a rich discussion in the next chapter about the identity and origin of these "star people" encountered by Amerindians.

The Abductions of Tiffany[31]

THE ACCOUNT

Ardy Sixkiller Clarke writes: "Tiffany was 17 when I met her for the first time. She told the following story: 'When I was 5 years old, I went into the woods near our home with my grandmother to look for wild plants. After a while, we came upon a clearing where we saw a circular metallic object resembling a huge spinning top. When we started going toward it, a door opened and we went inside. A woman was standing there. I don't remember much about her except that she shone as if she was surrounded by a bright light. She seemed to know my grandmother, because they greeted each other like friends and my grandmother held out a bag of herbs to her. They examined each one of the plants and discussed them one by one.

'Before leaving, I was lifted up and placed on a table by this strange woman. My grandmother stood by my side, holding my hand. I remember feeling quite ill at ease. The woman looked into my ears, [and] she took a sample of my hair and a piece of a nail. She scraped my arm and then[,] using something that looked like a pistol, took a bit of blood from me, which immediately left a bruise.

'After that, my grandmother took my hand and we left the vessel and continued picking plants. I was terrified by everything that had happened. Later, when I wanted to talk to her about it (I was ten), she told me that I was not to talk about "such things."

'I was abducted again the following year, when I was all alone. My father asked me to go and pick berries. Right when I started to pick some, I was taken away by two women. They made me board a vessel and put me in a room with other children, some of whom were crying. One after another of us was taken away, and when it came my turn, they took a sample of my hair, a piece of nail, and a little bit of blood.

'The next thing I remember was that my elder brother was there with me in the field, putting the berries in my bucket. He wanted to know where I had gone and I told him that I had gone for a walk with two friends. He told me that there wasn't anyone around other than him and me, and that I was dreaming.

'They would come back every year and go through the same routine. I was outraged. It's very annoying to be carried off like that when you don't have any say in the matter.

'They look like ordinary people except for this strange glow about them. Sometimes they float instead of walk. They all seem to be the same age, except for one person who is older. Later on I saw others who were different. If you look into their eyes, they hypnotize you. Their eyes are mesmerizing, and in spite of all of my efforts to avoid their gaze, it is as if I was forced to look them in the eyes.

'They wear protective coverings over their eyes that look like large glasses. Once I saw one of them without their glasses; they had eyes like those of a cat.

'Recently I had the feeling that their intentions were no longer well meaning. I am afraid of them. Their examinations are different. I think that they want to inseminate me. Their attention has become more sexual. This terrifies me.

'Once when they abducted me I felt a lot of pain. When I took a bath afterwards, my underclothes had blood on them—and I was not having my period. Every year since that time, I would feel the same pain, as if they were invading my body. I believe that they are raping me and there is nothing I can do about it. I fear that they want me to bear an extraterrestrial baby.

'Nothing stops them. They take me away right from under my family's noses. One night I was staying at my Aunt Helen's, and they came to get me. She woke up in the middle of the night and I was not there. She found me the next day wandering along the road more than 2½ miles from the house. I believe that they are capable of hypnotizing other people when they want to take you away, and no one remembers anything.'"

ANALYSIS

1. Entering the vessel of their own free will?

Unlike all the other cases reported previously where the victims were taken away by force (often from their bed or from their car), it could seem that in this case, Tiffany and her grandmother entered the vessel of their own free will. This was therefore not an abduction in the true sense of the term. The vessel was on the ground, and everything in this account leads us to think that it was a normal material object.

But we must remember that according to the information previously cited, the kidnappers have great telepathic abilities. They perhaps used these to push Tiffany and her grandmother to go inside of the vessel, without Tiffany being aware of it—since she was still quite young at the time. Also, it could be that the vessel, even though it had a material appearance, was actually in a parallel plane. Tiffany and her grandmother were thus led into this parallel plane without knowing it.

2. A friendly relationship:

It is noteworthy that the grandmother knew the person who welcomed them into the vessel. She had no reaction of fear and showed, on the contrary, that she had an amicable relationship with this person. We can deduct from this that the grandmother was used to these visits and that the visitors had never acted aggressively toward her.

And yet, when Tiffany reported later that her grandmother said she must not talk of such things, we can guess that the grandmother knew perfectly well that when Tiffany reached puberty, painful things were in store for her. She herself no doubt went through the same thing in her youth and had apparently come to accept it.

3. A parallel plane:

We can note that during her second abduction, when she was six, Tiffany was alone outside picking berries when she was approached by two women who took her inside a vessel where there were other children. This paradox leads us to think that the vessel was not in a material plane but in a parallel plane, and that she had been brought into this parallel plane along with the other children. This idea is reinforced by Tiffany's observation that "sometimes they float instead of walk" and the fact that her brother had not noticed anything.

4. The power of hypnosis:

The kidnappers have the power to hypnotize their victims. Tiffany noticed that in spite of her efforts to avoid their gaze, she was forced to look them in the eyes. This same observation has often been reported in a number of abduction cases and is always experienced as distressing.

5. A sexual plan:

Tiffany understood that for several years, her body had been used by the kidnappers to give birth to hybrid babies. As in all the abduction cases reported previously—again—the main goal seems to be a sexual plan involving human beings. The yearly abductions of Tiffany prior to puberty would have been a sort of preparation in order to get her used to these encounters. If Tiffany doesn't seem completely sure that her body was violated, it's probably because she did not remember all of the things she went through.

6. A physical abduction:

The last elements of this account clearly prove that Tiffany had definitely been physically abducted, since her aunt noticed that she was not in her bed and that she was found the next morning 2½ miles away from the house.

The Abduction of Russell[32]

Russell is a very solitary man marked by life's hardships. He hesitated before providing his testimony, in spite of the promises made to respect his anonymity and his private life. This Vietnam War veteran recounted the repeated visits he had from "star travelers," who gifted him with a power allowing him to survive not only the severe regimen of a Catholic boarding school but also the conditions of a prisoner of war in a camp in Vietnam. They also gave him tangible gifts.

THE ACCOUNT

"My distrust of people began at the boarding school. Before then[,] I had never been beaten or punished. When I arrived at the school, I didn't speak English[,] and the nuns and priest punished all those who spoke their Indian language by isolating them from the others. If you didn't know how to speak English, you were not allowed to play with the other children nor were you allowed to speak at all. For me, this was a very lonely existence[,] but I learned to get used to it. I decided then that I would never speak English while I was at that boarding school, so I spent eight years there without saying a single word.

"I hated them. It wasn't enough that they subjected us to boarding[-]school life, but they also forced us to learn a foreign language and a foreign way of life—and they claimed that they were helping us adapt to their culture. For this, you had to submit to them. They wanted to break me as if I were a wild stallion. I refused to submit, and they never broke my spirit. The hatred I felt gave me strength. I even learned English, but I refused to speak it. Finally, after eight years, I returned home and I never went back to the boarding school.

"My first experience with a UFO occurred when I was seven. The priest took me to the chapel and had me kneel down. He told me to stay there until I spoke English. When he left, I heard him lock the door. I still remember the salty taste of my tears. I was wondering to myself what I would do if I all of a sudden had to urinate, when suddenly a light appeared outside of the chapel window and I saw a being there. At first, I thought that it was one of the older boys coming to help me, but it was a star traveler. It took me, held me tightly against it, and we went through the wall as if the wall weren't there. It helped me escape.

"This star voyager looked like a robot. It looked more like an insect than a human, but I was so happy to be outside of this chapel and far from these nuns and this priest that it wasn't important. These star travelers taught me mental control. I don't know how they did it, but they taught me how to live with pain and to survive in isolation. After the first incident, I never felt pain again. I could stay forty-eight hours on my knees without feeling anything at all. When I left for Vietnam and was captured and tortured, I felt no pain. I learned how to dissociate myself from my body.

"I think that the star people could read my mind. They knew exactly when the pressure was becoming too much for me[,] and it was at that very moment that they would appear. I always went with them willingly, but not because I particularly liked them. I went with them because I was escaping situations that were even more unpleasant—whether it be at the boarding school, in the Army, or in prison. They made my conditions as a prisoner more tolerable.

"They taught me mental control, but before cooperating with them I had them do things for me. For example, when we were in a prison camp and there was very little food, I had them bring me fruit—real fruit—like oranges, apples, and bananas. When I hinted that I needed fruit, they appeared. My cellmates loved these apples, oranges, and bananas, and this was concrete evidence of their existence and my abilities.

"But in exchange for fruit, I had to submit to their physical examinations and allow them to take sperm specimens and all other samples that they needed. They experimented on my eyes and my nose. They exposed my eyes to diverse liquids and varying degrees of light. They took a lot of blood.

"These beings looked like mechanical insects. They were good to me and helped me[,] but they also had a bad side. I saw them hurt people, and this didn't seem to faze them.

"Many times I have seen other people kidnapped by them, mainly when I was in the Army. Several times they abducted everyone in our barracks. They even took our weapons just to examine them. When they brought us back to the barracks, none of the men had the slightest memory of the incident. I always found that strange.

"They go by certain principles that forbid them to interfere in human lives when it would change the course of history. I never told this story to anyone—only my companion. You are the second person I am telling this to. If I were to speak about this to someone else, they would have me put away."

ANALYSIS

Russell's very strong personality, fed by the hatred he felt toward the educators in his boarding school, led him to experience extraordinary things. His account is extremely valuable for our study.

1. Escape through the walls:

In his first experience, he saw a being come into the locked chapel. The being then held Russell tightly as he took him through the walls. According to this account, the "star traveler," as he calls it, had taken on form from a light appearing at the chapel window. It thus materialized right in front of Russell. Then, by holding him tightly against it, it was able to take Russell through the wall. This means that Russell's body underwent a transformation—apparently without him being conscious of it—in order to dematerialize—meaning to go into a subtle state of matter that did not interact with the dense matter of the walls. This is why he was able to go through the wall.

It is this same transformation that makes abductees—who in the classic abduction scenario are taken from their beds—capable of leaving their bedrooms through doors or closed windows. The only difference is that in these cases, the kidnappings are carried out against the will of the victims, whereas in Russell's case the act of abduction served him by freeing him from his confinement.

2. Robots in the form of insects:

The description of these "star travelers" is that they looked more like mechanical insects or robots than they do humans. This insect-like appearance has often been reported in other abduction cases.

Russell specified that he didn't particularly like them, but on several occassions they had made his prison life more bearable. He therefore benefited from their help in relieving his suffering.

3. Dissociated from his body:

The first gift the star travelers gave Russell was to teach him how to separate himself from his body in order not to feel what otherwise would have been intolerable physical pain. This allowed him to go through experiences of imprisonment and torture without too much suffering—physical suffering at least. This is not a natural ability. This serves as a clear example of the kind of protection these beings offered Russell.

4. Fruit in prison:

Among the most surprising and valuable parts of this story is the fact that in response to Russell's request when he was imprisoned without food, he received fruit by supernatural means: perfectly real fruit that he was able to share with his cellmates.

This shows the level of mastery that these "star travelers" have over matter. They can create material objects and even living things belonging to the vegetal world if they so desire.

This ability is of course beyond the grasp of people who do not know about this phenomenon, but it reminds us of an anecdote from a previous work (cited below) concerning the ability of Helena Blavatsky, who founded the spiritual movement called Theosophy at the end of the nineteenth century. She was able, in the same way, to manifest an abundance of grapes thanks to her ability to give orders to an elemental being who did her bidding:[33]

One evening, Colonel Olcott witnessed another wonder performed by Helena Blavatsky, showing perfectly well her absolute mastery of elementals. One winter evening when London was covered in a thick layer of snow, Olcott and Blavatsky had been working late on *Isis Unveiled*, a groundbreaking book of theosophy that came out in 1877. At around one in the morning, Olcott was thirsty and said, "It would be marvelous to have some grapes. Alas, it is not the right season." The good Helena retorted that she had the power to create grapes right then and there in the room if he really wanted her to. Intrigued, the colonel agreed. Helena asked him to turn out the light and then to turn it back on. Olcott recounts: "Look!" Helena cried, as she pointed to a bookshelf on the wall facing us. To my great surprise, two huge grapevines of good Hamburg Black Muscat grapes were hanging from the knobs of each side of the shelf, and we ate them right up. When I asked her how she did it, she said that it was the work of elementals who were at her service. Two more times during our stay, she repeated the exploit and got us fruit to refresh us while we were working on Isis.[34]

This anecdote, which could seem incredible to us, shows us the ability that elementals have to act on matter even when they are in an invisible plane. It also shows us that some rare human beings, such as

Helena Blavatsky, beyond having deep knowledge of elemental beings, gained the ability to give orders to elementals telepathically—either to get relief from certain domestic chores, to manifest material objects, or to act on matter.

The precious nature of Russell's account lies in the fact that it is very similar to the one about Helena Blavatsky, where it is clearly suggested that the beings who manifested themselves in bringing fruit are elemental beings, or elementals. We will come back to this very important point further along, in chapter 6.

5. Samples taken and experiments done on his body:

Another particularity of these "star travelers" is that they were quite interested in doing all sorts of experiments on Russell's body and, in particular, taking sperm samples. No information was given by the star travelers as to why they were doing this, but we find again here, without any possible doubt, the same sexual plan to create hybrid creatures from humans and these kidnappers of humans. This leads us to link the case of Russell with the other cases of abductions into UFOs, since the kidnappers are of the same nature. The difference here is that Russell "always went with them willingly because he was escaping situations that were even more unpleasant—whether it be at the boarding school, in the Army, or in prison," although, in all the other cases, the kidnappings are experienced by the victims as being a violation of their human liberty.

It is worth noting that even if Russell had not mentioned that the samples taken and the experiments done on his body took place inside a vessel (he has never been precise on this point), he did use the phrase "experience with a UFO."

6. Both good and bad:

It is interesting to detect that according to Russell's experience, the beings he was dealing with were understanding toward him and showed up to help him whenever he needed and "when the pressure became too much for him." They were, therefore, "good to him." But "they could also have a bad side too" and were capable of hurting others without any remorse.

7. All the soldiers from one barrack were kidnapped together:

Russell's account can imply that the abductions of humans are much more frequent than what is actually known, since he observed several times that the kidnappers had taken all the men from the same barracks without them having any memory of it and apparently without anyone noticing. Because of his previous experiences, Russell was the only one who was aware of what was happening.

8. Saving the earth is never mentioned:

Let's go back to what was explained at the beginning of chapter 2. The phenomenon of kidnappings into UFOs as we have known them since the 1960s has two specific features:

1. the implementation of a sexual/reproductive plan
2. Awareness-raising about the serious threats weighing on the earth, with apocalyptic images of a devastated planet as it would be after a nuclear war

But in the accounts of Tiffany and Russell, taken from *Encounters with Star People*, as in all the other accounts reported in the same book, the "star people" never show the slightest preoccupation with saving the earth. This seems logical since the Amerindians have always remained very close to nature and are not at all responsible for the alarming state of the world today. This again confirms that the kidnappers have a certain intelligence, albeit different from that of humans.

Jesse's Encounter[35]

The following account is not about an abduction into a UFO, but it is relevant because it is about an encounter with a nonhuman linked to a UFO.

THE ACCOUNT

"UFOs have always been in this area," relates Jesse, who has seen them ever since her childhood, and "they can change form right in front of our very eyes. When I was little, I would see them two or three times a year. The first time I saw them change form was when I was in my last year of high school—when I came here with five of my close friends to celebrate the end of the school year before the graduation ceremony. We put up tents and made a fire for cooking. At around midnight, we saw seven flying objects coming toward the hills. Before that, I had always seen only one vessel at a time. These objects did maneuvers in the valley below us and we were able to watch them. On top of that, while in flight, they turned into balls of light right in front of our eyes, before blending into each other. After that, we saw an enormous vessel in a completely different form—a sort of large triangle— shoot up at great speed toward the sky and disappear in just a few seconds.

"Later on I experienced something similar when I was alone at the ranch. Dusk was falling when I saw seven balls of light coming toward the ranch. I sat down on the edge of the porch and watched. Suddenly, one of the lights moved away from the others and started coming toward the house. It stopped about nine feet away and hovered in midair, about three or four feet from the ground. Right when I made a movement to get away, the ball of light changed into a human figure right in front of me. The being was wearing a lightweight one-piece suit. It told me not to be afraid. I felt myself starting to faint, and I don't know if it was because of fear or because of the odor that I smelled—a strong odor of rotten eggs or sulfur.

"Anyway, the 'man from space' came toward me and told me that he had been coming here for a long time and that he had watched me grow up and had always wanted to say hello to me. Then he asked me about the horses. He wanted to know all about their digestive systems. He was of average height, perhaps five-foot-six. He was thin, but it was too dark for me to make out any other features. His outfit glowed in the dark, and that is how I was able to see his silhouette.

"After we talked about the horses, it's as if he fell on the ground and again turned into a ball of light before flying away to join the other luminous balls. Later on I saw them all at the top of the hill. They turned into an enormous vessel and disappeared—and I never saw them again."

ANALYSIS

1. A ball of light turns into a human being:

The most important element of this account is of course the fact that these balls of light were capable of changing form and taking on a material appearance—even a human one. In the first account, they were described as "flying objects," conveying the fact that they seemed to have a material appearance. Then they changed into luminous balls that merged into each other to become an enormous vessel in the form of a triangle.

We can't help but see a connection with "black triangles"—a form of UFO that has been sighted very often over the past several decades. It seems clear that these black triangles are not to be thought of as ordinary material objects but rather as living, intelligent forms.

In the second account, Jesse reported seeing a ball of light turn into a being of humanoid appearance that materialized right in front of her. There was even real communication between this being and her. This change from an object appearing to be simply luminous into a living being of humanoid appearance is extraordinary and makes this testimony exceptional and quite valuable. It is, however, similar to Russell's account. Russell at first saw a light that was outside the room where he was, and then this light turned into a being once it was inside.

2. A demonstration of the ability to materialize:

This account is a demonstration of how the entities behind the balls of light really have the ability to materialize any object (a black triangle in the sky) and even a living, human being. The existence of this materialization is proven by the communication that took place with Jesse about horses. Of course, these accounts can never have the same value as scientific proof . . .

3. An intelligence connected to the balls of light:

It is significant that the ball of light moved toward the house and then toward Jesse. It appears that the reason for this appearance was to communicate with Jesse by taking on a human form. This behavior clearly showed that there is an intelligence attached to these balls of light, and even when they are not taking on other forms as they did here in Jesse's account, they are maneuvering in a conspicuous manner.

4. Rather illogical behavior:

It seems illogical that the entity would say that it "had been coming here for a long time" and that it "had always wanted to say hello to her." What would have stopped it from saying hello before? Furthermore, its interest in the horses' digestive systems doesn't seem coherent with the fact that the entity "had been coming here for a long time," because it could have already found the answers to its questions a long time ago. The way the entity casually ended its communication with Jesse by disappearing without any form of goodbye is also typical of odd behavior. The entity therefore appeared in the form of a human, but its behavior did not suggest anything about why it came, and therefore seems rather strange.

Abductions: A Modern Form of an Ancient Practice

What can we now conclude from the information given in this chapter? A large number of texts show that the practice of mating between men or women and nonhuman entities has existed throughout the history of humanity. These entities were called incubi and succubae in the Middle Ages, and later on demons by the Catholic Church. These practices were also known in certain popular traditions, and the people of northern Europe attributed these practices to trolls and elves. We have seen that in Celtic countries as far away as Scotland and Iceland, fairies were known for their abductions of human beings and for their amorous inclinations toward them. In the countries of Maghreb, the same practices were quite well known since they were explicitly referred to in Koranic texts and attributed to djinns. The word "djinn" in Islam corresponds to the term "elemental beings" in the Western world.

The nature of all these supernatural entities has never been well understood. But numerous examples have shown us that the way that these creatures of the past would disrespectfully enter the private lives of men or women to sexually unite with them reveals a connection with the entities of our day who abduct human beings into UFOs to—most often—impose sexual acts on them.

Several times we have made the parallel between the supernatural entities of former times and the supernatural entities of today who function in UFOs.

- We have seen that the objective was the same: to inflict sexual acts on the victims. In the past, this goal was reached through direct mating with these nonhuman entities, and in our day it is reached through the abduction into UFOs and forced insemination to produce hybrid beings.
- The incubi were capable of deceiving a woman by taking on the appearance of her long-deceased husband in order to achieve their ends. They therefore had the ability to assume the appearance of whomever they pleased. Similarly, those behind the modern-day abductions into UFOs are capable of taking on the appearance of an abductee's spouse and assuming other appearances as well.
- In L. M. Sinistrari's account we find other examples: the incubus appeared one night as a young man elegantly dressed in a Spanish costume in order to seduce his victim. Another time, he stole all her jewels from her without touching the locks on the jewelry case where they were kept. This showed his ability to master matter and that he could dematerialize and rematerialize these objects. Those behind the abductions into UFOs also have great mastery over matter since they are capable of entering a bedroom through a wall or a closed door. It is as if they dematerialize in order to go through the walls, then rematerialize once inside.

It would therefore seem that these sexual practices have always existed, but today, as in former times, such experiences are considered taboo in human society—so much so that they more often than not remain hidden and are very difficult to talk about. This is no doubt one of the reasons why today the phenomenon of abductions into UFOs is barely known.

It also would seem that the implementation of these practices has evolved over time. Although in the past the entities would appear in the homes of their victims and abuse them in their bedrooms, today the victims are kidnapped from their bedrooms and taken into a flying vessel. They find themselves face to face with a being who looks like a doctor, assisted by his personnel. This doctor performs a pseudomedical protocol on them before proceeding with sexual acts. All of this points to an elaborate staging, as if to correspond to our modern era and impress upon the victims the illusion that they are dealing with extraterrestrials.

But this parallel between ancient methods and those of today should help us demonstrate that this is indeed a setup to deceive the victims. It is probable that those responsible for the abductions of today are the same entities as the supernatural entities of yesteryear, since these entities are known for deceiving their victims by pretending to be who they are not. Those behind today's kidnappings are therefore perhaps not at all who they are pretending to be: extraterrestrials. They are, rather, masters in the art of deceiving humans and perhaps as terrien as human beings.

The question now is this: What is the real nature of these entities who kidnap human beings today? Using the analogy that we have drawn with the practices of former times, it is logical to think that they should be the same nature as that of incubi and succubae, and demons and nature spirits such as fairies and elves. We will again examine this question in chapter 6.

CHAPTER FOUR

TWO DIFFERENT SOURCES OF UFO PHENOMENA

In chapter 1, we listed the characteristics of the phenomenon of abductions of human beings into UFOs and clarified its two very distinct aspects.

In chapter 2, we showed that this second aspect is quite present in UFO appearances of our day, even when they do not involve human abductions. This observation leads to a logical connection between the entities carrying out the abductions and the entities who, conspicuously or not, control the UFOs: they are either similar beings or the exact same ones.

In chapter 3, we saw that throughout the ages, and practically up to our day in certain regions of the world, mysterious supernatural entities (demons) have invaded the lives of men and women to impose sexual relations upon them against their will. This phenomenon was relatively frequent in the past, giving rise to the tragic witch hunts that haunted the Middle Ages in Europe. It is logical to think that these mysterious entities could be similar or exactly the same as those responsible in our day for abductions into UFOs and the bodily violations that take place. This is all the more supported by Agobard's account, which showed that this practice of abduction had already existed in ancient times. The study of Celtic and Muslim traditions has also provided us with accounts supporting the reality of abductions of human beings in centuries past.

It would seem then that the sexual practices imposed on human beings in UFOs today have existed for a very long time, while the procedures over time have changed.

For a long time in the past, the entities known as incubi and succubae would mate with women and men. There were abductions of human beings in at least some regions, but we don't have any information about what actually happened during these kidnappings.

In our day, the victims are abducted and taken into UFOs. The procedures performed inside the vessels still seem to be aiming for sexual procreation but do not necessarily involve actual mating. It is through sperm samples taken from men and artificial insemination performed on women that procreation is achieved. The apparent goal is to create hybrid beings that are half human and half supernatural.

The Characteristics of the Kidnappers

We can now complete our list of characteristics of UFO abductions by describing those who are responsible for them:

Extremely preoccupied by ecology: The entities are quite concerned about the multiple sources of pollution that humans inflict on the earth in our so-called modern day, and the serious ecological imbalances that result.

Quite interested in sexual relations with humans: These entities intrude upon the lives of men and women without any respect for their dignity. They either impose sexual relations upon them or use their bodies for reproductive ends. Even though these violations of their bodily integrity most often leave deep psychological scars on the victims—all the more so when some of them undergo this repeatedly over a period of years—the kidnappers do not justify their behavior nor do they show any remorse.

Abductions of humans are very ancient: Even if, in our modern day, UFO abductions have been observed only since the 1960s, abductions of human beings have in fact existed for a very long time.

Sexual violence is very ancient: We have seen that the sexual violations imposed on human beings by supernatural entities, characteristic of today's abduction phenomenon, are far from being uniquely related to our day and have existed in different forms throughout the ages.

Very different appearances: These entities have the ability to take on very different appearances. Even though some of the entities on board today's UFOs look like humans, as they did in the past—whether associated with UFOs or not—they are also sometimes described as having a humanoid appearance but with all sorts of different traits that set them apart from humans beings. They are also sometimes described as being similar to robots, or looking like insects. Furthermore, we have seen that the same entity can take on very different appearances.

In the book *Encounters with Star People*,[1] we find several accounts, some of which were previously cited here, that are completely compatible with the descriptions above. But now we are going to see that a certain number of Amerindian testimonies are not at all like these descriptions and even have characteristics that are totally opposite. These accounts seem, therefore, to belong to another category of events even though the witnesses often refer to the appearance of a flying vessel. Indeed, we will suggest that there are two distinct categories of encounters.

Several Cases of "Encounters with Star People"[2]

The testimonies that follow are very rare, and some of them are even more priceless because they are quite remarkable. They were completely unheard of before the publication of Ardy Sixkiller Clarke's *Encounters with Star People*, and even though this book helped increase awareness of these accounts, they are still not known well enough. The reason why we know about them is due to two different factors:

The Amerindian people have always lived in close contact with nature and, as a result, live in conditions more conducive to UFO sightings. As a result, this type of observation is relatively common among their population, but the terrible oppression they experienced when their territories were invaded by Western civilization caused them to very rarely confide in others outside their inner circles.

But these witnesses agreed to confide in Ardy Sixkiller Clarke, who herself is an Amerindian. She grew up hearing stories about the star people directly from her grandmother. This is how she became passionate about the subject and strove to gather testimonies, convinced of the importance of making them known by publishing a book on this subject. Furthermore, she is an academic, with the social recognition that comes along with it. It is also by virtue of her profession that she visited most of the Indian communities and was able to come in contact with a great diversity of people among the different Indian populations.

The excerpts below are from Ardy Sixkiller Clarke's book and contain the most-significant information. Readers who wish to read the entire accounts can refer directly to her book.

Ross's Account[3]

I operate a snowplow in Alaska. It was two months ago in February when a horrendous snowstorm took us all by surprise. Winds were more than fifty miles an hour and the temperature fell to 76 degrees below zero. An hour after starting my night shift, I found myself suddenly facing a disk right in the middle of the highway. The disk took up two lanes of traffic. It was circular in shape with bright orange lights at its base. I stopped my vehicle at about 18 feet from it and flashed my lights. I wanted to call a colleague but my radio was silent. Suddenly, blinding white lights came on and the vessel rose straight up and disappeared. I watched it until it was out of sight, which didn't take long because visibility was nearly zero due to the storm. Once the object had disappeared, I was plunged in[to] darkness.

I stayed there for a while. I couldn't believe what I had just seen. It was then that I noticed that my snowplow motor was not running. I never turn off my motor[,] out of fear that it will not turn back on because of the extreme temperatures ... and yet, it was off. I held my breath as I turned the ignition key and[,] happily, the motor came on with the first try. I put my snowplow in gear and started to move forward. Right when I started to accelerate a bit, I felt a bump underneath my right wheel, as if I had run over something. I was terrified. I thought that it could be something coming from the vessel I had seen. I stopped the snowplow and got ready to get out. As I was lacing up my parka above my cheeks, I saw an outstretched hand up against the side window. Then a second hand appeared. It was the most terrifying thing I had ever seen. The hands had only four fingers each. I turned the light on inside of the cab, and a face suddenly appeared, watching me intensely. It was wearing a sort of face protection but I could see its eyes—large dark eyes that were staring at me. It quickly turned around and ran across the highway, disappearing into a row of trees.

I had no intention of following the creature. Leaving a vehicle in the middle of a snowstorm could have fatal consequences. I thought that the incident was over, but I was wrong. A second later, the creature reappeared in the middle of the highway, right in front of me. Somehow I understood that it was cold and needed shelter. I suggested that it climb up into my snowplow but it didn't want to. It told me that it felt cold and that it was my fault. The vessel had taken off without it; it was outside of the vessel when I happened upon it. In their haste to get away, the other crewmembers [sic] had left the creature behind.

I again invited the creature into my snowplow. I told it that I had to plow the roads and that I could not leave it outside in the cold. Even though it didn't want to, the creature came inside, but not in the way that you or I would have climbed in. It simply appeared. One moment it was standing in the middle of the highway, and a moment later it was inside the cab with me. I was terrified but I forced myself to stay calm.

It was the longest night of my entire life. During the trip, the traveler from space stood as straight as an arrow in the passenger's seat. It was short with a human form, but it was not a human. It could have passed for a 10-year-old child at a certain distance. Its ability to appear and disappear fascinated me. I asked about this, but it told me that in its world everyone could come and go in the same way. It told me that their engine had been damaged, and they had landed briefly in the middle of the highway to repair it. The creature was curious and left the vessel to take a look at the snow. Because of the storm, the occupants of the vessel had not realized that they were on a highway. When I came up to the vessel, my appearance was a real shock to them, and in their confusion, they took off without their fellow crewmember [sic]. They hadn't expected anyone to suddenly appear in the middle of the storm.

To make matters worse, the space travelers in the vessel were not authorized to come in contact with humans[,] and this is why the creature was not comfortable about being seen. So the others took off immediately, leaving their team member behind. By doing so, they violated several rules during their trip. The creature explained to me that they were a young crew and they would probably lose their rights as explorers if their superiors were to discover their error.

I finally arrived at the end of the part of the highway that I was responsible for plowing, but I turned around and went the opposite way. It was snowing heavily, and the roads were again covered with four inches of snow. On my way back, the vessel appeared again in the middle of the highway at the exact spot where I had seen it earlier. The space traveler suddenly disappeared. Several seconds later, I saw it in front of the vessel. I was able to make out its profile in the flashing lights, and in the pale light I could see it making a hand gesture in my direction . . . and in an instant it was no longer there. It disappeared at the same time as the vessel.

There's something else too. It was fascinated by the snowplow and the way it functioned. It considered it a rather primitive machine, but the plow got its attention. It told me that humans depended too much on machines that run on gas. It told me that they should put their energy into studying the use of magnetic propulsion for travel. It didn't understand why scientists had not been looking in this direction.

It also told me that it was the first time it had seen snow and experienced extreme cold; it had never been so cold in its entire existence. It said that on its planet, weather never changes.

ANALYSIS

1. A motor that doesn't function:

When Ross found himself close to the UFO, he first noticed that his radio did not work, and then that the motor of his snowplow had stopped. This is a very common observation: all motors and electrical devices stop functioning when UFOs are nearby. But all it takes is for the UFO to move away for everything to return to normal. This demonstrates that the rays emitted by the UFOs cause these problems.

2. Hands with only four fingers:

Ross finds himself suddenly in the presence of a being who has a human form but is not human. Its hands have only four fingers each. He can easily communicate with it as if they spoke the same language, even when the being is outside the vehicle. It explains to Ross that the vessel had taken off without it as soon as Ross's snowplow arrived. Even though this is not specified, we can understand that the communication took place by telepathy.

3. The creature reluctantly accepts shelter:

After the creature found itself alone and abandoned by the vessel in extreme weather conditions and in the presence of Ross, its first reaction is to hide in the trees. It then comes back but refuses the invitation to come and seek shelter inside the snowplow. Finally, the creature reluctantly accepts the invitation. This reaction of running away seems not to be out of fear, but rather out of the desire to avoid contact with Ross.

4. The ability to go through matter:

Ross was terrified by the way that the creature came on board the snowplow without having to open the door. It is also in this way that it left the snowplow to rejoin the vessel when it reappeared. We find here the same ability to go through closed doors and windows—an ability that is often reported in abduction accounts. It is as if the entity could dematerialize and then rematerialize instantly.

5. Not allowed to come in contact with humans:

This is of utmost importance because it indicates that the crew of this UFO must obey orders and is under the direction of a hierarchy that forbids contact with humans. This enables us to understand the behavior of the creature when it found itself alone and helped by Ross. The creature accepted temporary shelter in the vehicle with Ross, but reluctantly—and only because its life was in danger due to the harsh weather conditions. The creature left Ross as soon as it was possible, and after giving a simple explanation as to why it had to break the rule. This also explains that the vessel had taken off so quickly the first time because it saw the snowplow.

It is evident that this rule forbidding contact with humans is never applied by the kidnappers and seems to be unknown to them when they abduct humans. Here we see two completely opposite behaviors.

Chee's Account[4]

Chee is a jeweler whose magnificent jewelry sells in high-end jewelry stores throughout the world. During his interview, he said to Ardy Sixkiller Clarke: "I met the star visitor on a magnificent, warm, summer evening. The sky was filled with stars. I had gone out into the desert to spend the night, as I like to do. I got there right before dusk, made a camp fire[,] and set about boiling water to make tea.

"Suddenly out of nowhere, there it was. In the dark I took it for one of the young Indians who lived in the area. I invited it to sit down. When it was in the campfire light I could see its red eyes and its silver-blue uniform. At first I was surprised. It apparently noticed my reaction because it then introduced itself as a star traveler who had come a long way. It explained that its mission was to collect herbs, plant, soil, and rock specimens, but got tired from walking so much. Even if there is oxygen in its world, it is very different from ours. I offered it a cup of tea, but it didn't drink liquids—

at least not the way humans do. When I asked it about where it came from, it pointed to the far end of the Milky Way and said that its planet was in that area, but that it could not be seen by the human eye.

"It stayed about fifteen minutes—and I felt no fear. It was a kindly creature. I recall that the night air seemed mild to me, but that the star traveler was cold. I wrapped it in a saddle blanket and invited it to sit near the fire. When I asked it about its family, it said that it didn't have a family in the sense that we know of. It had already been to other parts of the earth, but it was the desert that it liked best. It said that its ancestors had visited this place thousands of years ago at a time when this territory was not suffering from such drought. Here on the Indian reservation, there was little chance that it would encounter humans[,] and it could accomplish its work without interfering with other forms of life on Earth. But it was nonetheless unable to resist speaking to a human and risked being reprimanded by its superiors if they were to learn of this violation.

"I don't remember if the star traveler spoke to me as you or I would. It was dark and there was only the firelight. All I know is that I spoke to it. I remember its eyes and its silver-blue outfit, which seemed so out of place in this land of red dust.

"I asked it if it were true that extraterrestrial races abducted human beings. It replied that its race did not practice abductions. It told me that there were many civilizations, many worlds up there. There are other star travelers who perform experiments and who kidnap humans without bringing them back to Earth. It didn't know why they did this[,] and seemed hesitant to talk about these things with me.

"I know others who have seen UFOs and who have even gone inside these vessels, but I don't know anyone who would talk about such encounters with a stranger."

ANALYSIS

1. A human appearance:

The "traveler" looked like a young Indian at first, but it was set apart by its red eyes and its strange outfit. Then it said that it was from a planet located at the far end of the Milky Way where the atmosphere was a bit different from the Earth's. Its physical makeup still allowed it to breathe and survive without a special suit or mask. It could easily communicate with Chee. We can assume that it directly read Chee's mind and didn't need to know how to speak his language—meaning that this communication took place through telepathy.

2. The rule to not interfere with other forms of life:

The "star traveler" explained that its mission on Earth was to collect mineral and vegetal specimens. This implies that it brought the specimens back to its planet for analyses and other reasons. It explained that in order to carry out this task, it chose a desert region so as not to interfere with other forms of life. The traveler had therefore been told by its superiors not to approach human beings. It explained that its curiosity got the best of it, and it decided to violate the rule to talk a little bit with Chee. The traveler was therefore supposed to obey a rule that forbids contact with human beings. In reply to Chee's question about abductions, it even said that its species did not abduct human beings.

3. The earth has been visited for thousands of years:

The space traveler explained that its ancestors had already visited this region thousands of years ago. This means that long ago, the extraterrestrial race it belonged to had reached a level of evolution that allowed it to travel in space. It seems obvious that this species didn't use material means such as rockets to travel from one end of the Milky Way to the other, but that they used their abilities of dematerialization and rematerialization, which we have seen in the previously cited accounts. It seems that their visits had always been discreet and respectful without interfering with the diverse forms of life encountered.

Darren's Account[5]

"My grandfather told me that once, in the 1940s, at around the time of Roswell, a vessel landed in New Mexico and some Indians hid an extraterrestrial. My grandfather said that he and some of his friends had come upon the extraterrestrial[,] who was wandering in the desert. They hid it so that the soldiers sent by the government wouldn't find it. The extraterrestrial nonetheless died and they buried it.

"I myself saw an extraterrestrial once. It came to my grandfather's house. I was seven years old and I was afraid of it, as I was of all strangers— but my grandfather told me that I didn't need to be afraid and that everything was fine. Tall with dark skin and dark eyes, the extraterrestrial wore a brown, tight[-]fitting[,] one-piece suit and a strange pair of boots with pointy toes, the same color as its outfit. Its hands were covered by gloves[,] and it wore a snug-fitting hood on its head.

"It communicated with my grandfather. We went down with it to the inside of the canyon. My grandfather stopped several times to check for footprints, and then we started following a path. The footprints led us to a large vessel, sitting on the other side of the canyon ridge. My grandfather explained that the extraterrestrial had gotten lost and that it was a member of a small group of explorers sent on a mission. They got separated from each other[,] and while the others went off in other directions, our visitor went up the canyon. It was carrying equipment that was supposed to guide it back to the vessel, but it was no longer working. This is why it came to our house seeking help.

"My grandfather and I accompanied the visitor back to its vessel. The others came out and welcomed it. I watched how the extraterrestrial turned to my grandfather as if it was introducing him to the group. The other extraterrestrials bowed and for a moment they remained standing out there talking to him, but I couldn't hear anything. I wanted to go toward the vessel[,] but my grandfather warned me not to and told me that I must not touch it. It was round and had a dull silver finish. There was no opening—only a door that, when it closed, you couldn't know where it was located. When they all climbed back into the vessel, my grandfather said that we had to move back to a safe distance. We then watched the vessel rise up. But it didn't even stir up any dust, and this was the thing that was the most surprising to me.

"My grandfather and I would often talk about this. He insisted that the extraterrestrials were all kind and that they wanted to do no harm. He said that they had been visiting the earth for a very long time.

"Neither my grandfather nor I saw another vessel after that, but I have seen the star visitor twice since then. It was at my grandfather's house ten years later[,] when I was seventeen. The same visitor showed up in front of the house—at least that's what I believed. It wanted to see my grandfather. They greeted each other like old friends. A bit later, the star man left and I followed him. He walked toward the canyon where my grandfather and I had guided him when I was a little boy. He must have known that I was following him because just before entering the canyon, he stopped. I understood that I was not allowed to go farther, so I returned to the house. My grandfather said that the star man had stopped by to simply greet an old friend. He also told me that he had given the star man a bag full of turquoise stones, which made him very happy.

"I saw him again five years later. My grandfather was almost 90 years old. He wasn't in very good health and I was worried about him. It was late at night when the star man suddenly appeared. He went directly over to my grandfather's bed and knelt before him. Shortly after, he left. Three days later, my grandfather died."

The following summer, when Darren went to spend a month in his grandfather's house, the first thing he noticed when he got there was a sack at the entrance of his grandfather's little workshop. It was the sack full of turquoise stones that his grandfather had given the star man. The star man had returned them.

ANALYSIS

1. A friendly relationship:

The amicable relationship that developed between the visitor and Darren's grandfather makes this account unique. The fact that this friendship lasted in spite of the passing years proves that the visitor felt real gratitude and great loyalty toward Darren's grandfather. This showed that the visitor had an honorable nature.

2. A simple man-to-man visit:

When the visitor came back ten years later (it was daytime), it took the trouble of going on foot to greet the grandfather while he left the vessel hidden in the canyon. On top of showing loyalty toward the grandfather, through this simple and discreet man-to-man visit, the visitor also showed great regard for the grandfather. The visitor did not want to risk disrupting its friend's tranquility with the imposing view of a space vessel or reminding him in any way that it may have been an extraterrestrial.

3. Telepathic communication:

During the first encounter, Darren was unable to hear the conversation between the visitor and his grandfather although he was standing right by his grandfather's side. This was also the case when the other visitors greeted them in front of the vessel. We can therefore conclude that the visitors were directing their telepathic communication to the grandfather and not to Darren, who was too young at the time.

Furthermore, during the second visit when Darren followed the visitor back, he understood that the visitor asked him to turn around, even though there was no exchange of words. Here again, we have telepathic communication.

4. Lost and alone in the desert:

It seems funny that the space visitor, lost in an unfamiliar region with navigation equipment that had ceased to function, was as helpless as any other normal human being would have been.

Brett's Account[6]

Brett is a policeman. "I remember the date of the encounter I had; it was April 13, 2004, my birthday. I had been driving around in the area[,] listening to the complaints of local farmers who were saying that something was frightening their cattle and their horses. It was late in the evening as I was driving back to the police station, when I saw a vessel fly over the road across from me and then disappear behind the buttes. The object was about sixty feet in diameter and about forty-five feet high. I could see flashing red lights at its base, and when it crossed the road, the entire area—the road, the rocks, and the trees—were all bathed in a reddish glow. There wasn't any noise, but when it crossed my path, the headlights of my patrol car started dimming and I thought that they were going to go out. But after that, the headlights were even brighter than before. I slowed down, waiting for the vessel to reappear, but I saw nothing more.

"So I stopped the patrol car on the side of the road and got out. I listened for the slightest noise as I inspected the night sky. I looked toward the ocean, searching for the slightest sign of what I had seen, but there was nothing. I decided to walk up to the butte to see if something was there. It was there that I saw the lights, and I continued to cautiously move forward until I had a direct view of the vessel. It was very large and had no windows. It was not touching the ground but suspended at about four feet from it. Its lights lit up the ground as if in broad daylight. There were four short creatures of humanoid appearance who were walking underneath the vessel as if carrying out an inspection. I stayed there a moment and observed this surprising scene taking place in front of me.

"Then I decided to show myself and call out to them. As soon as I did, they climbed immediately back into their vessel[,] using a trap door located underneath. The vessel disappeared quickly into the night. I have relived this scene thousands of times in my mind. I wonder if it would have been better for me to keep quiet or if I should have simply walked up to them without saying anything. In any case, that's my story. As I was going back home, I couldn't decide whether or not I should report the incident. I ended up deciding not to say a word about it. I have to take care of my family and I didn't want to risk losing my job, all the more because I am an Iraq war veteran and it could look like I am suffering from PTSD.

"I remember that these creatures were about four feet tall. Their one-piece suits fit tightly on their bodies, which were light colored and humanoid. Their heads seemed large for their bodies[,] and their arms were long for their height. The next day I went back to the same spot. There was no evidence at all that they had been there."

ANALYSIS

1. Creatures of humanoid appearance:

This account is all the more interesting because it is reported by a policeman—someone used to observing and investigating. He saw four creatures of humanoid appearance but short of height, with proportions slightly different from those of humans: large heads and long arms.

2. They flee as soon as they are discovered:

While the four creatures are quietly going about inspecting their vessel, they become aware of Brett's presence and immediately get back into their vessel and disappear into the night. They didn't take the time to gesture a greeting, let alone introduce themselves and give any explanation. This behavior of fleeing as soon as a human being approaches is perfectly coherent with what has been previously reported. Everything happens as if these "space travelers" are subject to a strict rule forbidding all contact with human beings when they come to visit the earth.

3. A policeman who decides not to file a report:

It is worth noting here that a policeman, though conscious of the importance of discipline in following procedures, still decided not to file a report about what he had seen. His reasons are easily understandable, but this example leads us to think that such extraordinary encounters are most likely more numerous than we think.

Harrison's Account[7]

"My grandfather was living on a very isolated ranch on the Indian reservation when a spaceship crashed near his home in November 1944. During the summer of 1945[,] when I was twelve years old, I had just arrived to spend the summer with him when he took me to see the ship … and I was able to climb on board. Today we can no longer see it because the butte was covered with water when a dam was built there.

"The crash had shaken the ground so violently that grandfather believed his log house would collapse. The horses were so frightened that it took a month to round them all back up. At first, my grandfather believed that it was an earthquake, but when he ran outside, he saw an enormous dust cloud covering up the sky. When the dust cleared, he saw the vessel. It had crashed into the butte with such force that only a small part of it was visible. My grandfather sat there a long time on the butte[,] watching for the slightest sign of life. He stayed there on the lookout for several days, but in vain. Finally after a week, he set out to take a look at the crash site.

"It was later on that several times my grandfather saw star travelers collecting rocks and plants. At first, they would disappear right before his very eyes as soon as they saw him. He never found an explanation for it; they simply disappeared. Then, as time passed, they realized that he meant no harm[,] and they no longer disappeared when he came toward them.

"One day he brought them some food but they said that they didn't eat meat. They were white, and taller than he was. They must have been more than six and a half feet tall. They had white hair and thin fingers that were longer than those of humans. Their eyes changed color with the light. They all seemed to be the same age and looked so much alike that my grandfather had a hard time telling them apart. They were all wearing light-green one-piece suits. My grandfather told me that several times he saw them wading around in the river[,] and when he got closer to them, he saw that their clothes were dry. He told me that he really would have liked to have the same kind of outfit. There were fourteen of them. Grandfather was never able to tell if one of them had died in the crash, but when I got there to spend the summer with him, I climbed aboard the vessel and saw that there were seventeen seats and no signs of anyone having died in the crash.

"My grandfather understood that they were worried about their vessel. They didn't want it to be discovered. They lived there from the end of November 1944 to April 1945. According to my grandfather, another vessel appeared on April 17, 1945, and he never saw them again. He knew that they had been waiting for a rescue vessel. He told me that their ship belonged to a fleet of four vessels that were exploring the earth, and that they had left a larger vessel that was in orbit. During the five months that they waited to be rescued, they were not afraid of being discovered because they could make themselves invisible, but they could not do the same thing with their ship.

"Grandfather was watching them prepare for their departure when the rescue ship landed in the field to the west of his house. It was exactly like the one that had crashed. Before leaving, each one of the stranded star travelers came up to my grandfather and bowed to him. He understood that they had appreciated his discretion.

"The crashed vessel was not an ordinary machine. Grandfather said that it was able to change form and then take on its original form again. When it crashed, the vessel was severely damaged, but it took on an appearance that made it blend in with the landscape. Grandfather said that when he saw the ship for the first time, there were bumps and scratches all over the backside of it, as well as a large crack. The ship changed form and took on the appearance of a huge tree trunk. He never knew how that happened. He again said that the travelers had dug a tunnel in the butte in order to hide the vessel so that only a part of the trunk could be seen by the naked eye while blending into the landscape. This I saw with my own eyes. The ship was silvery, but the section of it where the entrance was and the backside of the ship both looked like the butte's desert ground. The travelers were capable of changing the outer part of their ship, but they were unable to get its navigation system up and running again.

"The star travelers told my grandfather that they were from a star system belonging to a constellation that they showed him, and my science teacher taught me that it was the constellation of Taurus. They told my grandfather that they were voyagers who traveled the Universe in order to observe life in other worlds. They had been coming to Earth for thousands of years in order to observe, collect data, and record changes. One day, they had him come on board their vessel and showed him pictures of their home planet. Their homes were subterranean. In their world, water was underground; there was none on the surface.

"When I arrived at the ranch at the end of May 1945 to spend the summer at my grandfather's, the star travelers had gone. At the time, the entrance to the vessel had been camouflaged, but grandfather showed me how to get inside through an invisible door that had been so cleverly concealed that even the most perceptive person would not have noticed it. I entered through this door and inspected the vessel. I sat down in one of the seventeen seats on board and felt enveloped in it as if the material it was made of melted around me. I also felt restrained, but it "freed" me as soon as I wanted to leave, as if it could anticipate my desire to get up. Everything inside of the vessel was made of the same dull, silver metal, including the seats. The interior surface of the vessel was smooth[,] and the walls, the seats[,] and the floor were rather austere. I noticed some screens, buttons, and handles, some of which had inscriptions on them. In a smaller section of the vessel, I saw an enormous cylinder inside of a ball that looked like it was made of glass. I never knew what it was.

"The vessel had been hidden so cleverly that anyone passing near it would have missed it. But if someone had brushed away the dust, they would have come upon a dull, metallic surface just underneath. The object wasn't round like flying saucers. It was long and had the shape of a rocket. It was a long cylinder that was thirty feet wide and sixty feet long. I measured it with my steps.

"The fact that this was an isolated area far away from the center of the Indian reservation[,] with very little comings and goings and twenty miles from the highway, explains why the crash had been able to remain a secret for all these years. At the time of the crash, the nearest ranch was uninhabited and ten miles away. Furthermore, the vessel was perfectly hidden by the rocks and the dust[,] and one would have had to walk on top of it to notice it. My grandfather never spoke about this to anyone other than myself and two of his childhood friends. We all swore to keep the secret. Later on, in the 1950s and in the early 1960s, the Whites moved tons of land in order to build the dam. We couldn't even find the place where the butte used to be[,] and grandfather thought that they had discovered the vessel and taken it. One of the engineers came to see my grandfather one day and asked if he had seen anything strange. My grandfather played dumb but understood the reason for this question. Today the site is under water.

"Concerning the relationship between the star travelers and human beings: they told my grandfather that while they were not our enemies and didn't want to cause any harm to the earth's inhabitants, they didn't want to be friends with earth dwellers either. They never interfere with the forms of life they find in the Universe. It's their way of going about things. Apparently, this is the reason why they were so obsessed with hiding their ship; they didn't want to leave any trace on the earth. Anyway, this is what grandfather thought."

ANALYSIS

1. "Men" who are different from us:

The "space travelers" are described as men with light skin, but also with features differentiating them from human beings. All of them are tall, with long fingers, white hair, and eyes that change color. Furthermore, their physical makeup allowed them to survive the collision of their vessel, a collision that must have been extremely violent considering the terrible effects witnessed by the grandfather and the extent to which the vessel was embedded in the ground. Human beings would not have survived, while the star travelers were not even scathed.

Short as it is, we can see how this description differs from the previous accounts when mentioning the height of the beings. This shows that there can be large differences in the features of the space travelers, even though they all have a humanoid appearance.

2. Avoiding contact with humans:

For more than a week after their crash, they avoided showing themselves to the grandfather and went so far as to play dead. Then when they saw that the rescue ship did not come right away, they left their ship to collect rocks and plants. We can understand that in order to collect material objects from the earth, they had to be present in the material world and, therefore, be visible. But as soon as they saw the grandfather, they became invisible—they dematerialized—to avoid contact with him.

It is only over time, with their stay on Earth lasting longer than planned, that the space travelers understood the grandfather's isolated position and his trustworthy nature. They were thus able to accept that he approach them and accepted to communicate with him. Later on they made it clear that they never interfered with the life forms they found in the Universe, that this is why they didn't want to do anyone harm, and that they were not looking to establish friendly relationships with earth dwellers.

3. Trying to hide the remains:

The beings were visibly quite worried about the remains of their ship, and they did all they could to hide it from the eyes of humans passing through the area. This is consistent with their worry about being seen by humans and not leaving any trace of their presence so as not to disturb them. It is indeed easy to understand that the discovery of the remains of a space vessel could potentially greatly disturb humans, as with the Roswell crash in 1947. But in this case, it was impossible for the space travelers to completely hide their vessel.

4. A futuristic technology:

During his visit inside the vessel, Harrison saw the star travelers' technological marvels with his own eyes, such as the shape retention properties of the materials or the way in which the seats adjusted to the person who was sitting in them.

Sam's Account[8]

Sam is an Amerindian elder. He is ninety-two years old and well known by those around him for his traditional knowledge. Concerning "space travelers" who kidnap people and take them against their will, he says: "There are different groups of star travelers. Some of them look human, and others that look somewhat like humans, and still others that don't look at all like humans. Those who kidnap people and perform medical tests on them against their will are no longer human, and no longer have any moral conscience. This is no doubt the reason why the ancestors avoid them. But there are others who are quite advanced and who are mainly content to just observe. They say that in the universe there is a law of noninterference."

Commentary

In Sam's view, there are different categories of "star travelers":

- "those who look human or look somewhat like humans"
- "those who are not at all human"

He also pointed out that the ones who kidnap people and carry out medical tests on them against their will "have no moral conscience and are no longer human."

On the other hand, others are "quite advanced," meaning in an evolutionary sense. "They are content with mainly observing" and do not intervene in the lives of human beings according to "a universal law of noninterference." Logically this must be about the space travelers he describes as "looking like humans."

This distinction was already evident in the testimonies reported above, and very clearly conveyed by Sam.

All the Amerindian accounts are extremely valuable for two reasons:

1. They describe the behavior of "space visitors" who as much as possible avoid all contact with humans, therefore respecting a universal law. Clearly, this behavior is totally opposite that of the kidnappers who abduct human beings, and this is why we distinguish between two categories of "visitors."

2. They mention certain cases of limited contact between these visitors—who must respect this law of noninterference—and humans. In certain circumstances, the reason is clear as to why this law was broken.

Thanks to the reported dialogues and descriptions of the behavior of the visitors, we have an idea of what state of mind they have when visiting the earth. This information is essential for us to understand the nature of who we are dealing with.

Other Cases of "Close Encounters with Avoidance"

It appears that in a number of well-known cases in Europe, this behavior of avoiding humans has been observed without there being any communication. These cases are part of the category known as "close encounters of the third kind" according to the classification proposed by the American astronomer, J. Allen Hynek. Passionate about UFOs, Hynek has greatly left his mark on UFO research in the United States in the second half of the twentieth century.

According to this classification, there are three levels of close encounters:

1. **close encounter of the first kind** (CE-1): A UFO is sighted at a distance of less than 500 feet.
2. **close encounter of the second kind** (CE-2): The UFO leaves behind material evidence, such as marks on the ground.
3. **close encounter of the third kind** (CE-3): Both the UFO and its occupants are seen, or the supposed occupants are seen without the UFO.

Over the last few decades, a very large number of witnessed events have been classified as close encounters of the third kind, but they don't all have the same characteristics. Many of them, for example, involve luminous phenomena and intrusions into the lives of the witnesses, leaving them extremely traumatized. This is particularly the case when there are abductions into UFOs. On the other hand, a behavior of avoidance of human beings has been observed in a very small number of these "close encounters of the third kind," leading us again to distinguish—as we did before—two different subcategories of occurrences:

1. close encounters of the third kind where nonhuman beings are encountered, and UFO occupants who exhibit a behavior of avoidance of human beings as soon as they realize that their presence has been discovered

2. other close encounters of the third kind where there is no behavior of avoidance

In this chapter, we have described events only of the first category, similar to the previous cases experienced by Amerindians. These cases make up the very small number of cases of "close encounters of the third kind."

We suggest that we name this category "close encounters of the third kind with avoidance."

We shall name the other category "close encounters of the third kind without avoidance" or, even more specifically, "close encounters of the third kind with abduction."

The four accounts that follow had widespread media coverage and left a great impression on thousands of ufologists. They were included in the famous COMETA report.

The Famous Case of Valensole, France

Valensole is a small Alpine community in the region of France known as Haute-Provence. It is July 1, 1965, and forty-one-year-old Maurice Masse leaves his home at five in the morning and sets out for his lavender fields located on a plateau near the village. Before starting his tractor at around 5:45 a.m., he lights a cigarette and at that moment hears a sort of whistling sound coming from his lavender field. He goes toward the spot and sees, at about 300 feet from him, a sort of machine sitting in the middle of his lavender plants. Its shape reminds him of a rugby ball with a transparent dome on top. He estimates the object as being around nine feet high and eleven feet wide, supported by a central tube surrounded by six smaller support poles.

Maurice Masse approaches it cautiously and comes upon two small beings bent over some lavender plants. He describes them as being of humanoid appearance, but not even three feet tall—and wearing dark-gray one-piece suits. They have large, bald heads that are disproportionately big compared to the rest of their bodies. When the beings spot Maurice, who had managed to get to less than thirty feet from them, they immediately stand up and remain still, with expressionless faces. One of them then takes a tube out of a satchel hanging on his left side and points it at Maurice. Maurice Mass is then instantly immobilized on the spot—completely paralyzed—but perfectly conscious of what is going on in front of him. The two small beings seem to be talking about something, even though their mouths do not move. But Maurice very distinctly hears sounds like the buzzing of bees and concludes that this must be some sort of speech. Maurice would go on to say that he was not afraid and that he felt relaxed in spite of being forcibly paralyzed.

He was thus able to observe the strange beings as they went back to their ship and entered through a door that silently opened and closed. He could see them behind their transparent cockpit. Maurice heard a sort of "thud" as the ship rose three feet from the ground—with not a bit of smoke or the stirring up of dust. The central tube underneath went back up into the vessel, as did the six support poles. The ship shot straight upward before veering off and disappearing faster than a jet.

Maurice estimated that he stayed immobilized for about fifteen minutes before gradually recovering the use of his arms and legs. He got back onto his tractor and tilled his soil until 8 a.m. But when nine o'clock came around, he went back home. Quite shaken, he recounted his adventure. News got around and the local police showed up to conduct a first investigation.

The Valensole Police Department, followed by the investigation squad of the nearby town of Digne, investigated this case for several days. The investigations revealed that at the spot indicated by Maurice Masse, there was a cylinder-shaped hole about seven inches in diameter and fifteen inches deep. At the bottom of this hole were three other holes, one of which was vertical and the other two slanted.

After several days, the lavender located within a radius of about twenty feet around the site of the vessel started to wither. This phenomenon would last several years, during which Maurice Masse tried in vain to grow other plants. For several months after his adventure, Maurice Masse suffered from hypersomnia, sleeping from twelve to fifteen hours a night.

COMMENTARY

This story contains several significant things (some of which have been mentioned in the previous accounts).

The visitors were obviously interested in the lavender stalks and were observing them. We can hypothesize that they were intending to take a sample back with them.

They arrived very early in the morning. They needed to make their observations in daylight and chose an early hour when the fields are normally deserted. But Maurice Masse had decided to begin his workday very early, and this allowed him to have this extraordinary encounter.

As soon as the visitors were aware of Maurice's presence, they ended their observation and—after a brief discussion—got back into their ship and disappeared into space. This behavior shows that they were surprised by the presence of a human being, and it particularly reveals that they wanted to avoid all physical contact and communication with him. Showing up suddenly like this in the lives of humans and then running away without any kind of explanation can be interpreted as rudeness and even insolence, but it can also be seen as a resolute desire to avoid all contact.

Maurice had gotten quite near to them at less than thirty feet, and to be sure that he could not get any closer, the creatures decided to immobilize him by using an instrument they had on them as a precaution. This act had most likely been planned to prevent any aggressive reaction or simply anyone getting too close.

The Case of Cussac, France

On August 29, 1967, around 10:30 a.m. on a beautiful sunny morning on the high plateaus of the region of Cantal in the center of France, a boy and a girl, aged thirteen and nine, were sitting watching over their herd of cows in a prairie that bordered a local highway. Their herd dog warned them of a cow getting ready to jump the low, stone wall that served as a fence. When the little boy got up to go fetch the cow, he saw on the other side of the road four children whom he did not recognize. Surprised, he called his sister over, and both of them saw an extremely bright object in the form of a sphere near the four children. They then realized that the "children" were actually short beings whose clothing and faces both were black. Two of them couldn't have been more than three feet tall, while the two others must have been about four feet. Two of the beings were standing next to the spherical object, and one of them was waving something around as if to alert their companions. The boy would later say that the object looked like a mirror. Another one of the beings was kneeling as if searching for something on the ground, while the fourth one was standing up as if to observe things around it.

Right when the boy cried out to them, "Do you want to come and play with us?," the little creatures, who didn't seem to have seen the children, ran quickly back to the spherical object. The first creature flew straight up into the air and went headfirst into the object. The second and third creatures flew up the same way, disappearing into an invisible opening on top of the sphere. Finally, the fourth creature flew straight up, too, but quickly came back down to pick up something that was on the ground— the little boy thought it was its "mirror"—and then flew back up and went into the sphere, which had started to take off and was about forty feet from the ground. As the sphere went upward, it gave off a whistling sound and traced a spiral in the air. The brightness of the light emitted by the sphere became so intense that it was hard on the children's eyes. Finally, the luminous ball rapidly disappeared into the sky.

During the whole time, the children smelled a strong odor of sulfur. Both their own cows and those of the neighbor's started to moo and nervously thrash about, while the dog barked and seemed very agitated.

The little boy specified that the little creatures were all black, but they gave off a sort of silklike glimmer. We can suppose that they were wearing a kind of tight-fitting suit that enveloped both the head and the body. Their arms were long and thin.

A counterinvestigation was carried out in 1978 by a team of investigators from GEPAN (a unit of the French Space Agency, CNES, whose mission is to investigate unidentified aerospace phenomena and make its findings available to the public), as well as other qualified advisors, including a former investigating judge. The noteworthy facts revealed by this counterinvestigation were not taken from the children's eyewitness account itself, but from the testimonies of secondary witnesses who showed up afterward, providing additional evidence that reinforced the credibility of the case. A local police officer, in particular, came to the site immediately after the occurrence and found marks on the ground where the children told him to look, and noticed a very strong smell of sulfur there. Also, another witness reported that he was in a hayloft nearby and remembered perfectly well the whistling sound—a sound that was quite different from that of any helicopter of the time.

The reconstructions of the event carried out on the site in the presence of the two primary witnesses confirmed both the descriptions of what had taken place and the circumstances following the event. At the time, the children mentioned a strong odor of sulfur, but they most of all experienced physical ailments for several days afterward, such as watery eyes. These facts were observed by their family doctor and confirmed by their father, who was then the town mayor. The judge, upon concluding his investigation, gave his opinion of the eyewitnesses and their accounts: "There are no flaws or discrepancies in the diverse facts presented that cast any doubt on the sincerity of the accounts or lead us to imagine any kind of dishonesty, trickery, or hallucination. Given these conditions, and in spite of the young age of the primary witnesses and the extraordinary nature of the facts related, it is my belief that they really saw these things."

COMMENTARY

Several years later, it was considered necessary to confirm the authenticity of the extraordinary, incredible facts reported by the additional witnesses, since there had been no soil analysis done in 1967.

The two main witnesses, who were children at the time of the occurrence, were adults when the counterinvestigation was carried out in 1978. This, along with the confirmation of the secondary witnesses, allows us to consider their account in its entirety in spite of some of its seemingly impossible elements.

In this case, as in those we have previously seen, the visitors showed their concern about being spotted by humans, even though they seemed to act as observers who were interested in knowing more about the environment in which humans lived. As soon as they realized that humans saw them, they quickly got back to their ship—in a rather peculiar way—and disappeared into the sky. The fact that the vessel was already forty feet above the ground when the fourth traveler managed to get back inside plainly shows how much in a hurry they were to leave. This behavior clearly demonstrates that they wanted to avoid all contact with humans and not even let humans get near them.

The Case of Trans-en-Provence, France

This is another famous case of the landing of a flying vessel, which occurred in the center of France on January 8, 1981, at around 5 p.m. Renato Nicolaï, a mason, was in his garden, building a cover for his water pump. It is a typical end of the afternoon with sunny and clear skies. Renato's attention is suddenly drawn to a metallic object in the sky, reflecting the sun's rays. He observes the mysterious, silent object's descent as it lands on a piece of land below his house, about 240 feet from him. Oval in shape, the vessel looks like two upside-down dishes glued together. There are no windows, nothing is written on it, and it makes no noise. It is metallic in appearance and measures about five feet high and eight feet in diameter.

According to Renato Nicolaï, the vessel remained on the ground for a minute before taking off again—still without any noise—and at an incredible speed. If this story had such an impact in France even though there was no "close encounter," it was because the police station was alerted as early as the following day. The investigation team took soil and vegetation samples and then informed GEPAN three days later.

The samples taken on the ground underwent numerous biochemical and physiochemical tests in different specialized laboratories. Examined and verified by GEPAN, these analyses concluded that all the samples had anomalies, thus confirming the exceptional event that had occurred near Renato's home. In addition to the effects on the soil and the ground's surface caused by heat and mechanical pressure, the biological effects noted were premature aging of the surrounding young alfalfa plants and a change in the photosynthesis process.

GEPAN concluded its report by saying, "An unexplained physical phenomenon really did take place." According to a technical report published in 1990 in a scientific review: "Something out of the ordinary really did happen, and this could be, for example, the effects of an electromagnetic source."

COMMENTARY

Even if the event that took place in Trans-en-Provence weighs little in the context of this study because there was no encounter with a nonhuman creature and no abduction, numerous analyses still confirmed that there was the landing of an exotic vessel. This event would go on to be classified as a CE-2 according to the system of Allen Hynek, but the vessel, in fact, was seen up close by the witness, which makes it more of a CE-3.

The confirmation that the event took place provided by the analyses of the soil allowed the investigators to take into account the testimony of Renato Nicolaï, who affirmed having watched the landing of a spaceship near him, and its almost immediate takeoff before disappearing into the sky.

This exotic spaceship had to have been piloted by an intelligence—intelligent beings who did not show themselves.

The nonhuman origin of this vessel seems to be unquestionable, since its takeoff at an incredible speed without any noise is beyond what any known aircraft can do. Furthermore, it is not realistic to imagine that the vessel had been made by some human being possessing a secret, advanced technology. Indeed, in this case, the pilot, by landing in an inhabited region, would have been taking a great risk of being seen.

We can therefore suppose that these nonhuman beings had some sort of unknown motive for landing in this particular area—perhaps to observe a specific object—but when they saw that they were being watched, they abandoned their plan and left immediately.

Here again we find that the occupants of the vessel didn't want to show themselves to a human being. They were visibly surprised to notice that they were being watched, and gave up their plan to explore on the ground. The case of Trans-en-Provence can therefore be considered similar to those of Valensole and Cussac. All three of them show us nonhuman entities who pilot vessels, who land on Earth, and who avoid humans.

The Case of Socorro, New Mexico

This event occurred on April 24, 1964, in Socorro, New Mexico. The American authorities considered it to be credible enough to start an in-depth investigation. Several declassified FBI and Strategic Air Command documents attest to the reality of the facts, but it was declared as "unexplained"—even for the Blue Book Project (one of a series of systematic studies of unidentified flying objects conducted by the United States Air Force), and it remains unexplained to this day.

The witness, police officer Sergeant Zamora, is driving alone in his police car at around 5:45 p.m. He is pursuing a vehicle that had committed a traffic violation, when he suddenly hears a sort of screaming sound and sees a red-orange flame up in the sky about a half mile away. The region is semideserted, but he does know of a cabin close by that has dynamite. He gives up his car chase and starts driving toward the hill where he saw the flame drop, and then he turns onto a dirt path. At the top of the hill he sees a metallic object, shiny like aluminum, and next to it, two figures dressed in white one-piece suits. From 600 feet, Sergeant Zamora takes them for strangers involved in an accident. He speeds up to go help them.

The land becomes so rocky that he has to leave his car and continue on foot. He radios his sheriff to let him know that he is going toward the unknown metallic object. He barely gets out of his car when he again hears a sort of rumbling and screaming, which is getting worse. He then sees the object go upward, as if pushed by an orange-and-blue flame with a cloud of dust forming around it. Out of precaution, he goes back to his car. The oval object positions itself horizontally and moves over the car. On the completely smooth surface of the object, Sergeant Zamora makes out a sort of red insignia. He is then stricken by panic and runs for safety behind the hill. The rumbling stops and is replaced by a sort of grinding sound, going from low to high pitch before ceasing.

Finally, all is quiet again and Sergeant Zamora sees the metallic object go very high up into the sky, head off toward the mountains, and disappear. His colleague, Sergeant Chavez, shows up shortly afterward, and they both observe several bushes on the landing site that are still smoking, as well as marks on the ground. Many people are quickly alerted and arrive at the scene: an FBI agent, investigators from APRO (the Aerial Phenomena Research Organization), officers from the US Air Force—and Allen Hynek himself, then acting as advisor for the Blue Book Project.

The official investigators found four identical holes sitting on top of a diamond of diagonal lines of 19½ and 17½ feet, and four burn marks. The amount of pressure necessary to produce such holes was estimated at over a ton per hole.

COMMENTARY

The UFO first appeared with a loud screaming sound and a red-orange flame, and then, at the time of takeoff, another screaming sound followed by a grinding noise, accompanied by a blue-and-orange flame. It seemed that the machine was experiencing some kind of serious damage, which could explain why it had to land. But this did not keep it from hastily taking off again.

The landing did not last very long, because the vessel took off when the sergeant was 600 feet away. It seems clear that given the sequence of events, the reason for taking off in such a hurry was connected to the police car approaching. The UFO's occupants apparently decided to leave the site in spite of the apparently alarming condition of their vessel, in order to avoid the police officer approaching and thus being seen more.

Mysterious Disappearance of Apples

Lucy Pringle, a renowned specialist of the crop circle phenomenon, recounts a strange occurrence in one of her books.[9] The event was experienced by a farmer in the region of Kent, England. While he was getting ready to harvest apples in his orchard, the farmer noticed that all the apples inside a large circle had mysteriously disappeared, along with the leaves of the trees (except for the leaves at the ends of the thinnest branches). This circle was very large, with a surface of about 43,000 square feet. More spectacular yet, the circle was so clearly defined that the farmer could see that the trees that were sitting right on the line of the circle were still full of fruit on the portion outside the circle and were completely stripped of apples on the portion inside the circle. The mowed grass inside the circle had also been as if suctioned up. Yet, all had been normal in his field the night before.

At nine in the morning, while the farmer was assessing the loss of his harvest, he noticed three men walking among the trees. They were all the same height and were wearing gray one-piece suits. He went up to them and called out, but they did not answer. He moved closer to within about twenty-five feet and realized all of a sudden that he was unable to breathe, and he felt a pressure come over him as if an invisible wall kept him from moving forward. This "wall" pushed him backward, and he felt as if he were in a dream, trying to move but unable to. Then the three men vanished. When the farmer came to his senses and looked at his watch, it was noon. He had no idea what had happened over the past three hours, nor who the three men were.

COMMENTARY

This account of the disappearance of apples—given that one accepts its validity—is the result of a supernatural force. The force aspirated the apples along with the leaves and the mowed grass on the ground, all of which were inside a circular area. Humans are incapable of harvesting fruit in this way.

Furthermore, the humanoid-looking creatures demonstrated abilities that were beyond those of humans. They immobilized the farmer by using an invisible force and then suddenly disappeared. These beings were not human.

We can sum up things in this way: three nonhuman, humanoid-looking beings physically showed up on Earth and removed apples from an orchard by what appeared to have been supernatural means, and as soon as they realized that the farmer was quite close to them (about twenty-five feet or so), they kept him from coming closer by using a mysterious means to temporarily paralyze him, reminding us of the tube used in Valensole to immobilize Maurice Masse. They then disappeared out of sight, as if by magic.

This sudden disappearance out of the sight of the farmer leads us to think that the creatures went into another dimension. We can also imagine that they went back to their vessel, which was also in this other dimension and thus invisible to the farmer.

We can therefore conclude that the three beings were of extraterrestrial origin. Their interest in apples shows that they had come to Earth to observe things and to take this fruit. They allowed themselves to take samples of vegetation but avoided all contact with human beings, apparently so as not to directly interfere in their lives.

Mysterious Beings next to a Crop Circle

In the *Daily Telegraph*, a well-known English newspaper, the following account was published on October 20, 2009. On July 6 of the same year, an off-duty police officer was intrigued by the presence of three men in a field near Silbury Hill in the South West England county of Wiltshire, where every year a large number of crop circles are found. Tall and blond, the three men were wearing white one-piece suits and seemed to be examining the crop circle that had appeared in the field on May 25 of that same year.

The police officer reported that he stopped his car and went toward them. When he got to the edge of the field, he heard a crackling noise, like that of static electricity. The sound moved around although the topography of the field was almost flat around its source. He cried out to the men, but they didn't even look up. It was when he walked onto the field that they looked up and started to run "faster than any man." The police officer looked away for a split second, and when he looked back again, they were gone. He then became frightened because the noise was still there. For the rest of the day, the police officer suffered from a severe headache.

COMMENTARY

In this last account, we again have creatures of humanoid appearance that are not human: they run faster than humans and suddenly disappear as if dematerializing. They were obviously interested in a crop circle because they were examining it very closely. They refused to have any contact with the farmer who tried to communicate with them, and they hastily left the area.

Given their behavior, it naturally comes to mind that these nonhuman entities came from space and were extraterrestrials. They came to observe what happens on our planet, all the while avoiding contact with humans.

It is somewhat pleasant to note that these extraterrestrials, when confronted with a crop circle, are much like humans; they are intrigued by it and examine it closely.

Two Different Origins of UFO Phenomena

Let us again define the two very specific characteristics of abductions of human beings into UFOs, which form a common thread among the large majority of abduction cases:

1. the UFO occupants' implementation of a sexual/reproductive plan whose apparent objective is to create a hybrid species
2. Awareness-raising about the serious threats weighing on the Earth, with apocalyptic images of a devastated planet as if after a nuclear war

It is clear that the two characteristics mentioned above are totally absent from all the accounts of close encounters with avoidance reported in this chapter. These accounts have other, very different characteristics:

The occupants of the flying vessel exhibit a clear desire to avoid contact with human beings so as not to interfere in their lives. They show this by fleeing as soon as they notice they are being approached or observed by humans.

The occupants of the flying vessel show their interest in plant and mineral life by observing and taking samples.

Only two aspects appear in both categories, but they are significant:

The entities appear as passengers of a flying vessel who seem to come from space.

They have the ability to dematerialize and rematerialize in order to go through walls. The kidnappers use this ability to kidnap their victims, and we saw this in the exceptional testimony of Ross in his close encounter with avoidance. We also saw that Harrison's visitors were capable of becoming visible or invisible at will. Finally, we saw that visitors who were interested in apples and a crop circle were able to instantly disappear upon being seen by a witness.

But outside of these two common aspects, the two descriptions are of totally opposite behaviors coming from two totally different mindsets. This opposition leads us to think that we are dealing with two completely different types of entities. The fact that in these two cases, the entities show themselves to humans as occupants of vessels from space—as if they were extraterrestrials— of course creates confusion between these two categories. In order to facilitate the distinction between the two categories, it is therefore necessary to use their behaviors to better describe and distinguish the entities.

Description of the Two Different Categories of UFO Occupants

We will make a distinction between the two categories of beings by using the terms "abductors" (for those who carry out abductions) and "visitors" (for those who do not kidnap humans and who avoid all contact with them). The following two chapters will show us what identity we can attribute to the beings of these two categories.

THE ABDUCTORS

Based on the testimonies in the first chapter and in addition to what we have previously shown as a common denominator, this is what we can say for sure:

Intrusions and trauma:

The abductors of human beings are entities who intrude upon the lives of their victims without any respect for their dignity as humans. They have no moral conscience and do not measure the trauma they inflict on their victims. The only thing they seem to care about is carrying out their plan of genetic manipulation against the will of those they kidnap.

Activists in protecting the Earth:

The abductors show themselves to be quite concerned about the earth and make sure their victims adopt a lifestyle that develops ecological awareness among human beings.

Transported into another world:

The kidnapped people are most often taken from their beds or their cars through doors or closed windows, or through the roofs of their cars, showing that they are no longer of this material world and are taken into another dimension. Indeed, they really express the impression that they are transported into another world.

Initiated by the abductors:

The encounters are always initiated by the abductors and are always against the will of their victims.

Taken on board a vessel:

Every time, the victims are taken inside a vessel to undergo the same protocol.

Absurd experiments:

Inside the vessel, the abductors perform what seem to be absurd experiments on the bodies of their victims: experiments on eyes (Russell), and samples taken of nails, hair, blood, and tissue. There are also relatively numerous cases of implants placed under the skin, whose final objective has never been clearly established, but that we can say for sure violate the bodies of the victims.

Very diverse appearances:

The abductors sometimes have a human appearance (often that of the "head doctor") but sometimes look like insects or even robots. The most common appearance and the one that we see the most in the media is that of a short humanoid between three and four feet tall with a large head that is out of proportion with the rest of the body, and very large almond-shaped eyes. Using physical appearance as a basis, some researchers have categorized up to eighty different species of extraterrestrials.

A changing appearance:

Another significant element is that according to some accounts, these beings can change appearance right in front of their victims, which can be considered as rather deceitful and rude. We saw this in the story of the incubus that was infatuated with a lady of the Renaissance. The incubus one day took on the appearance of a young, elegant, and seductive man, and this led us to make a clear connection between the ancient accounts of incubi and succubae and the modern-day abductions into UFOs. We also saw this in the encounters experienced by Russell and Jesse, where a being of human or humanoid appearance appeared first in the form of a ball of light.

Simulations of different environments:

The abductors tend to modify the appearance of the environment—such as simulating a conference room or a forest—inside a UFO. Such staging without any explanation implies that they want to deceive their victims.

Erasing the victims' memories:

Most often, the abduction victims remember nothing of what they went through during their abduction, or they have only a partial recall. It is only after a long, effortful process, usually through hypnosis, that they manage to bring their memories back up into their conscious mind. They then realize that their memories had been erased by their kidnappers.

Note: In Russell's account, we saw that his abductors seemed to be subject to a principle of noninterference in the lives of humans when it could change the course of history—but this does not prevent them on an individual basis from profoundly upsetting the lives of humans whom they use as guinea pigs in a laboratory.

THE VISITORS

A rule of noninterference:

The rule of noninterference in human lives was explained several times by some of the visitors themselves who, for diverse reasons, found it necessary to deviate from this rule and communicate with humans. In all other cases, however, the rule was strictly observed.

The rule is either strictly applied or at least it is intended to be:

In several cases this rule of noninterference was not applied to the letter, and information was exchanged with the witnesses, but in all accounts there was an explanation as to why this rule was not respected:

- The visitor's life was in danger when it found itself all alone in the middle of nowhere in a snowstorm and in extreme cold (Ross's account). But the visitor left again as soon as it found its vessel. Here we have a case of life or death.

- The visitor was lost due to the malfunction of its navigation device, and it needed the help of Darren's grandfather to get back to its vessel. Here we have another case of its life being in danger.

- The visitor, out of curiosity, spoke with Chee for fifteen minutes before disappearing.

- The visitors had to stay for a while—five months—near Harrison's home after their vessel crashed and they had to wait for help to arrive. But they accepted contact with a human only because their rescue was late in coming, and only after taking a week to make sure that Harrison lived an isolated life and that no other human being came to the deserted area. Only then did they show themselves.

Given the above exceptions—which are minor ones—we can still consider that at least the idea of this rule of noninterference in human lives was respected. Furthermore, in all of these exceptional cases, the visitors always showed goodwill and respect toward the witnesses and always thanked them before leaving.

Three visitors explained this rule:

It is interesting to note that in each one of these cases, this rule of noninterference was explained by the visitors themselves because it just so happened they had to violate it. These cases are very rare and thus even more precious. It is no doubt significant that these accounts came from Amerindians.

Ross's visitor said, "They were not authorized to have contact with humans, and this is why they were uncomfortable about being discovered."

Chee's visitor said, "It couldn't resist the temptation to speak to a human despite the risk of being reprimanded by its superiors if they were to learn of this violation."

Harrison's grandfather's visitors, who were in contact with him for several months, said, "They never interfered with life forms they found in the universe. They were not our enemies and did not want to harm the earth's inhabitants, but they also did not want to be friends with earth dwellers. They did not want to leave behind any trace on Earth."

Unplanned encounters:

The encounters with the visitors always happened by chance and were never initiated by them. The only exception is that of Chee. The encounters seemed to respect a law of randomness, in keeping with the law of noninterference.

Never taken into the vessel:

The witnesses were never invited into the vessel, even when there was contact with the visitors. This is consistent with the rule of avoidance. The case of Harrison's grandfather was an exception. It was precisely thanks to the amicable bond that was created over a period of several months—a rather long time—that the visitors invited Harrison's grandfather into their vessel to show him pictures of their home planet.

Never taken into another world:

The witnesses always remained in their natural, material environment. They never had the feeling of being taken into another world.

Respect and goodwill:

In all the cases where there was physical contact between the visitors and the witnesses, these contacts were characterized by mutual respect and goodwill.

Noble qualities:

Darren's case is exceptional because the visitor, whom Darren saved when it was lost, came back twice several years later to personally greet his rescuer. This behavior reveals noble qualities of gratitude and amicable loyalty.

Cautious attitudes:

In several cases, such as those of Valensole and Kent, we saw that the visitors immobilized the human beings who were present. We could interpret this as aggression, but the context tells us that it was more an attitude of caution than anything else. They wanted to prevent the witnesses from coming any closer and therefore respect the rule of noninterference. Furthermore, the witnesses did not experience any lasting effects.

Differences between the Two Categories of UFO Occupants

Our objective is to shed light on a very sensitive subject influenced by many different points of view, so at the risk of sounding repetitive, we will now highlight the differences between the characteristics of these two categories: the abductors and the space visitors.

Voluntary intrusions vs. chance encounters:

Abductors: They are the ones who initiate the encounters. They intrude on the lives of their victims without any respect for their dignity.

Visitors: The encounters occur by chance, respecting the law of randomness. When certain circumstances provoke these encounters, the visitors do all they can to limit the duration of the contact and to avoid any close contact, out of respect for the rule of noninterference in the lives of humans.

Violation vs. goodwill:

Abductors: The abductors violate their victims. They have no moral conscience and do not measure the trauma they inflict.

Visitors: When circumstances force them to violate the rule of noninterference, they are always perfectly neutral and kind toward human beings, in keeping with the spirit of the rule of noninterference. They show total respect for human beings and never do them any physical harm.

Activists for the earth's future vs. neutral observers:

Abductors: The abductors are quite concerned about the earth's ecology and try to raise ecological awareness among humans.

Visitors: The visitors always act as perfectly neutral observers and don't want to leave behind any trace of their visit to Earth.

Taken inside a vessel vs. not being taken inside a vessel:

Abductors: The victims are always taken inside a flying vessel to undergo the same medical protocol.

Visitors: The witnesses are almost never invited inside the vessel. The only exception is that of Harrison's grandfather, due to the amicable relationship that arose out of a long, five-month period of cohabitation.

Taken into another world vs. remaining in their own environment:

Abductors: The abductors take their victims into another world and bring them inside the vessel by using supernatural means. They can also simulate different environments.

Visitors: The witnesses always remain in their natural material environment. They never have the impression of being taken into another world.

Diverse appearances vs. solely a human appearance:

Abductors: According to the accounts, the abductors have different appearances: human, insect, robot—or humanoid with a large number of possible variations. They can even change their appearance in the course of one abduction experience.

Visitors: The visitors always have a human appearance and are dressed in tight-fitting one-piece suits that can be of various different colors.

Memories erased vs. memories intact:

Abductors: In general, the abductors, using methods only known to them, erase the memories of the kidnappings they inflict on their victims.

Visitors: The visitors, who in all cases display a neutral and respectful attitude, never interfere in the lives of the witnesses. On the contrary, in the several cases where contact did take place, the visitors ended the contact by expressing their gratitude, either through gestures or words.

In conclusion, we can sum up the opposing differences between these two categories by pointing out their most important differences:

Abductors: They use supernatural means in order to abduct their victims into a vessel and violate them through sexual practices with no moral conscience or respect for their dignity. They are concerned about the earth's ecological imbalances.

Visitors: They act as neutral, noninvasive observers. They avoid encountering humans as much as possible and do not want to leave behind any trace of their visit to Earth. When at times they are taken by surprise near their vessel, their reaction is always to run away. When exceptional circumstances require contact with humans, they are always very respectful toward them.

At this stage of our study, on the basis of everything that has been presented, we can conclude that *we really are dealing with two totally different types of entities.* Our next step will be to try to uncover the identity of (1) the beings who commit abductions and (2) the beings who are sometimes encountered at the foot of their space vessel.

CHAPTER FIVE

WHAT CAN WE SAY ABOUT THESE VISITORS?

Let's start by taking a closer look at these visitors—these visitors who claim that they come from faraway stars and who seem like the extraterrestrials that we have always imagined. But we really don't know that much about them. Indeed, before the recently published Amerindian testimonies, never in known human history have there been verified accounts of contacts with representatives of extraterrestrial civilizations. These accounts, some of which are cited here, are therefore of capital importance. What do they teach us about these visitors?

What "Close Encounters with Avoidance" Teach Us

In the several accounts where there was brief communication with Amerindians, we noticed that the visitors demonstrated noble qualities of respect, kindness, gratitude, and loyalty. To these qualities, we can also add their unobtrusiveness when observing life on Earth and their respect for the rule of noninterference—which we saw in all other cases where there was no communication but only simple, visual contact. We can also notice that never did the visitors exhibit the slightest sign of aggression or a feeling of superiority. We can therefore reasonably credit the visitors with being honest and sincere. On the basis of what they themselves have explained about their species, we will reflect on this information more closely in order to get to know them a bit better.

Ross's Account

According to Ross's visitor, "They were a young team and they would probably lose their rights as explorers if their superiors were to learn of their error." They were not authorized to come in contact with human beings, and this is why they were uncomfortable at being discovered. Furthermore, "On its planet, the weather never changes," and it had "never seen snow before or experienced such extreme cold." The visitor therefore introduces itself as belonging to a team of explorers from a faraway planet who are visiting planet Earth. It is on a mission to explore Earth and is under the supervision of its superiors.

Moreover, this visitor "had a human form but was not human. From a certain distance it could be mistaken for a ten-year-old child." Its hands had only four fingers each. Its normal way of moving around was to become invisible (dematerialize) and visible (rematerialize) in another place. Its physical makeup is therefore comparable to that of humans but with significant differences and a mastery over its physical body largely beyond that of human abilities. It can thus be described as belonging to an extraterrestrial human race with abilities that are different from those of our own terrestrial human race.

Chee's Account

Chee's visitor introduced itself as "a star traveler who had come a long way." To explain where it came from, "it pointed to the far end of the Milky Way and said that its planet was in that area, but that it could not be seen by the human eye." It specified that "there was oxygen in its world, but it was very different from ours." We can suppose here that the visitor meant to say that either the atmospheric pressure was different or that the composition of the air was different, with a different proportion of oxygen. It explained that "its mission was to collect specimens of herbs, plants, soil, and rocks."

This visitor also introduced itself as a traveler from a very faraway planet but also specified that the planet is part of our galaxy. It is a planet similar to Earth since it also has an atmosphere made up of oxygen, and thus is conducive to life that is comparable to the one we know on Earth. Their minerals and vegetation, however, must have developed differently than ours, since its reason for visiting Earth was to collect samples of vegetation and soil, which, we can imagine, are different from what can be found on its planet. Concerning its physical makeup, it indicated that "it didn't drink liquids like humans do." We can understand from this that their bodies are also different from ours.

It specified that "there were many civilizations or worlds up there," thus expressing that many other developed life forms live on many planets throughout our galaxy and that many other space travelers can come and visit the earth. It also said that "its ancestors had visited the same place thousands of years ago." This indicates that a long time ago, its race had attained a level of evolution allowing it to travel in space, and as a result, these visits to Earth were not at all recent.

Darren's Account

Darren's visitor simply indicated that it was part of a small team "on a mission of exploration" and that its species "had been visiting the earth for a very long time." This supports the information in the previous accounts.

Brett's Account

Brett provided very little information about the visitors, saying only that these creatures had a human appearance and were short. He did specify that they were about four feet tall and were fair skinned.

Harrison's Account

Harrison's grandfather saw fourteen visitors who were all very tall: more than six and a half feet. "Their fingers were longer than those of humans," and they looked so much alike that Harrison's grandfather had a hard time telling them apart. This tells us that he had closely observed them, but he had not pointed out any large differences between their faces and those of humans, other than to say that their "hair was white and their eyes changed color with the light." They were therefore very similar to us, except for their height, their eye color, and their hair.

"At first, they disappeared right before his eyes as soon as they saw him," which means that they also were good at making themselves invisible, or dematerializing, at will. This certainly shows their high level of evolution and also perhaps has something to do with being able to travel long distances in space. We will address this later on.

Concerning their origin: "The star travelers told my grandfather that they were from a star system belonging to a constellation that they showed him, and my science teacher taught me that it was the constellation of Taurus. They told my grandfather that they were voyagers who traveled the Universe in order to observe life in other worlds. They had been coming to Earth for thousands of years in order to observe, collect data, and record changes." This is perfectly coherent with the previous accounts. These travelers came from another planet in the Milky Way, but they were of a different race than the previous visitors—and their physical makeup was very similar to ours.

The Other Accounts

In these cases, there wasn't any communication with the visitors, and we have only some vague information about what they looked like.

Maurice Masse (the Valensole case) described his visitors as small beings of human appearance. They were short in height—not even three feet tall—with big heads that were disproportionately large for their bodies.

The children of Cussac described little beings who seemed to be wearing black outfits that covered their heads and bodies. The shortest ones were no taller than three feet, while the other two were no more than four feet tall. What is noteworthy about this episode is the way they got back into their vessel: they flew straight up in the air and then went headfirst into the ship.

In the case of Socorro, the police officer saw only "two silhouettes."

In the case of the disappearing apples in England, the witness said he saw "three men of equal height" and then described the three beings who were observing the crop circle as "tall, blond men." When it came time to run away, they "started running faster than any man," which seems to distinguish them from our human race. Then they suddenly disappeared, which clearly confirms that they belonged to another, more evolved race.

These last observations are consistent with the previous information and provide no additional elements. They confirm that in all the reported cases, the visitors had a human appearance even though there were some differences. They showed a manifest interest in observing vegetation and even in taking samples. When they were surprised by the presence of humans nearby, they did all they could to avoid contact.

Where Science Stands Today

We are living in a time where, thanks to the improvement of astronomical instruments of observation, we know that more than two hundred billion stars, similar to our sun, make up our galaxy: the Milky Way. In addition to the Milky Way, there are several hundred billion galaxies of significant mass in the observable universe. We also know that each one of these stars is potentially surrounded by a number of planets that revolve around it. Moreover, in recent years, an ever-increasing number of exoplanets have been observed in the Milky Way. Several thousand were detected in 2018, and today it is estimated that there are more than two hundred billion in our galaxy alone. Astronomers think that many have physical characteristics similar to those of Earth, making it possible for comparable evolved life forms to inhabit them.

This being said, it has pretty much been since the beginning of time that humans have been watching the sky and asking themselves if there is life elsewhere in the Universe and if other civilizations have developed on other planets. The nearly infinite number of stars and planets in the sky leads us to think that this is highly probable. And even though this seems more and more likely, this is still just a hypothesis for today's scientists, physicists, and astronomers.

Analysis of Electromagnetic Signals Coming from Space

In recent decades, projects one after another have tried to find proof of the existence of extraterrestrial civilizations. For example, American projects such as SETI (Search for Extraterrestrial Intelligences) detect and analyze electromagnetic signals coming from space that could be attempts by other civilizations to make contact with us. The first project of this nature was launched in 1960. Others have taken over in recent years and are ongoing. Since the beginning of these observations, several unexplained signals have been detected, but none of them have been identified as being from an extraterrestrial civilization.

The Chilbolton Crop Circles (2001)

We also know of the famous message emitted in 1974 toward faraway stars by using the radio telescope of Arecibo, Puerto Rico, within the context of a SETI project. It received a lot of attention when, in 2001, two crop circles appeared near the Chilbolton observatory in England. One was an image of a human-type face. Located near it was another crop circle that consisted of a message composed by using the same code as the one used to send the message in Arecibo, but it contained some information that was identical and some that was different. The message sent by the Arecibo astronomers in 1974 was in the form of electromagnetic pulsations and used coded information. It consisted of a succinct description of what a human being is. The crop circle in 2001 can be considered a response, since the code was the same and likewise provided a description of its sender.

Most specialists attributed the origin of the Chilbolton message to an extraterrestrial being because the information contained in the message was incomprehensible to them. This conclusion seems logical, even though an extraterrestrial origin has not been formally proven. As for the scientific community, it has never taken this type of response seriously, since it is not at all interested in the crop circle phenomenon and therefore does not recognize its authenticity.

However, the author of the current work has proposed a different interpretation based on esoteric knowledge of the veritable nature of human beings. This allows us to make sense of the Chilbolton message.[1] According to this interpretation, the creator of the Chilbolton crop circle would belong to the terrestrial human race while being at a very high level of evolution in the spiritual plane.

The Absence of Scientific Proof of Extraterrestrial Intelligences

The scientific point of view today is that no extraterrestrial civilization has ever contacted us, although the age of our galaxy—ten billion years—should have allowed some extraterrestrial civilizations to engage in interstellar travel. These civilizations should have left behind some traces in our solar system—traces that we should be able to detect. Consequently, scientists' efforts continue to focus on the reception and analysis of extraterrestrial radio and optical signals, which could be from such civilizations.

But scientists have never envisioned the idea that extraterrestrials are already present on our earth—among us, unbeknown to us. However, we are now going to show that "close encounters with avoidance" can be considered as a proof of this. It is true that the large majority of the scientific community is not interested in UFO phenomena or crop circles, nor is it interested in other forms of material manifestations unexplained by science—material manifestations that are thrown into the category of "paranormal" phenomena. Through such indifference, today's science is cutting itself off from a large part of the reality of the world in which we live, and is depriving itself of a very important source of knowledge.

Discussion

This discussion will be based on the information contained in the ten accounts of "close encounters with avoidance" previously described in this work. This number of ten could perhaps appear derisory, yet it is quite significant because all the testimonies are different and independent of each other. Perhaps there are even more accounts—accounts that are less known? Ardy Sixkiller Clarke's book contains several other accounts that do not tell us much, so they have not been included here. All this being said, the metaphysical implications of the revelations we do have are immense.

BEINGS WHO ARE TRULY EXTRATERRESTRIAL

Building on the distinction that we have been able to make between the two categories of UFO phenomena, we know that these ten accounts report contact between humans and beings of human appearance claiming to be representatives of diverse extraterrestrial races on a mission to explore the earth. But the kidnappers also claim to be extraterrestrials; that is, beings coming from faraway stars aboard their flying vessels. Can both affirmations be equally trustworthy?

In order to answer this question, we can rely on the basic descriptions of the beings along with their main characteristics described at the end of chapter 4. The abductors are beings who kidnap their victims and violate their bodily integrity without any consciousness of the suffering they inflict, and, therefore, without any respect for human beings. Some of them can change appearance right in front of their victims, which reveals a deceitful attitude. Marie-Thérèse de Brosses recounts the case of a famous abduction that took place in Rhodesia, where, in response to a question that a pair of kidnapping victims asked their abductor, the abductor had said: "We have no form. We can take on whatever appearance suits you. If you want me to look like a duck because that's what suits you best, I will take on the appearance of a duck."[2] This deceitfulness is accentuated by the fact that they make a point of erasing these scenes from their victims' memories. Such base behavior does not inspire us to trust such beings in what they do or say.

We have, however, detected several noble qualities in the attitudes of the visitors: tact, respect, kindness, gratitude, fidelity, and loyalty—and all of this without any aggressiveness or sense of superiority. This is why we can also attribute to them the qualities of honesty and sincerity. All these traits reveal a high level of evolution and inspire us to trust such beings and believe that what they tell us is true. We can therefore envision that they are really of extraterrestrial origin. The discussion that follows will reinforce this interpretation.

In our discussion, we will remain firmly rooted in rational thought while as much as possible avoiding the influence of the limitations of today's science and the conditioning that we have unconsciously been subjected to. Consequently, this may seem like science fiction.

Neither Mask nor Spacesuit

In each one of these cases of close encounters, we have noticed that the visitors had a human appearance with some physical traits that are different from ours. At least from far away, they look exactly like us, with a physical makeup and outside appearance similar to ours. But they are not humans like us—first of all because they are capable of becoming invisible or visible at will, and second of all because they are able to travel in space vessels. Humanity, not yet having acquired this mastery over the physical body or such technology, is led to accept the idea that these visitors do indeed come from extraterrestrial planets and that they belong to a type of being that we can call human. But they are humans from space.

Meanwhile, each one of us possesses a mental image of astronauts setting foot on the moon, encased in their spacesuits—and we can't help but be influenced by this image. But in these accounts we have neither a spacesuit nor a mask; these beings do not need such equipment in order to live on Earth. They are adapted to life on this planet although they come from space. Because their bodies are evidently adapted to our form of life, we can easily believe that they were born and grew up on a planet similar to our earth.

Setting aside for a moment the fact that the visitors are able to travel between their home planet and the earth, these encounters show us that life exists elsewhere than on Earth.

They show us that other developed civilizations exist—and through the visitors' ability to travel in space and their consistently peaceful, respectful, and kind behavior, these encounters also show us that their civilizations are more developed than ours.

But we also discover that all these beings, with no exception, appear to be human as we know it. They are similar to us except for some details.

This implies that their civilizations have developed on planets apparently similar to that of Earth, and although belonging to other star systems, they have the same physical conditions favorable to our form of life: temperate climate, oxygen, average gravitational pull, the same basic chemical elements, etc.

Yet, minor differences exist, since, depending on the visitors we have encountered, some physical details distinguish them from our human race. Their interest in observing and collecting mineral and vegetal samples shows that these things probably do not exist on their home planets. Furthermore, Harrison's grandfather pointed out something that was concretely different on his visitors' planet: "In their world, water was underground; there was none on the surface."

The reality and implications of these extraterrestrial presences on Earth obviously create a considerable upheaval for human thought and glaringly reveal the limits of scientific thought, which remains trapped in its materialist dogma.

A "Subtle Physical" Body and a "Dense Material" Body

We have noticed in several situations that the visitors are able to make themselves invisible or visible at will, which seems incredible to us.

We saw this with Ross's visitor. It was able to enter and then leave from the cab of Ross's snowplow by using this ability: "One moment it was standing in the middle of the highway, and a moment later it was inside the cab with me." And then when it came time to part ways, even though the visitor was sitting beside him: "The space traveler suddenly disappeared. Several seconds later, I saw it in front of the vessel." And then right before the vessel took off: "I was able to make out its profile in the flashing lights, and in the pale light I could see it making a hand gesture in my direction . . . and in an instant it was no longer there."

We also saw this in Harrison's testimony. His grandfather noticed that "At first, they would disappear right before his very eyes as soon as they saw him." And then he said later: "During the five months that they waited to be rescued, they were not afraid of being discovered because they could make themselves invisible, but they could not do the same thing with their ship."

We again saw this in the incident of the disappearance of apples: "Then the three men vanished."

And finally, in the case of the Wiltshire crop circle visitors: "The police officer looked away for a split second, and when he looked back again, they were gone."

Dimensional Shifts

This ability to become invisible and then visible can be explained in terms of the ability to dematerialize and rematerialize. But this dematerialization does not mean that the physical body is reduced to nothing. It disappears only from sight, since the same body can reappear afterward. Its structure is thus preserved during the dematerialization process. We encountered this same process in the accounts of the temporary disappearances of Corporal Valdès and Jeff in chapter 2. We explained that Corporal Valdès had undergone a dimensional shift. Under the influence of his captors and due to invisible forces, he left the material world of humans to enter a world in another dimension, before an inverse dimensional shift brought him back into the material world, still under the influence of his abductors.

A Subtle Physical Body and a Dense Material Body

We can describe this same process, this dimensional shift, in different terms by using spiritual science, since it is obviously impossible to understand this on the basis of modern science.

Spiritual science teaches that at the beginning of time, because the process of materialization of the earth involved a gradual densification of matter, conditions were not yet conducive for human incarnation, and human beings therefore were still living on a spiritual plane. They had a physical body with a subtle nature. Then, when this process of materialization was advanced enough, human beings "came down to Earth" to be incarnated. Biblical texts allude to this descent to Earth. In order to live in matter—a material world—human beings had to take on a material body made in the image of their subtle body but composed of dense matter.

The principle is that for an individual to be able to manifest and evolve in a world—in our case in the material world of the earth—they must be present in this world and possess a body made of the same substance as this world. It is thus that human beings were able to "live in matter" by taking on a material body. Over time, human beings have completely identified themselves through their material body and completely forgotten their origin and their spiritual nature to the extent that they are in contact today only with their material body. But the veritable nature of a human being is their subtle physical body.

Thus, this esoteric knowledge explains the distinction between a human being's "veritable physical body," which is by nature subtle, immaterial and therefore invisible, and a human being's "material body," made of dense matter and therefore visible, which is a copy of the "veritable physical body."

"OUT OF BODY" EXPERIENCES AND "BILOCATION"

Some men and women experience this subtle physical body when, according to the often-used expression, they "go out of their body." This can happen, for example, during deep meditation. This can also happen spontaneously during an accident, while under anesthesia, or when in a coma. This subtle, physical structure, which carries our consciousness, can therefore face the material body and look at it and even move around and observe its surroundings, while the material body remains immobile.

It is also possible to understand this aspect of esoteric knowledge through the phenomenon of bilocation. This ability consists of being present in two different places at the same time and has been manifested by those who have attained a very high degree of evolution. The Catholic tradition reports numerous eyewitness-confirmed cases. Whereas the material body obeys the laws of matter and science, the subtle physical body does not. It can travel guided by the thoughts of an individual and eventually take on a material appearance and appear in any given place, depending on the amount of energy the person was able to produce in order to attract matter. The subtle physical body can therefore appear, change, and disappear at the will of the person who has this bilocation ability.

In order to better understand that the subtle physical body can thus move about and travel, guided by an individual's thoughts and therefore without limits, we can draw a parallel with what is most commonly known as a human being's astral body. According to spiritual science, the astral body is the other component of the human being; it is the part that allows us to feel emotions and to have thoughts (we will study what spiritual science says about the different components of a human being in chapter 6). It's the astral body that allows one to take astral trips, to transport one's consciousness anywhere in the world and to go observe, for example, what is happening "at the other end of the earth." And this is accomplished instantaneously without the material physical body and the subtle physical body moving at all.

Human beings who are capable of "leaving their material body" with their subtle physical body can travel with this body, because the astral body and consciousness are joined. They can move about physically wherever they wish—but not only astrally—and materialize their subtle physical body if there is enough energy available. This is what bilocation is.

THE SEVEN LEVELS OF DENSITY OF MATTER

There is yet another way to understand this delicate notion of subtle physical body. According to another element of esoteric knowledge—which we will come back to in chapter 6—matter has several levels of different densities. Each one of us knows about the three states of matter known as solid, liquid, and gas, in their order of decreasing density, which modern science describes very well. But spiritual science adds four other levels of density that are more subtle—known as ethers. Ethers are invisible to most human beings, and only acutely perceptive individuals have the ability to see these subtle levels of matter. We can put forth then the idea that the subtle physical body has a density that corresponds to the levels of these ethers, which are invisible to ordinary humans.

Subtle Physical Body and Interstellar Travel

Humanity's current level of evolution does not allow humans to engage in interstellar travel, and current science does not allow us to understand how these visitors from space were able to travel to Earth.

The theory of relativity's inherent limitation:

According to the theory of relativity (developed by Albert Einstein), the mass of a material object increases with its speed so as to attain an infinite value if its speed reaches the speed of light. By virtue of the fundamental relationship of dynamics, the larger the mass, the more energy is needed to move it. We therefore see that these fundamental principles of physics lead to the inherent impossibility for any material object to go faster than the speed of light—or even get close to it.

But it so happens that the stars that are closest to the earth are located light-years away, such as the closest one, Proxima Centauri, at 4.24 light-years. And if we are to believe Harrison's grandfather's visitors, they came from a planet belonging to the constellation of Taurus, located sixty-five light-years from us. This means that it takes light around sixty-five years to cover the distance from their home planet to Earth.

Chee's visitor claimed that it came from a planet located "at the far end of the Milky Way." Since the length of the Milky Way is estimated by astronomers as being between 100,000 and 120,000 light-years, the distance between the visitor's home planet and the Earth adds up to tens of thousands of light-years. At the speed of light, then, the visitor would take tens of thousands of years to get to us.

According to modern science, these distances are completely absurd when it comes to engaging in interstellar travel to visit the earth, even though we have read about the presence of space visitors in all of these preceding testimonies. This implies that in order to travel from their home planets, these visitors were not subject to the limitations of speed that the theory of relativity places on material objects. Spiritual science allows us to envision that they traveled with their subtle physical bodies, which do not obey the laws of matter. Once at their destination, the visitors then densified or materialized their subtle physical bodies in order to become visible on Earth.

Furthermore, it appears coherent that these visitors, whose presence on Earth shows their high level of evolution, have the natural ability to densify their subtle physical body—an ability already mastered on Earth by humans who are capable of bilocation.

Subtle body and travel in space:

According to the above explanations, if the space travelers want to land on a planet far from their home that belongs to another star system, they can travel only with their subtle physical body because such a trip is not possible within a reasonable time frame if they were to travel with their material body. It is only with their subtle body that they can break through the constraints and limits imposed upon dense matter—limits to which our astronauts are currently subjected to.

But if space travelers wish to visit a planet, they must apply the general principle explained above—that is, in order to manifest themselves in a given world, it is necessary to be present in that world. To illustrate this, let us imagine that we wanted to see fish living in the sea. In order to do so, we would have to enter into their world. By the same token, space travelers who want to observe material life on Earth must take on a dense material body in order to collect vegetal or mineral specimens. But in return, they must let themselves be visible to us human beings and thereby allow us to be aware of their presence.

Unharmed after the crash of their vessel:

Let us remember that the fourteen visitors encountered by Harrison's grandfather remained invisible for more than a week, and yet, they were present. We also notice that none of them were harmed when they arrived, even though their vessel had undergone a shock when it crashed—a shock whose intensity was comparable to that of an earthquake—which almost completely destroyed the vessel. Right away this appears to be impossible, at least for us human beings. We can propose the idea that they were still in their subtle physical bodies and therefore did not suffer the effects of the enormous physical shock of the vessel's crash. They did not suffer the devastating effects of the crash because they were not subject to the laws of material science.

But if the travelers had been in their subtle physical bodies—necessary for interstellar travel (and thanks to which they were protected from the crash)—the same could be said of their space vessel. The vessel also had to have been in a state of subtle density of matter at the etheric level in order to go beyond material limitations and undertake the trip. It is probable that as it approached landing time, the vessel materialized, or densified, but due to its malfunction was unable to land normally.

This reasoning supposes not only that the visitors from space had the ability to control the density of their physical body upon their arrival on Earth—to densify or materialize it to adapt to the world they were in—but that they could also do this for any object. Thus, spiritual science's concepts of subtle physical body and levels of etheric density—unrecognized by modern science—can enable us to understand that extraterrestrial visitors were able to travel in space and that they were able to easily disappear out of sight when surprised by the presence of witnesses.

Telepathy

We have observed that in each one of the cases where there was a conversation with the visitors, the communication took place spontaneously and easily, without any problem of language. In fact, the witnesses didn't realize right away how effortless it all was. They did not know whether or not the visitors were really speaking to them, since the conversations happened so naturally.

It appears obvious that these conversations were taking place via telepathy, even if the men weren't always aware of it. The visitors were capable of reading the minds of the men when they expressed themselves in words, and they were also capable of conveying their thoughts in a way that the men understood them, without having to translate their messages into words.

This practice of telepathy should not come as a surprise, since evolved human beings also have the ability to use it. We know that in our day, a number of people notice that this ability is developing in them.

Immense Philosophical and Spiritual Implications

THE CRAZY NOTION THAT HUMANS ARE THE ONLY INTELLIGENT BEINGS

The discovery of these extraterrestrial presences on Earth obviously has immense philosophical and spiritual implications. Science teaches us that we human beings are the most developed species on Earth, that we are the only ones who are intelligent, and that there is no proof of the existence of other intelligences in the Universe since scientists have never detected any presence of these supposed intelligences. But we realize how illusory this thinking is—this thinking that has over the years fed our human pride and inflated our ego.

In these Amerindian accounts, we have proof that this statement is false. It is urgent that we develop our sense of humility concerning these other human races whose level of evolution is clearly superior to ours. It is urgent, when we consider these extraterrestrial presences, for us to become aware that the level of evolution of our human race is still quite limited. Right now our human race is going through a real adolescent crisis, a crisis characterized by overinflated egos and inordinate pride, by disrespect for Mother Nature—whom we depend on for life—and by incessant fighting.

THE LIMITS OF CURRENT HUMAN CIVILIZATION

The history of research on UFOs since the Second World War has amply shown us that humans have interpreted these unidentified objects first and foremost as enemy threats during WWII and at the beginning of the Cold War. Later on, they saw these as threats of invasion from supposed extraterrestrial beings who were never identified. The study presented in this work shows that the reality is completely opposite. First, we have seen that there is a dual origin of the UFO phenomena, and if the presence of some representatives of extraterrestrial races is now certain, their behavior is always perfectly respectful of humans, on the basis of the principle of noninterference.

Furthermore, the number of sightings of these extraterrestrial presences on Earth is very small and does not take into account the millions of reported UFO sightings. We can therefore conclude that it is the other category of UFOs that accounts for the large majority of sightings, and that this category comes from a different origin, which we will examine in the following chapter.

When we compare the space visitors' attitudes of respect and kindness to the pervasive, conflictual attitudes of human beings here on Earth, especially at this time in history, we clearly see how limited our level of human civilization is today on this planet.

Extraterrestrials in Our Midst?

Continuing on with our sci-fi story—based on the extraordinary information given above—we see that reality can go well beyond fiction. The descriptions of the visitors showed us that they had, in all cases, a physical makeup that was similar to that of human beings—with differences that were sometimes large (heights of four feet) and sometimes small. We can therefore think that, given their blanket attachment to the principle of noninterference, the number of extraterrestrial races that visit the earth and the number of their visits could be much higher than the number of cases reported.

As a result, we can reasonably think that some visitors can be very similar to us and can perhaps be capable of blending into a group of human beings without anyone noticing.

Concerning this, Ardy Sixkiller Clarke wrote: "A large number of independent sources provide proof that extraterrestrial visitors of human appearance have blended into large urban areas, and this is known by a small number of government agencies and military structures. A number of highly classified government documents confirm this phenomenon, revealed by some whistleblowers."[3]

She continues: "In addition to the accounts of whistleblowers, a number of private citizens affirm having encountered extraterrestrials who have taken on the appearance of ordinary citizens in large cities throughout the world." She then cites the accounts of two women who lived incognito in the middle of human society but also described their own stellar heritage.

RETHA'S ACCOUNT[4]

Retha was a retired officer in the United States Air Force. Known as an emotionally, mentally, and physically strong woman, she was also gifted with an exceptional intelligence.

Ardy Sixkiller Clarke, on the suggestion of a close friend, went to see Retha at her isolated home, where she confided this: "I was not born on this planet. Everyone thinks that I am Amerindian, and this is what I put on all of the documents that I fill out. But the truth is that I was brought up by an Indian who passed me off as her granddaughter. I was on board a vessel that crashed on the earth. A 70-year-old woman, Mary Blevins, found me. The crash site was close to her house. When she heard the crash and came to take a look, it was there that she found me. From what I could tell, she hid my origin from everyone and claimed that I was her granddaughter.

"Everyone knew Mary, and when she insisted that I was her granddaughter, no one questioned it, even though they knew that it wasn't true. Revered for her medicinal knowledge, she had authority within her tribe, and no one brought up the subject of my birth. As she was the local midwife, it was easy for her to go to the court and ask for a birth certificate. This is how I became a human being known as Retha Blevins.

"I know little about my arrival on this planet, nor do I know much about where I came from. When I was a young woman, Mary spoke to me of my origins, but she did not have much information to share with me. She took me to the crash site of the vessel; it was a marshy area that was frequently submerged due to rain and stagnant water. Here I saw absolutely no evidence that proved her story. She claimed that when she found me, I was in the arms of a female that was still alive. The creature asked Mary to take care of me. I didn't have any reason to believe that Mary wasn't telling me the truth, and in fact I had always known that I was different from the other children at my school. At the time I still had no idea to what extent.

"When I was a teenager, I dreamt that one day my people would come and get me. At night I used to go out and sit under the stars and wait for them to show up, but they never came. I never got along with the other children, but this is a problem that many children have. I only felt comfortable with Mary, who had a special understanding of the Universe.

"I have a physical particularity in that I don't have a navel." She lifted up her shirt and revealed soft skin where the navel should have been. "I don't need much sleep—around two to four hours a day. It has been this way since childhood. Grandma said that she would wake up in the middle of the night and see me sitting in my bed playing and talking. I just didn't feel sleepy. My heart beats twice as slowly as that of a normal human being, but in spite of this I was able to pass the military medical check. Also, I age slower than humans. These are small differences, but when you consider them altogether, they do set me apart physically. I don't cry either—and I heard people say that it's because I am an Indian, but that has nothing to do with it. I simply am incapable of crying. I never went through the hormonal changes that human teenagers do. As a result, I was never attracted to men nor [sic] to women. I learned to read at the age of two. I skipped several grades at school, which made me look even more strange to others. At school I was always put with a group of students older than me, and I was too young for everyone. Thus in all of these subtle ways, I am different from you all, and yet I can pass for a human because these differences can be swept aside as being simple oddities.

"Mary died when I was at college. At first I was completely undecided about what I was to do with my life. Mary was my protector, my guide, my only family. It was then that I learned of the Air Force. It became my family and I remained there until I retired."

Retha never married and never had children. She died after falling off a horse. On her gravestone it is written: "Retha Blevins, granddaughter of Mary Blevins and Daughter of the Stars. She was not of this earth."

ANALYSIS

1. No navel:

The most noteworthy part of this account is obviously the fact that Retha had no navel. If the account's reliability is certain—and there isn't anything that says it is not—this fact allows us to conclude that Retha did not belong to our human race. All human beings before birth, without exception, gestate in the uterus of a woman and are fed through an umbilical cord, connected to the fetus by a navel. Without exception, all human beings on this earth have a navel.

2. A different reproductive system:

The reproductive system of beings belonging to Retha's race was therefore different from that of human beings on Earth. The fact that Retha had not gone through hormonal changes when she was a teenager and had not had a puberty phase, and the fact that she was not attracted to men or to women—while not being proof—nonetheless converge in the same direction. We can even ask the question if, in spite of the identity given to her by her "grandmother," she was not as much man as she was woman.

Retha never married and never had children. After being raised by her "grandmother," who was not her grandmother, the only other family she knew throughout her whole life was the US Air Force. She therefore always lived outside the realm of humans.

3. A woman not like the others:

The sum of these minor differences setting Retha apart from human beings gives weight to the conclusion that Retha was not a woman like the others. She did not belong to our earthly human race. Furthermore, the fact that since her childhood she needed only a little sleep and the fact that she could read as early as the age of two represent very significant differences in relation to human beings and must not be ignored.

GIRTY'S ACCOUNT[5]

Girty described herself as one-eighth black, three-eighths Cherokee, and half extraterrestrial. Ardy Sixkiller Clarke describes her as a tall, thin woman, with light coffee-colored skin. Her long black hair framed her face with its high cheekbones, evoking her Indian heritage. Her gray cat eyes with yellow reflects gave her an exotic appearance. She lived on a houseboat.

"It is not easy to grow up knowing that you are different. My father was from a star near the Seven Sisters constellation. My mother never knew how to pronounce the name of it. My parents had a strange relationship.

I often wondered how I was conceived, but my mother swore on her deathbed that the man she called Joe was my father and that he was indeed an extraterrestrial who came from another world. I don't think that my mother would have lied to me about this." She then showed me a picture of her parents, taken the day of their wedding, showing a woman of mixed race and a white man. According to Ardy Sixkiller Clarke, the general silhouette of this man was human, and it was difficult to make out any atypical features. "He was very tall and looked like a white man."

Girty continues: "My father's vessel had crashed in Lake Michigan. This was where he met my mother. She was working in a car factory in Detroit[,] and she ran into him in an alley on her way home from work. He was wounded and she took pity on him. She brought him home with her[,] and three weeks later they were married. My mother got him a job at the factory. At the time, it was easy to get a social security number; all you had to do was request one. My mother told everyone that he was deaf and dumb and that he couldn't speak. At the time, no one dug into people's lives like they do today . . . and all the factory needed was someone to place cylinders on the assembly line. When I was four, my parents moved outside of the city and settled on a small piece of land. My father would sit outside on summer nights looking up at the sky. I always thought that he was hoping that his people would come to get him, but they never showed up.

"He was a caring father; he loved me in his way and watched over me a great deal. He warned me of danger and picked me up when I fell, but he never spoke to me. We had a little garage with the house[,] and he spent most of his time there working on electrical appliances—mostly radios— but he could repair anything. People would bring him small household appliances, lawn mowers, and other things . . . and he repaired them all.

"He had a four-gallon bucket where he would put the money that people paid him. He said that the money was for me and that it was our secret. When he died, there was nearly $10,000 in it. At the time it was a good amount of money that could buy a nice house.

"I knew that he was an extraterrestrial because he was different from a human being. He slept no more than several hours a week. He never learned to speak, even if he and my mother seemed to have certain capabilities allowing them to communicate. I never saw him eat or drink, but my mother said that his stomach was different and that he mainly ate applesauce, sliced peaches, and baby food. She would also prepare bananas for him by crushing them and heating them up with honey and milk to obtain a sticky substance.

"My mother told me that shortly after their wedding, the crash of Roswell was announced. My father became very upset and thought that his people had sent a rescue ship. When my mother took him in, his vessel had sunk to the bottom of Lake Michigan. Several hours later, a fisherman helped him out of the water. I imagine that the cold had nearly killed him. He wandered aimlessly about and went in the direction of Detroit, to the alley where my mother ran into him. He was very weak. She took him to her apartment and offered him a warm place to stay. He never liked the cold. My mother told me that in his world the climate was always temperate. I remember that he liked flowers, and in the spring when the flowers started to bloom, he seemed happier. He liked to see my mother with a flower in her hair. He really couldn't take the cold, and during winter nights he would huddle next to the gas stove in the kitchen and wrap himself in thick blankets. He is now deceased."

ANALYSIS

1. A father who never spoke:

The most noteworthy element of this account is that Girty's father never spoke. He never even spoke to his daughter when she was an infant. Yet he was not deaf. He was also highly sensitive and quite the handy man as well. We recall that in the previous accounts, the visitors seemed always to communicate by telepathy. It is plausible that they had developed this means of communication to the extent that they did not need to use words and, therefore, had no vocal chords. The fact that Girty's father had never spoken goes along with this assertion.

2. Hardly any need of food:

The other particularity is that Girty's father had hardly any need of nourishment; it is indeed remarkable that his daughter had never seen him eat or drink. He ate only fruit and baby food, which reveals that he had a digestive system very different from ours, which did not require much food. We also recall that Harrison's grandfather's fourteen visitors, all accident victims from space, remained five months with him before being rescued, and during that time they apparently had nothing to eat. They also had refused all meat—most likely game—offered by the grandfather. It seems that they had no need of material nourishment, or if they did, it was only a small amount.

Along these same lines, we can evoke the fact that some highly spiritual men or women of this earth are capable of living without eating and drinking for rather long periods of time, even years. This is called breatharianism.

3. Little need of sleep:

A third particularity about Girty's father is that he hardly ever slept: barely several hours a week. Indeed, there is no human being who can content themselves with such a small amount of sleep in order to regenerate.

4. Not adapted for cold temperatures:

Another noteworthy element is that he couldn't stand the cold. His physical makeup was not adapted to Michigan's winter cold, a cold that did not exist on his home planet.

5. Biological compatibility:

Finally, it is remarkable that, if we are to believe Girty's account, a man coming from a planet other than Earth (the Seven Sisters) was able to conceive a child with a human woman. This biological compatibility shows that Girty's mother and father had similar genetic characteristics. This means that we can refer to the extraterrestrial race of Girty's father as a human one—but different from our earthly human race in some of its characteristics.

6. Unaffected by the aging process:

Yet, Girty did not inherit all of her father's traits, since she had a "normal" vocal system and a "normal" digestive tract. Ardy Sixkiller Clarke, however, was struck by the fact that as the years went by, Girty still kept the same svelteness, suppleness, and beauty, as if unaffected by the aging process.

Conclusion

The analysis of some of the Amerindian accounts chosen from among those published in Ardy Sixkiller Clarke's book has led us to some remarkable conclusions—conclusions that we can qualify as extraordinary because they refer to details containing great philosophical implications that are still unknown to the public and contrary to what today's science understands to be true.

Extraordinary Discoveries

Not only have other civilizations—most likely in large numbers—developed elsewhere than on Earth and reached a level of evolution more advanced than on Earth, and not only have these civilizations developed on extrasolar planets with conditions that seem to be very near to what we have on Earth (oxygen-based atmosphere, similar gravity field, etc.), but representatives of these extraterrestrial civilizations have also been visiting us on Earth for thousands of years—and quite regularly at that.

We have also seen that all the beings from these extrasolar planets have, without exception, a physical aspect that is similar to that of human beings (not like reptiles or insects, or "little grays," or robots). This leads us to group all these civilizations into one large category of human species, since the term "human" is no longer limited only to our planet. There are differences that exist between these species, and we can speak of different human races just as we speak of different races here on Earth. But these differences are minor when compared to the common traits that they do share, including the biological compatibility that we have seen in Girty's account.

Even more extraordinary is the fact that, thanks to two of the accounts (Retha's and Girty's), we have evidence of the presence of these "beings from space" on Earth, beings who have blended in among our humanity. This does not contradict the principle of noninterference in human affairs because Retha's and Girty's fathers' presence on Earth was the result of space vessel accidents, and neither of them were able to be rescued by extraterrestrials of their own races.

Another Amerindian testimonial from Ardy Sixkiller Clarke's book (not included here) goes even further, because the witness says that "groups of human beings from space" sometimes land in deserted areas and immerse themselves in urban populations without the witness seeing them return. We still don't know if these visits are temporary or not.

Until proven otherwise, what we can take away from all these discoveries is that the "human being" in the broader sense of the term seems to be the most evolved physical form—at least in the physical universe. This assertion refers only to the physical realm and does not pretend to include what occurs in the spiritual worlds.

The Limits of Modern Science

These discoveries expose the limits of the materialist view of the Universe as offered to us by modern science. Even though modern science is open to the idea that other advanced civilizations have been able to develop in our universe, it remains trapped within the concept that interstellar travel is subject to the theory of relativity, which imposes that material space vessels cannot go faster than the speed of light. Thus, there cannot be travel between faraway stars. This is why astronomers, open to the idea of the existence of other civilizations, are content with looking for signs of their presence through possible electromagnetic messages that these civilizations could be sending into space. But if we were to apply the reasoning of modern science, a message from a planet connected to, let's say, a star 100 light-years away (a very short distance compared to the length of the Milky Way), and eventually reaching Earth today, would have, in reality, been sent 100 years before being received. This would make answering the sender impossible.

Beyond the fact that this way of seeing things is based on false ideas (the world is not only material), this research has very little chance of yielding positive results since the "human beings from space" adhere to the principle of staying totally neutral during their trips in space and never interfering in other civilizations. They behave as observers who are as noninvasive as possible by avoiding being seen by the intelligent beings they encounter and by taking pains not to leave behind any trace of their passage. Sending messages into space in the aim of contacting other civilizations would be against their principles.

Our difficulty in understanding all of this is related to the fact that we are unconsciously conditioned by a materialist vision of science, according to which the human being is made of a material body and therefore is subject to the laws of matter. The theory of relativity asserts that material objects cannot travel at a speed faster than the speed of light. Even if we were to take into account that according to this theory, the aging process of a space traveler would take place more slowly than on the earth, this law prevents us from realistically envisioning the existence of interstellar trips between faraway stars. Not only do our current rockets move at speeds quite slower than that of the speed of light, but the current length of stay of the astronauts in the International Space Station is less than a year. This means that interstellar travel is not adapted to the human beings that we are: beings connected to our material bodies.

Models of More-Advanced Human Beings

The discovery of these extraterrestrial presences on Earth strikingly reveals the limits of scientific thought, enclosed in its materialist dogma. These discoveries should result in reducing the pridefulness of humans on planet Earth, who take ourselves for the most-intelligent beings of creation even though we are living in a state of continual conflict. These discoveries should lead us to develop our humility when faced with the reality of these extraterrestrial beings, who can be considered as other representatives of a larger human race. We can therefore see in them "models of more-advanced human beings" who show us what our earthly human race should become in the far future.

We can indeed consider that in the world, everything is evolving toward a form of perfection, even if there still are forces that oppose this evolution. Furthermore, we have seen that all these visitors demonstrate noble qualities that are still in their fledgling stages on Earth, such as kindness and unconditional respect for others.

For those among us who wonder about the meaning of life on Earth, and who because of this take pains to broaden their vision of life in the Universe—as much in space as in time—this idea that the world is moving toward perfection can be the basis for a profound reflection. It can bring us to give human life a meaning and a mission: a mission that would be to develop noble qualities such as respect and kindness while eradicating all aggressive behavior toward others. This is still a vast project in the making for our earthly human race of today.

Do we still need to remind ourselves that in all the cases analyzed in this work, none of the visitors showed the slightest sign of aggression toward the human beings encountered, and their behavior was, on the contrary, always dictated by the principle of noninterference? This observation is a response to all people who fear UFOs and extraterrestrials and see them as potential invaders of planet Earth. In light of this difference in levels of evolution between these visitors and ours, and in light of the amount of time they have been visiting us, these advanced civilizations would have already crushed our own civilization a long time ago if it had been their plan. It is therefore futile to remain attached to these false beliefs, just as it is futile to hold this fear inside us.

Finally, we need to remind ourselves that given that these human beings from space are more evolved than us human beings on Earth, it is illusory to claim that we can precisely describe them and really understand them. Because, by definition, an inferior being cannot understand a being superior to them. We cannot envision, for example, that a child can have the same vision of the world as an adult and understand their behavior. And even in our own human society, each one of us can accept the idea that some men and women possess an understanding of the world that is more advanced and more enlightened than others, and that these others are incapable of understanding them. It is the same thing for these extraterrestrial beings.

CHAPTER SIX

WHO ARE THE ABDUCTORS?

Flaws in the Extraterrestrial Hypothesis

The extraterrestrial hypothesis is strongly rooted in the minds of most people, probably because it is the only one that is considered compatible with today's science. This hypothesis bases itself on the fact that the abductors portray themselves as nonhuman beings. They take their victims into a space vessel, and in a large number of kidnapping accounts, they tell their victims that they are from such and such a star or such and such a constellation of our galaxy. They therefore intentionally come across as extraterrestrials.

We have seen in the previous chapter that in all the cases studied, the behavior of the visitors was based on the principle of noninterference, which was demonstrated through their prudence and avoidance of all contact with human beings—and in the cases where this was not possible, their attitude was one of absolute respect. This behavior is totally opposite that of the kidnappers, who behave as beings devoid of any respect or morality. They are also deceitful, which does not inspire us to have any confidence in what they say. It is clear that if the kidnappers were also representatives of extraterrestrial civilizations, these civilizations would stand out as being quite different from those of the noninterfering, pacific visitors. Is this extraterrestrial hypothesis therefore a realistic one when applied to the abductors?

THE CORRELATION BETWEEN THE LEVEL OF EVOLUTION AND THE ABILITY TO TRAVEL IN SPACE

It is natural to accept that a civilization coming from another star system and capable of traveling through space to visit the earth would be necessarily more advanced than and superior to our own earthly human civilization. The ability to travel in space requires a high level of evolution—a level that is definitely higher than ours.

THE CORRELATION BETWEEN THE LEVEL OF EVOLUTION AND NOBLE QUALITIES

From what we have observed on Earth over a long period of time, we can see that a superior principle is at work in all forms of life, a principle that shows everything evolving toward perfection, even if opposing forces are visible at the same time. This principle applies not only to a civilization's individuals, but also to a civilization as a whole. Do we not say that a person capable of remaining serene in all circumstances and always good toward others has reached a high level of wisdom and is a person who is evolved? On the other hand, a person who is always angry and in conflict with others is considered as not being very wise or evolved. It thus seems natural to correlate the level of evolution of a being or of a civilization with the noble qualities it is capable of showing: noble qualities such as respect, kindness, and goodness.

THE CORRELATION BETWEEN THE ABILITY TO TRAVEL IN SPACE AND NOBLE QUALITIES

From these two observations, we can suggest a direct correlation between the ability to travel in space, which reflects a high degree of expertise, and a superior degree of emotional intelligence, which reflects the ability to exhibit the noble qualities of kindness and respect, among others. A civilization, therefore, in order to engage in space travel and encounter other civilizations, should have attained a sufficient level of evolution, should have gone beyond the stage of conflicts, and should have developed respect for others. This is what we saw in all the cases of "close encounters with avoidance" in chapter 5. But when we look at our own civilization, it is still quite marked by egocentrism—egocentrism that is so developed that it has led to exploiting other human beings. Our civilization of today is also marked by incessant conflict and, therefore, lack of respect for others. Indeed, it is evident that our civilization is not ready to undertake interstellar travel, since it is still at a rather low level of evolution.

What stems from this reasoning is the idea that these abductors— who show up without any respect for their human victims—demonstrate an inferior level of emotional intelligence and consequently would not really be representatives of extraterrestrial civilizations.

The Abductors Are at an Inferior Level of Evolution

In chapter 4, we revealed that

1. the abductors intrude upon the lives of their victims without any respect for human dignity,
2. the serious trauma that the abductors inflict upon their victims without any apparent remorse shows that they have no moral conscience, and
3. the abductors attempt, more often than not, to erase the memories of kidnapping from the minds of their victims. This can reveal that they are conscious that these practices are contrary to ethical behavior and disrespectful of humans, but they nonetheless continue with their practices, most likely to satisfy their own interests.

These three observations reveal an inferior level of evolution.

A Species That Is Apparently Inferior

Furthermore, a contradiction appears between the extraterrestrial hypothesis—related to a high level of evolution—and the kidnappers' apparently absurd behavior. Indeed, the final aim of the pseudomedical protocol, consisting of sexually violating their victims, is incomprehensible to us. From a certain perspective, this procedure calls to mind a species that is at an inferior level to a human species, an inferior species who would be trying to improve itself through the implementation of a plan of mixing or genetic manipulation. Their insistence on performing kidnappings over and over again in large numbers shows that the kidnappers' species would need the human species to ensure its own survival, or at least its evolution.

Nothing here is compatible with the idea that the abductors would be representatives of supposedly superior extraterrestrial civilizations; the extraterrestrial hypothesis is not at all coherent with these observations.

Too Many Kidnappings

The inconsistency of the extraterrestrial hypothesis is still accentuated by the very large number of estimated abductions. Taking into account that this phenomenon is not well known, that the victims are not always conscious of what they experience, and that they rarely dare talk about them out of fear of not being taken seriously, certain studies have estimated that the number of human abductions over these last decades could be in the millions—and in the United States alone. This estimate would be even greater if we took into account that the UFO phenomenon dates back at least to antiquity, as explained in chapter 3. Why would an extraterrestrial civilization—supposedly more evolved than us—need to abduct human beings in such large numbers and practice pseudomedical protocols on them? No—the large number of kidnappings taking place is not compatible with the extraterrestrial hypothesis.

Never Any Explanation or Communication

Furthermore, we have seen in the accounts in chapters 1 and 3 that the abductors very rarely answer their victims' questions. When they do, it is just to provide some "words" to calm their victims down, while claiming that, anyway, they will not remember anything of their abduction. Even though in the cases reported in chapter 5, where witnesses encountered visitors from space, the visitors are always very caring and respond clearly to all questions asked—there is never, on the other hand, any real communication between the abductors and their victims.

Thus, the disrespectful behavior of the abductors reveals their inferior level of evolution. Their insistence on showing up in large numbers and intruding on humans with their apparently absurd procedures is not coherent with the extraterrestrial hypothesis. In fact, the extraterrestrial hypothesis is by "default": proposed by ardent supporters of science who cannot envision any other explanation. This hypothesis is, in fact, compatible with the materialist vision of the world that dominates humanity today. But it is not at all coherent with the characteristics of the abductions.

Deceit and Lies

Thus, if we are to disregard the extraterrestrial hypothesis, two conclusions must be made:

1. The abductors, pretending to be extraterrestrials with their space vessels, are intentionally deceiving us and lying to us.
2. The abductors are of earthly origin, or at least connected to the earth. They would therefore be nonhuman, intelligent beings—but related to the earth. In this eventuality, we are necessarily led to envision that they are present in a world—another plane—that is parallel to that of humans and, although invisible, is near enough to interfere in our own world.

To answer the question as to the identity of the kidnappers, let us begin by taking another look at the two main studies previously mentioned: the study carried out in Celtic countries by an ethnologist, and the study based on the compilation of all of the Koranic texts from the Maghreb.

The Hypothesis of Fairies in Celtic Countries of Yesteryear

In chapter 3 we examined the hypothesis of fairies. We described the kidnappings that took place in the Celtic countries of medieval times— incidents that at the time were attributed to supernatural entities, or fairies.

We recall that Walter Yeeling Evans-Wentz (1878–1965) was an anthropologist at the University of Los Angeles. For two years, starting in 1907, he met with dozens of witnesses—often elderly people—to collect their last living testimonies about the "little people" (the name given to gnomes, fairies, and other creatures) throughout Ireland, Wales, Scotland, and Brittany. He then compiled all these accounts into a book about the folklore of Celtic countries called *The Fairy-Faith in Celtic Countries.*[1.]

In our modern day, fairies and gnomes, and generally all the creatures known as "the little people," are considered to be the figment of human imagination. The idea is widespread that fairy tales are nothing but fabulation based on no reality whatsoever. Yet, in the past, this was not at all the case. In the historical data that W. Y. Evans-Wentz collected, one can indeed see that "Both learned and unlearned Celts alike affirm that the fairy world exists. It is an invisible world in which our environment is immersed, like an island in the middle of an unexplored ocean, peopled by innumerable species."

FAIRIES ABDUCT HUMANS

"The belief that fairies are capable of kidnapping humans was widespread and still exists in a large part of Western Ireland." To prove this, Walter Evans-Wentz met with people who either knew or had known victims of these abductions attributed to fairies. He added that people who had returned from the fairy world after being abducted generally did not remember what they had seen or what they had done. This is also the case today with a large number of people who are victims of abductions into UFOs.

FAIRIES ARE ANTHROPOMORPHIC BEINGS

According to the study by Walter Evans-Wentz, fairies would be anthropomorphic beings. They can therefore take on an appearance that is human, or at least humanoid. We know that this is the same for the kidnappers into UFOs. He also wrote: "Fairies can either be good or evil. They enter a house without opening the door." This way of entering homes is completely consistent with the way that the kidnappers of our time enter the bedrooms of their victims in order to take them into a flying vessel.

STRIKING ANALOGIES

The four parallels we can draw between kidnappings attributed to fairies of yesteryear in Celtic countries and modern kidnappings into flying vessels are striking:

1. In both cases, it is indeed kidnapping—that is, temporary disappearances of human beings without their consent.
2. The kidnappers of today—just like the fairies of the past—are capable of entering the homes of their victims without opening doors or windows. They are therefore immaterial supernatural beings, but their victims can see them. We can deduct that since they are visible, they must be present in a parallel plane that is very near our own.
3. Fairies manifest themselves by taking on anthropomorphic appearances, just as the kidnappers appear as humanoid and even sometimes as humans.
4. In both cases, the recollection of the kidnappings is erased from the minds of the victims after the ordeal.

We cannot continue any further with our analogy because the people whom Walter Evans-Wentz met with had their memories erased. He therefore was unable to find out what had happened during the abductions—and at the time, hypnosis was not a practice.

DO FAIRIES EXIST?

Walter Evans-Wentz, continuing with his research in Brittany at the very beginning of the twentieth century, observed: "The general belief deep in Brittany's countryside is that fairies did exist, but they disappeared when the province became transformed by the conditions of modern life. In the department of Ille et Vilaine, it is said that fairies have not existed for more than a century, and on the coast, where it was firmly believed that the fairies dwelled in the caves of cliffs, the opinion is that they disappeared at the beginning of the nineteenth century. The oldest of the Bretons say that their parents or grandparents would often speak of the sightings of fairies that they had heard of, but very rarely did they say that they saw them themselves."[2]

The loss of contact between the populations of Celtic countries and the "little people" or fairies therefore coincides with the development of industrial and technological society and the changes that ensued in the lives of men and women. Popular belief holds that the fairies disappeared when this happened. This corresponds to today's conviction held everywhere that the fairies, just like the gnomes, elves, sylphs, and all of the creatures making up the "little people," existed only in the imagination of the elders, who were excessively influenced by folkloric tales and legends.

An Enigma and Its Solution

A large number of ancient texts and a number of enlightened individuals from the past and present declare that these elemental beings really did exist and still exist today. This assertion has been developed in a previous work.[3] Further, if elementals really did exist and were perceived in the past by the elders—as shown in the research of Walter Evans-Wentz and in numerous ancient texts and accounts—and are no longer seen today by human beings, to the extent that the knowledge of their existence has been almost completely lost, logically we are led to two possibilities:

1. Elementals really have disappeared from the regions where they used to be seen. If this is true, the reasons for this remain to be developed—and would require a better knowledge of these beings, their origin, their way of life, etc. and would therefore require further study. The question would be this: How can it be that all these creatures—who have left a strong imprint on the minds of human populations of the past—have completely vanished?
2. Elementals continue to exist today as they did before, but humans have forgotten them because they have lost the ability to see them due to their own evolution over time. According to this hypothesis, elementals would still be present around us in a parallel plane and invisible to most of us.

The second possibility seems to be the most plausible.

Walter Evans-Wentz himself suggests a key to this enigma when he observes that the sightings of fairies ceased when modern industrial and technological society gained ground at the beginning of the nineteenth century. The development of this modern society brought with it a change in the lifestyle of human beings by distancing them from nature, and it was from this point on that their vision of the world became more materialist. This evolution in lifestyle was coupled with the diminishing ability to see into the subtle planes and, therefore, to see elementals—an ability that people had in ancient times. This ability ended up disappearing in our modern day; human beings ended up forgetting the very existence of "the little people."

We now have a new hypothesis for identifying the abductors, a hypothesis that draws on the knowledge of fairies, or elemental beings. But because the very existence of these beings has been either forgotten or eclipsed, it is important to be able to confirm their reality by using other knowledge sources, and we shall begin by studying the relationships between human beings and djinns in the countries of Maghreb.

The Hypothesis of Djinns in the Countries of Maghreb

In chapter 3 (the "Djinns in the Countries of Maghreb" section), we explained that there appeared to be a direct link among humans, djinns, and fairies. Indeed, even if this can seem unbelievable for those who are only now discovering this information, djinns have lifestyles very similar to those of humans. In fact, experts on elementals (or nature spirits or fairies) say the same thing about them. This allows us to draw a very clear analogy between djinns and elementals, to the extent that djinns can be considered as a species of elementals specific to Maghreb countries.

In Walter Evans-Wentz's study, we have indeed seen that fairies lead lives similar to those of humans. The "little people" or fairies make up a society that models that of humans and is complete with women, men, and children, even if their supernatural powers set them apart.

Likewise, according to Koranic and traditional knowledge in the countries of Maghreb, the life of djinns is very similar to that of humans: they eat and drink, they are born, they grow up, they marry, they have children, and they die. Gordon Creighton wrote: "The best way to understand djinns is to see them as beings who are very much like human beings while at the same time being very different. In other words, they live in another dimension, a parallel world, or another space-time." "There is a close relationship or a sort of link between the destiny of djinns and the destiny of humankind."[4]

Regarding the abduction phenomenon, Gordon Creighton's work shows us that there are nine characteristics of djinns that we explicitly find in the behavior of today's abductors. As shown earlier:

Dj1: In their normal state, they are invisible to the ordinary human.

Dj2: They are nonetheless capable of materializing and appearing in the physical world. They can thus make themselves visible or invisible at will.

Dj3: They can change form and take on any aspect, whether it be large or small.

Dj4: They also have the ability to appear in animal form.

Dj5: Incorrigible liars, they take impish pleasure in disorienting and confusing humans in all sorts of absurd ways.

Dj6: They love to abduct humans.

Dj7: They love to incite humans to have sexual relations and liaisons with them.

Dj8: Djinns have the habit of grabbing humans, transporting them, and leaving them—if they so choose—miles away, in the wink of an eye.

Dj9: They also possess immense telepathic abilities and the power to easily seduce their human victims.

An Inevitable Answer

Thus, Koranic knowledge holds that the abductors of humans in the countries of Maghreb have a name: djinns. Gordon Creighton could not help but point out that this conclusion was self-evident after he had compiled the list of djinns' characteristics. These characteristics are definitely consistent with the behavior of today's abductors during kidnappings:

Djinns deceive humans through all types of absurdities. The first deception is that they portray themselves as extraterrestrials by making space vessels appear and claiming to their victims that they come from faraway stars. We have also seen that the pseudomedical protocol carried out in the UFOs seems absurd and resembles more of an elaborate staging to provide the classic image of a respectable medical exam.

They can materialize and take on any form, including that of animals. Here we can understand that they can also take on a human or humanoid form, but also that of an insect or a robot, as has been reported in modern abduction cases.

They "love to abduct humans," in the words of Gordon Creighton. This characteristic is crystal clear, and the djinns are the only creatures we can say this about in the countries of Maghreb.

They have the power to seduce their human victims through their great telepathic abilities, meaning they can communicate simply through thought without their victims being aware. These telepathic abilities are also used by today's abductors, in particular when they teach kidnapped humans about the ecological issues on Earth.

They also take pleasure in having sexual relations with humans. This is very important because it can explain the sexual violations that are systematically practiced today on abduction victims, whether they be women or men, in an apparent aim to produce hybrid beings.

Thus the answer to the question "Who are the abductors?" is incontestable and comes immediately if we accept the results of Gordon Creighton's work. The abductors are djinns, the very same supernatural beings that are so named in the countries of Maghreb.

Whether Fairies or Djinns, They All Are Elementals

This response is all the more evident because it is perfectly consistent with what was said previously: fairies and djinns have different names in different countries—but they are both supernatural beings who are invisible to humans and who today are referred to as elementals.

The challenge for us twenty-first-century humans is that we have lost consciousness both of the existence of these beings and their abilities to show themselves. Yet, spiritual science teaches us that they are present everywhere in nature and that they are living forces of nature—and it is for this very reason that they are called nature beings. They are also called "nature spirits," a term that clearly expresses that they are not material, but spiritual—and therefore invisible.

An Evolution of the Phenomenon over Time

If we have been able to establish that the identity of the kidnappers is elementals, thanks to the study done by Walter Evans-Wentz, we have also been able to confirm that the abduction of humans must have been relatively frequent in Celtic countries up until the end of the Middle Ages. There are very few abductions reported today in these regions.

Likewise, if we have been able to establish that the identity of the kidnappers is elementals, thanks to the study done by Gordon Creighton (elementals are called djinns), this seems to imply that the same phenomenon was relatively frequent in the Maghreb countries of the past. There are few if any abductions reported today in these countries.

Today, the abduction phenomenon has spread above all to the United States in the form of abductions into flying vessels. These incidents started to appear in the 1950s. Never in Celtic countries or in the Maghreb of the past have there been reports of abductions into vessels. Moreover, there was never any precise detail as to the manner in which the abductions took place. The victims simply disappeared. This shows that there has been an evolution in the form of the abduction phenomenon.

An Elaborate Staging

In spite of this evolution in form, we can clearly see that it is all about the same phenomenon, whether it be in the past or today. Human beings disappear from their material environment and are taken elsewhere—"into another world"—against their will and then are brought back to their original environment. We can therefore conclude that this same phenomenon is being perpetrated by the same species. This means that the beings known in the past as fairies in Celtic countries and djinns in Maghreb countries, and now called elementals, are continuing to practice abductions today. They make themselves look like extraterrestrials by taking their victims into flying vessels. Have we not already made note of the abductors' deceitful behavior?

This also means that the kidnappers have set up an elaborate staging to deceive humans and make themselves look like superior beings, although in reality they are "little people": elementals present on Earth in a plane that is parallel to ours. Fairies, like djinns, were indeed known for often deceiving humans. It would seem that the extraterrestrial, spaceship "mise-en-scène" has been a common one since the 1960s. The first known kidnappings into UFOs were those of Antonio Villas-Boas in 1957 and Barney and Betty Hill in 1961.

Yet, we can recall the medieval kidnapping case where Archbishop Agobard was called in to free the four people persecuted by the crowd. In this account, these four people, although not providing much detail, claimed to have fallen from vessels flying among the clouds. This description seems to be very close to that of UFOs. We can also note how the account given by Nicolas P. Henri de Montfaucon in 1715 describes the occupants of these vessels as being sylphs. Sylphs are none other than elementals associated with the element of air. He therefore had the same understanding, and the same knowledge of what is being suggested here.

Elementals: Forgotten Supernatural Creatures

Let us broaden our analysis by using the conclusions made in chapters 2 and 3 to call to mind the two specific characteristics of the abductors of human beings into UFOs:

They implement a sexual plan in the apparent aim of creating a hybrid species by taking sperm from abducted men and artificially inseminating women before removing their fetuses several weeks later.

They convey information about the crazy behavior of human beings threatening the earth's future by destroying its ecological balance, through the projection of apocalyptic images of a devastated planet as if after a nuclear war.

Urgent Ecological Concerns

ECOLOGICAL CONCERNS ARE
ASSOCIATED WITH UFOS IN GENERAL

We showed in chapter 2 that ecological concerns about the future of the earth have been a constant in UFO phenomena since the 1940s. We have clearly shown that UFOs (or the intelligence associated with them) are quite concerned by nuclear technology and by everything related to pollution. This observation leads us to the idea that the abductors could very well be the same as those associated with UFOs in general.

A previous study already cited[5] and based on the analysis of sixteen different cases of UFO sightings showed that these unidentified flying objects are the work of elementals, nature spirits, or nature beings. In these sixteen cases studied, there was no "close encounter with avoidance," which is the main characteristic of the extraterrestrial visits we saw in chapter 5.

Because the existence of elementals remains unrecognized by science, the study was based on several sources of knowledge left behind by science and, therefore, unknown to most people. Some of this knowledge has already been mentioned in this work: ancient knowledge from the Celtic countries, modern-day knowledge from Africa (which we will see below), religious knowledge from Islam (djinns), and spiritual knowledge. All this information is completely coherent and allows us to paint a precise picture of elementals. It is from this picture that each one of the sixteen cases of UFOs can be analyzed closely and rationally, and in each one of them we find the characteristics of elementals.

ECOLOGICAL CONCERNS ARE PRESENT IN MESSAGES RECEIVED THROUGH AUTOMATIC WRITING

We have also seen in chapter 2 that a new practice has appeared in recent years to incite human beings to take ecological problems seriously and to correct their actions. Through automatic writing, certain people with psychic-medium abilities receive messages in which they are told that it is a "teaching destined to save the earth" that they are encouraged to share with others. This new practice still seems to be infrequent, but it corresponds perfectly to the concerns expressed by the abductors. This leads us to think that the messages could be coming from beings of the same nature. But the technique of automatic writing, which is sometimes erroneously attributed to the souls of deceased humans, is, in fact, according to spiritual science, a manifestation of nature spirits—of elementals.[6] Thus, this new practice again confirms the validity of the hypothesis that the abductors are indeed elementals.

An Ancient Sexual Plan

Furthermore, we have shown in chapter 3 that the mating between humans and nonhuman creatures is an ancient practice largely widespread throughout medieval Europe and perhaps dates back even as far as antiquity, even if this is not at all common knowledge. In the Middle Ages, these practices were attributed to beings called incubi, succubae, or demons.

THE PRACTICES OF INCUBI, SUCCUBAE, AND DEMONS

We have cited a certain number of ancient accounts describing these practices. On the basis of these accounts, we can describe incubi, succubae, and demons as beings that are capable of

- flying through the air,
- entering homes through closed doors, and
- taking on the form of a victim's loved one, even if they have been dead for years. They can therefore take on any form, even human.
- They have mastery over matter, which enables them to move objects and even people, to make them disappear and then reappear.
- They even have the ability to manifest any object from nothing at all (a table covered with fine dishes) and then to make it disappear.

According to traditional and spiritual science, all these abilities are precisely those of elementals. We can thus say that the entities called incubi, succubae, or demons, whose nature has never been understood, are in fact elementals according to the term used today.

Therefore, the same sexual practices imposed on men and women have traversed the centuries and are still happening today during abductions of humans into UFOs. We are again led to the conclusion that the abductors of our time are not extraterrestrials, but elemental beings. These supernatural creatures normally live in a world that is parallel to ours, and this is why they are invisible to us. But they are connected to the earth just as we are, and they are able to interfere in our world.

Elementals: Present Everywhere and throughout Time

When we sum up the appearances of

- fairies in Celtic countries of the past (kidnappings),
- djinns in the countries of Maghreb (kidnappings and sexual practices),

- incubi and succubae in medieval Europe (sexual practices), and
- elementals of today (kidnappings),

we realize that elementals seem to have existed pretty much everywhere in the world and in all time periods. Actually, this realization is only natural if we refer to spiritual science, which says that nature would not exist at all were it not for nature spirits, who embody the earth's four elements. But this vision of things is not shared by modern science.

A 2013 work, *Dwarfs and Elves of the Middle Ages*,[7] based on texts from medieval French literature, shows that elementals really existed in the Europe of bygone days. Indeed, according to its author Claude Lecouteux, "One thing is certain: dwarfs and elves are not only literary creations; the medieval French really believed in their existence." The way he uses the word "believe" shows clearly that the author himself does not believe in dwarfs and elves, and that for him they exist only in literature. But it is precisely the aim of this current work not only to show what the ancients knew well—that the "little people" really did exist—but that they still exist today in a parallel world.

The Elementals' Trademark: Based on Spiritual Knowledge

An additional argument that demonstrates that the kidnappers are elementals can be found in Russell's account. Here we saw that in exchange for undergoing their physical examinations, Russell managed to obtain a sort of "cooperation" from his kidnappers. When he was imprisoned and suffered extreme deprivation, his kidnappers would bring him fruit on demand—real fruit that he was able to share with his cellmates. We also saw that the Theosophist Helena Blavatsky had the ability to make fruit appear at will, and that she explained to her friend Colonel Olcott that it was the work of elementals who did her bidding. Thus this supernatural ability to make real fruit appear—which looks to us like magic—is in fact a trademark of elementals. Since we have shown that the extraterrestrial hypothesis is not valid, it is only elementals who have this ability to create any object. Russell's kidnappers were therefore elementals.

This ability was also demonstrated by the incubus who used nearly every imaginable strategy to win Hiéronima over in L. M. Sinistrari's seventeenth-century account. We saw how, one evening, this incubus made an entire table of food disappear. Then, a bit later, another table appeared, covered with new place settings, glassware, silverware, and plates filled with succulent foods and fine wines, all of which were enjoyed by the guests. At the end of the evening, the first table reappeared, covered with the dishes that had originally been prepared by the cook. This account does indeed seem incredible, but the fact that it was provided by L. M. Sinistrari guarantees its authenticity. Sinistrari was an eminent scholar who was one of the highest authorities serving the Catholic Church. As a philosopher and theologian, he wondered how to judge this case while being faithful to the tenets of Catholic law.

As mentioned previously, humankind has become distant from nature and has lost all ability to perceive nature beings since the onset of industrial and technological civilization. We can support this statement by looking at what is happening in the regions of the world that have remained on the periphery of Western civilization, particularly some of the isolated regions of Africa.

Knowledge from African Traditions

In this twenty-first century, certain regions of Africa south of the Sahara are still partially protected from the influence of Western civilization and have not yet been influenced by Islam. Their local cultures indeed know of the existence of little people, similar to humans, who are normally invisible and live in an "invisible world" or in a space-time other than ours, but who sometimes show themselves. These beings are described as "very intelligent and very powerful" and "living in a dimension close to ours." These very little beings are similar to those who in Western mythology are referred to as elves," meaning elementals or "beings from a subterranean world." It is even possible sometimes to encounter them physically in caves—to the point of touching them and even communicating with them. This description reveals a large similarity to the elemental beings we know of in the West.

Two books have shared this information with the world. The first, called *African Wisdom*,[8] was written by Malidoma Patrice Somé, an African who grew up with the traditions kept alive by the ancients of his village, and who went on to pursue higher education in several prestigious universities in France and in the United States. This dual educational experience allowed him to build an extremely valuable bridge between traditional African culture and modern Western culture. His account is exceptional.

The second book, *Encounters with Beings from Another World in the Heart of Africa*,[9] was written by a Frenchman named Maen. Maen is no doubt the first Western man to have directly encountered elemental beings. These elemental beings, whom he saw on several occasions, showed themselves in the material plane. This was possible thanks to the special relationship he had with a traditional African healer.

It is no doubt significant that in these two accounts, the encounters with "these beings of another world" took place in relatively isolated villages of Burkina Faso, one of the world's least developed countries.

Beings from Another World

In this country where Western civilization has only slowly penetrated, the native tribes far away from the cities have remained in contact with these "beings from another world" since very ancient times. They have maintained this contact as well as their knowledge of these beings thanks to their way of life, characterized by a close contact with nature. Even if these "beings from another world" live in nature like the elementals everywhere else in the world, their role in this region is to provide support and comfort to human beings through the intermediation of traditional healers. These healers are regularly in contact with these beings and are responsible for establishing the link between them and humans. When a sick person consults a healer, the healer gives the person a remedy concocted on the spot by these "beings from another world," who remain invisible and are in constant contact with the healer. This treatment practice is obviously incredible for uninformed Westerners. But it clearly means that we are in the presence of two parallel worlds that are in communication with each other: the world of human beings and the world of "other beings." In fact, these same practices are frequent in Asia among the traditional people, who, still relatively untouched by Western influence, have been able to preserve a close bond with these beings

The firsthand accounts provided in these two books teach us how these "beings from another world" have the ability to manifest remedies; that is, to create medicinal substances from completely ordinary materials (such as soil), and from the energy they put into the process through strong intention. This is of course outlandish for Westerners but is consistent with what we learned in the preceding paragraph: Russell's kidnappers bring him fruit in prison, and the incubus makes a feast appear for a group of guests. Furthermore, it is consistent with the subject of UFOs, where objects suddenly appear and disappear.

These two books also explain that "these spirits try hard not to intrude upon our world, as if there were laws forbidding them to interfere with our normal development out of fear of disturbing the natural course of our evolution."[10] This is the reason why appearances of these beings are so few. It is interesting to note that this attitude is equally found in nearly all the UFO manifestations, which remain mysterious and incomprehensible to us. It is as if their operators wanted to attract our attention and establish contact with us, all the while remaining firm in not wanting to show themselves so as not to disturb our way of life.

But we have seen that in the kidnapping phenomenon, the abductors overtly and uninhibitedly intrude upon and interfere in the lives of their victims. It would therefore appear that while there is an analogy between the kidnappers and these "beings from another world," we can also notice that there is a large difference in their behavior toward humans. This can lead us to think that there could be different species of these beings, all of which belong to the same large family. It is true, though, that they present themselves to humans that are very different: on the one hand, inhabitants of Africa, where people live as in olden times, highly respectful of nature, and on the other hand, Americans who are completely representative of modern civilization, distanced from nature and imbued with feelings of superiority.

A Powerful Personal Story

The following personal account of the African author Malidoma Patrice Somé is very helpful in understanding the considerable difficulty we have in reconciling the vision of the native peoples with that of the modern Western one, and, as a result, in accepting the knowledge of native peoples as truth. The same problem exists in accepting as reality the knowledge from Celtic traditions and from Islam, both of which are consistent with the African traditions.

When he was young, Malidoma Patrice Somé felt torn between the native culture he was born into and the Western education forced upon him between the ages of four and nineteen by white missionaries. He relates that "because of this Western consciousness, I acquired grandiose notions of superiority, and it took me a long time to accept any interference or intrusion coming from a native perspective. It was as though a certain type of knowledge coupled with an extremely vicious territorial instinct had colonized my thoughts. For example, the education I received gave birth to a way of thinking in me that wanted to brandish the sword of analysis. When my mind was unable to organize certain things into its diverse rational categories, it quickly dismissed them as primitive illusions that were unworthy of civilized thought. Each time a new piece of knowledge did not meet the necessary requirements for making an appropriate analysis, my Western-trained mind considered it as something foreign and hostile, and it fought it with patriotic pride. Now I realize that what I believed to be a civilized mind was in fact a rather unrefined one."[11]

RECOGNITION OF GORDON CREIGHTON'S WORK

A parallel can be drawn between the above testimonial and the way in which Gordon Creigton's article on Islamic knowledge and djinns was welcomed by the ufologist community in 1983. Because the information in his article was so radically opposed to the Western, materialist vision of the world, we can understand how it was, and is still, very difficult for Westerners to accept what the article put forth as reality. Westerners consider Islamic knowledge either as belonging to the domain of the paranormal and magic, or simply as primitive beliefs. It is therefore immediately rejected. This is what happened to Gordon Creighton's article after its first publication and again after its republication several years later. It is very important that the reader become aware of this difficulty, which for all of us is inevitable. As a result, we must make a substantial effort to free ourselves of our Western conditioning if we are to hope to finally understand what is hidden behind the abduction phenomenon and get closer to the truth on this subject.

Excerpts from *The Healing Wisdom of Africa*[12]

"If I had not encountered such beings on several occasions throughout my adult life and if I had never conversed with them and, with their permission, recorded their voices for my personal use, I think that I would have rejected my very first experience as being some sort of hallucination. Still today[,] something about them leaves me perplexed: it's the fact that they do not want to let me see their entire world, on pretext that it could be dangerous for me."

"In Africa, particularly in the region where I come from, no one shows any surprise upon hearing about these highly intelligent, powerful beings who live in a dimension that is close to ours."

"This encounter made me truly aware of the existence of beings hidden behind nature's veil, and who are, in all likelihood, closely observing everything humans are doing. Every time I go for a hike outdoors, I can't help feeling as if I am being watched[,] and wonder how many pairs of eyes are spying on me without me knowing it."

Concerning the abduction phenomenon: "My mother was quite worried when I disappeared after following a rabbit-like kontombli (fairy) into the thicket, not only because she had lost her son for a whole day, but also because she knew of people who had gone to that very same spot and who had never returned."

Two significant elements are contained in this excerpt:

The kontomblis that he followed as a little child had taken on the appearance of a rabbit. We have already seen this in other contexts when we saw that fairies, djinns, or elementals could take on any form, including that of an animal.

People who had gone to a certain spot in the forest never returned. We can understand by this that the kontomblis also have the ability to make things disappear and thus to abduct people. This very same ability has been seen in fairies in Celtic countries and djinns in Islamic countries.

Moreover, Malidoma Patrice Somé clearly wrote that these supernatural beings who are present in the heart of the African forests, whom the natives call kontomblis, are nature spirits. But we also refer to them as elementals. Indeed, these supernatural beings have different names based on their different regions and time periods, and they show themselves in slightly different ways—but they are all intelligent beings that are present on Earth in a world that is parallel to that of humans.

ANALYSIS

Once we have become aware of how hard it is for a Western mind to accept traditional African knowledge, it can be useful to reiterate several things:

1. Meetings with "beings from another world":

Malidoma Patrice Somé encountered on several occasions these "beings from another world." He even recorded their voices, which means that they are capable of speaking like humans and do not (only) use telepathy.

2. Well known in many regions of the world:

The power and intelligence of these beings are known by all natives in the regions of world isolated from Western civilization.

3. A dimension close to ours:

These kontomblis live in a dimension that is close to ours and are normally invisible to us, but they can see us at all times because our bodies are denser than theirs.

4. The appearance of an animal:

Malidoma Patrice Somé affirms that the kontomblis, like elementals, have the ability to take on the appearance of an animal. He experienced this firsthand.

5. The ability to make someone disappear:

They also have the ability to make a human being disappear. Here we can understand that they can take the person into another dimension—meaning to dematerialize them and then, if they so desire, to rematerialize them.

6. A clear connection between kontomblis and elementals:

All this information about the kontomblis known to the native peoples of Africa has already been explained regarding elementals in the preceding chapters. Malidoma Patrice Somé explicitly makes a connection between kontomblis and elementals.

Highlights from *Encounters with Beings from Another World*[13]

It is remarkable that Maen was able to create a real, lasting relationship with these beings from another world. On multiple occasions, they made themselves visible to him for a short period of time so he could touch them; exchange documents, objects, and gifts; and accept these things directly from their hands—just as if he would have with human beings. But they looked more like elves with very small bodies. They manifested themselves through dense material bodies so that Maen—who so wanted to meet them, and who lacked psychic medium ability and the acute perception that goes along with it—could see them and communicate with them.

In order to show themselves to him, these beings would generally use a borrowed physical body that was not really theirs. They also showed themselves several times in their real bodies, which were also anthropomorphic, but this was always either in the darkness of their cave, or outside . . . and only at night, so that Maen was never able to make out the details of their faces.

Over the course of the first years of this relationship, the communication always took place in the beings' own language. This language was known only by the healer and a few others like him. The communication could take place directly and orally but also in writing. Indeed, this language was particular in that it used specific characters that are different from what we humans know.

What can seem even more extraordinary is that for the past several years, the communication with Maen has taken place in French. Maen, who is French, continues to visit with them about once a year, and on several occasions he has received letters from them written in French.

It appears, again through this account, that the description of these "beings from another world in the heart of Africa" is quite close to the descriptions of elementals. But the descriptions are set apart by the fact that these beings show themselves regularly to Maen in their own physical bodies—quite different from humans—and also through the way in which they communicate with him. This leads us to think that we are dealing with a particular species that is obviously different from those who show themselves in human abductions, since these beings have a relationship with humans that is very different.

The Twelve Reasons We Can Say Elementals Exist

In spite of the total consistency between the conclusions drawn in the previous paragraphs, all which converge toward an interpretation based on the existence of elementals, the difficulty remains that the people of today are often unconsciously subject to the conditioning of a society that makes us believe that elementals do not really exist, and that it is all superstition. Let us examine some evidence of the reality of these creatures, all the while keeping in mind that they can be real—not in our material world but in a parallel one.

Concerning superstition, let us quote the work of Edouard Brasey in *Enquête sur l'existence des fées et des esprits de la nature* ("Investigation into the existence of fairies and nature spirits"):[14] "Is it not pretentious to treat as superstitions the convictions that served as a foundation of the cultures of the past and that are still alive today in all of the animist peoples, from the Africans to the Japanese? Must it be a given that the rationalist, materialist ideal of the nineteenth and twentieth centuries has to take precedence over several millenaries of beliefs?"

Edouard Brasey also said, "The official churches and their monotheistic dogmas worked very hard to cast aside or demonize those who defended the Little People. By representing elves as demons and fairies as witches, the inquisitors of the Middle Ages and the Renaissance made it easy to chase down, condemn, and burn humans who were suspected of maintaining contact with the Little People: those who were known as witches, soothsayers, alchemists, and other enthusiasts of the Cabal. The relentless fight that pitted burgeoning Christianity against ancient paganism in the Western world succeeded in breaking the bond that existed between humans and nature spirits."[15]

1. Many tales and legends:

The existence of tales and legends in countries all over the world in which we see the involvement of similar supernatural characters called gnomes, dwarves, elves, fairies, undines, nymphs, et al. shows that this has to be based on reality. The pervasiveness of these tales and legends reveals the fact that these characters were known in the past as real beings who lived in nature— in forests and rivers. Today, most people "believe only what they see" and have lost this knowledge of the spirit world.

2. Experiences that are not often spoken of but are relatively numerous:

Men and women of today hardly ever speak of these nature spirits; first, because the majority of people are unaware of their existence, and second, because—as a result—the subject is considered to be irrational and phantasmagoric. Yet, when we happen to bring up their existence—to explain the mysterious disappearance of something, for example—we realize that a rather significant number of people, in particular circumstances, have had fleeting encounters with beings clearly represented as elves, gnomes, fairies, or nature spirits. In fact, some people still possess acute perceptive abilities and are capable of physically or psychically sensing subtle presences in certain instances (such accounts can be found in another book by this author).[16]

3. Young children can see them:

If we look closely enough, we realize that often, young children are capable of seeing beings who are invisible to us adults. But in order to understand this, their parents must have an open mind, and this is rarely the case. Children are then necessarily influenced by those around them and conditioned by the society such that they not only lose their abilities but block out the memories of their past experiences. But sometimes it happens that, as adults, these children can recall their visions and in retrospect recognize that they did indeed see elves or fairies, et al.

Dogs and cats are equally capable of perceiving nature spirits. In some instances, we can see a defense reaction in them as if surprised by a presence that to us is invisible.

4. An example from Iceland:

This knowledge of the invisible world is still quite prevalent today among the people of Iceland. A recent documentary (*Investigation into the Invisible World* by Jean-Michel Roux) reveals that a majority of people of this region think that they are surrounded by invisible beings, and a large minority affirm being in contact with them. For them, these beings are gods, deceased ancestors, or nature spirits. A large number of children declare seeing elves, gnomes, dwarves, et al.

As a result, the inhabitants of this region are much more respectful of nature and of elementals. Indeed, they are so respectful of nature and elementals that when the office of public works decides to make a new road, the route initially planned can be modified to bypass a site known to be occupied by nature spirits.

The former Icelandic president comments on this unique aspect of her country when she says, "Catholicism didn't leave any room for other beliefs in countries such as France or Spain. When Catholicism came to Iceland in the Middle Ages, the Icelanders adapted it to their pagan heritage and continued to maintain contact with the invisible beings."

This singularity can be linked to the geographic isolation of Iceland and the low density of the island's population, which allowed its inhabitants to remain in contact with nature. Here we can also see proof that human beings of the past were indeed in contact with the spiritual world. We can also confirm from this that the materialist vision of the world has been in the West only for the past several centuries—partly as a consequence of the harshness with which religion established itself and of the development of material technologies.

5. Seen by psychics:

Furthermore, elementals can be seen by people who have developed acute perception and have acquired psychic gifts. These people are therefore capable of truly communicating with elementals and, if skilled enough, can even command them to do their bidding. But these men and women are scarce.

6. Seen by blind people:

It even so happens that a person blind from birth can possess psychic abilities and see elementals. This is the case of Ursula Burkhard, who has published several books recounting her experiences.[17] This also serves as confirmation—as if we needed it—that these beings, although not made up of the same matter as we are, do indeed exist. They are made up of a matter that is more subtle and etheric—a matter that cannot be detected by our eyes—and can be perceived by those who are blind.

7- Eyewitness accounts:

In spite of the decline of awareness of the spiritual world, which intensified in the West at the time of the Renaissance with the gradual development of technological society that today dominates humanity's way of life and thinking, some people have resisted the domination of materialist thinking and have preserved this awareness.

In Europe, Paracelsus, the famous doctor and psychic, published in 1535 the first book devoted to different sorts of elemental beings, called *The Book of Nymphs, Sylphs, Pygmies, Salamanders, and All Other Spirits.*[18] He wrote: "Experience proves it: everyone knows that there are undines in the water and gnomes in the Earth, as there are also elves in the element of air. The role of true science is not to deny the facts that have been observed—its role is to explain them."

Later on, in 1670, the French writer Nicolas-Pierre-Henri de Montfaucon, abbot of Villars, developed a theory about the genies of the four elements.[19] "The air is full of a countless multitude of peoples (sylphs) of human form. They are rather proud in appearance, but are actually very gentle. Great lovers of science, they have great finesse, are helpful to the wise, and are enemies of fools and of the ignorant. Their wives and daughters possess a handsome beauty, like that of the Amazons. Know that the seas and rivers are inhabited just like the air is; the ancient wise men called this species of people undines or nymphs... The Earth is filled nearly to its center with gnomes: people short in height who are guardians of treasures, of mines[,] and of precious jewels. As for the salamanders—they are passionate inhabitants of the land of fire and are of service to philosophers."

In Scotland, Robert Kirk, a church authority of the seventeenth century, published another book devoted to elementals, *The Secret Commonwealth of Elves, Fauns and Fairies.*[20]

Today, more and more books are being written by people who perceive and sometimes communicate with nature spirits. Thus, even if there are still not enough of these people, accounts of direct communication with nature spirits are on the rise,[21] and this allows readers to retrieve the awareness that they once had.

8. Renewal through successive spiritual currents:

After the end of the Middle Ages and its ensuing loss of contact with the subtle worlds, it took until the beginning of the nineteenth century for spiritual currents such as the Rosicrucian Order, and then Theosophy (Helena Blavatsky), to restore a spiritual vision of the universe by reintegrating elemental beings. These beings make up and have always made up the creations of the universe. In the twentieth century, this restoration continued, thanks to Rudolf Steiner's Anthroposophy, and continues today thanks to the Psycho-Anthropology of Selim Aïssel.

9. Agricultural experiments:

Furthermore, agricultural experiments in places that are now famous, such as Findhorn in the north of Scotland,[22] or Perelandra,[23] a center for nature research in Virginia, can be considered as concrete proof of the existence of nature spirits. Indeed, thanks to real communication and the resulting collaboration between humans and elemental beings—who represent the forces of nature—the gardens of these places were able to produce vegetables of well-above-average size and flavor. In the 1960s in Findhorn, for example, the land was originally practically uncultivable and in an unfavorable climate—and agricultural engineers recognized that the results obtained could definitely not be thanks only to classic agricultural knowledge.

10. Biodynamic agriculture:

The biodynamic agriculture movement, born from the guidance given by Rudolf Steiner, is based on the principle that these elemental beings intervene explicitly in the development and growth of plants. We can call upon their know-how if we show that we are respectful in meeting their needs.

11. Shamanism:

Here we must mention the shamanic approach, which is thousands of years old and is enjoying a resurgence of popularity today. Since the dawn of time, humans have collaborated with nature spirits to acquire knowledge and expand their healing principles. The shaman enters a modified state of consciousness to communicate and interact with spirits. In our day, each native population living in North and South America, Siberia, Australia, Asia, Africa, and the Arctic has shamans among them. These practices are increasing in the West, with the aim to help people live in harmony with nature.

12. Intervention in the Chernobyl nuclear disaster:

The nuclear disaster that took place in 1986 at the Chernobyl nuclear facility was the largest industrial tragedy of all time. The information coming out in recent years reveals that things would have been much more serious—serious beyond measure—if UFOs had not intervened. The study previously cited[24] leads us to the interpretation that the UFOs are interdimensional manifestations controlled by elementals. The analyses developed previously in this work have led to the same conclusion concerning close encounters of the third kind, at the very least when there is no "close encounter with avoidance."

The nuclear reactor in Chernobyl got out of control during an experimentation that had been insufficiently prepared in 1986, and all physical conditions came together to potentially create a nuclear explosion complete with an atomic mushroom cloud. But none of this happened, thanks to the intervention of elementals, who, thanks to their mastery over matter, were able to

- immediately open the nuclear reactor by moving aside its cover,
- release some of the combustible uranium into the atmosphere, and
- transform most of the remaining uranium.

These actions, observed by several independent, indisputable sources,[25] went way beyond human capability.

For example, the UFOs that were above the reactor were seen by hundreds of witnesses, and their immediate effects on the radioactivity were observed by two engineers and recorded on the nuclear facility's computer.

This intervention is exceptional and extremely significant. But this information was shared years after the disaster—and only in certain milieus. It is therefore still unknown to many people.[26]

We must therefore confront the evidence. Elementals really exist and have always existed—even if with time they have become invisible to a large majority of us. This reality opposes today's science but has to be obvious to us if we take into account the observations and numerous testimonies detailed above. Our world is not limited to its material part, the part that we perceive with our physical senses. We have to distinguish the visible, material world from the real world—the world that englobes the visible, material one but also includes the subtle, ultrasensitive, spiritual worlds. Furthermore, the visible and invisible worlds are interrelated.

A Psychic's Account

A psychic tells his story: "My name is Antoine, and I am a lithotherapist. I also do activities for children. After meeting Daniel Harran and talking with him about the mysterious phenomena he is so passionate about, we very quickly saw that there was great convergence between his research and my own personal experience, and I understood that the time had come for me to share my secret.

"My 'secret' isn't really a secret, of course! I have been seeing and communicating with nature beings since I was a little child. I also know many people who have the same abilities as I do, and they communicate, in their ways, with different worlds that are in proximity to our material world. Therefore, for mediums, shamans, and other healers, it's an open secret.

"When I was very little, I saw the energy that surrounded people's bodies—what we normally call auras. When I closed my eyes after having looked at a person or a beautiful landscape, I would still perceive an energetic outline of their contours, like a sort of light. When I was a child I thought that everyone saw the same things as I did, and were also able to leave their bodies during the night to go play with the stars or do other fantastical things.

"There are a lot of people—a nearly infinite number—who are on the other side of the veil, beyond the physical world in which we live. Some of these beings come to give us the help that we need. Others strive for the good of all and work in a spirit of love and joy for everyone's well-being. There are others though who are not always kind toward humans and who can play tricks on them without them being aware of it.

"As I grew up, the distance between me and those around me grew as well, and at the age of about seventeen, I had to deal with other, inferior perceptions—perceptions that one could refer to as lower astral. Under their influence, which I was unaware of, I lost my way and fell into darkness. I thus experienced the hardest years of my life, up to the age of twenty-three. This is when I learned to distinguish between the dangerous, malevolent energies that would invade and dominate me against my will, and good, benevolent energies that were always available but that I had to summon. I was thus able to free myself little by little from these evil influences. Kind friends helped wake me up and they taught me to open my heart.

"At twenty-three, I experienced what shamans call a rise of kundalini, and this was the beginning of a new life for me. Already before this I was beginning to have contact with goodly beings again. I hardly saw them at first, and as I continued on the path of purification of my body and spirit, they would bring me different changes and energetic forms of treatment during the night or during different rituals.

"After coming a long way with them, I came to know these beings well. I had more and more contact with them, and today it has become completely ordinary. Now, when I garden, little beings like to show themselves to me. They are very quick, very playful, and they look like little goblins. They help me place certain rocks or plants based on energy flows and other entryways they set up. The result is that my floral compositions are remarkable every time—both vibratory and visually. They love to work with us when it's possible.

"It is, however, important to point out that for a lot of mediums, the path can sometimes be very difficult, like what I myself experienced between the ages of seventeen and twenty-three. Indeed, I understood that the medium or psychic abilities that are naturally present in some men and women are associated with 'flaws' in their energetic bodies. Certain subtle, malevolent beings take advantage of these flaws to enter the energetic bodies of their victims. Not only does this cause loss of energy, but it especially allows these beings to attach themselves to their victims and direct their lives according to their own desires. In other words, they use the weaknesses of these men and women— weaknesses that they can see very clearly—to possess their bodies and use them for their own ends, which can sometimes be very dark and even sordid. The influence of these beings can also be felt by those close to the victims. Becoming free of these presences that occupy us against our will can be very long and arduous. It is only the power of love and a great faith in life that can protect the hearts that are wounded by these unwanted, evil presences, along with the help of friends who know these processes well.

"People who manage to make it through these traps and free themselves of these presences can then help those around them and sometimes bring relief to those stricken with certain illnesses such as schizophrenia, insanity, and other types of depression. I think that humanity would be more evolved if, with humility, it could have a more open mind about these subtle presences that are sometimes called elementals, demons, or many other names. Too little is known about this subject in today's society.

"I am grateful to Daniel for all of his valuable research, because thanks to the testimonies that he has gathered together in this book and the accuracy of this information, I was able to shed light on and free myself completely of the influence of these other subtle beings who, posing as guides, were pumping me of energy. In fact, they were not guides at all; they were simply satisfying their curiosity."

—Antoine Moyenin

Two Responses from Spiritual Science

The objective of this paragraph is to again find the answer to the question "Who are the abductors?" But this time we will use knowledge from spiritual science. Our initial answer to this question is that these kidnappers are nonhuman, intelligent beings who manifest themselves in the physical world by abducting human beings. The extraterrestrial hypothesis not being satisfying—can we ask if there are such beings here on Earth? It is indeed rational to look for an answer to this question among the beings that are present here on Earth, before envisioning an extraterrestrial origin.

The knowledge that is about to be described is based on two major spiritual movements: anthroposophy, founded by Rudolf Steiner (1861–1925), and psychoanthropology, developed by Selim Aïssel. These teachings are—or were—conveyed by remarkable men, who, thanks to their authentic abilities of acute perception, could directly perceive the beings of the spiritual world who are in contact with this world. Such people, who have access to true knowledge, are very rare in each generation.

These two spiritual teachings are interested in the spiritual dimension of human beings (*anthropos* in Greek). These teachings therefore propose a spiritual vision of the universe that goes beyond the scientific vision and its materialist thinking. These two opposing visions are juxtaposed below:

Scientific knowledge holds that the human being is made up of a material body that is capable of thoughts and emotions and totally disappears upon death.

Spiritual knowledge holds that the human being is a spirit embodied in a physical body, and that the spirit is the immortal part of the human being.

It is therefore clear that the spiritual vision of humanity cannot be proven using the experimental scientific method. We invite the reader to look at the coherence of this spiritual knowledge and then compare it against their own experiences—using their own "knowledge of the heart" —and then do their own soul-searching to finally either validate this vision and make it their own or cast it aside.

The Four Components of a Human Being

According to spiritual knowledge, the human being is made up of four components:

1. a physical, material body
2. An etheric body or life-giving body that gives life and structure to the physical body. Vegetables and animals are living things and also have both a material and an etheric body.
3. An astral body that allows us to experience emotions and feelings. Animals also have emotions. They have a physical body, an etheric body, and an astral body.
4. a mind or an "I" that allows us to think

THE FOUR COMPONENTS OF A HUMAN BEING		
Component		**World**
Mind ("I")	Thought	Spiritual
Astral body (soul)	Feelings, emotions	Astral
Etheric or (life) body	Life force, structure, form	Etheric
Physical body	Matter	Material

At the moment of death, a human being sheds its different bodies: First, it leaves the casing of its physical body, which decomposes and returns to dust. It then passes into the etheric world, with its etheric body, its astral body, and its mind. Around three days later, all of its energies are dissolved and it leaves its etheric body. It then passes into the astral world, with its astral body and its mind. Later, it leaves its astral body, and its mind goes into the spiritual plane, the spiritual world.

For those who believe in reincarnation, human beings, after a certain amount of time, take the opposite path to prepare for a rebirth. To put it another way, death is not an end but, rather, just a step. Only the physical body dies—but a human being does not. It continues on to live its life in other worlds.

By limiting their vision to the physical body and the material world as modern science suggests, human beings have a fragmented vision of life and the world. They have forgotten that a large part of human life takes place in other worlds, in particular after the physical body dies.

Human beings have therefore forgotten that other worlds exist. As long as human beings are incarnated in physical bodies, these other worlds are usually invisible to them. But these worlds nonetheless exist and are inhabited by deceased human souls as well as other beings—some of whom can manifest themselves in the material world. These are the beings that we are seeking to know in order to answer this question: "Who are the abductors?"

A General Principle

The general principle is that only beings present in the physical plane can manifest themselves in the physical plane. For example, if we want to see fish and be seen by them while they live in the sea, we need to go into the sea—into their world. Consequently, only beings who have a physical body can show themselves in the material physical plane. The question is this: Who are these beings on Earth who are not living human beings and who have physical bodies in order to show themselves in the physical plane as the kidnappers do? When we add the fact that these are intelligent beings, the question then becomes this: Who are these intelligent beings on Earth who are not living human beings and who have physical bodies?

First Response: Wandering Human Souls

We have seen that at the moment of death, after leaving the material plane when the physical body dies, human souls spend about three days in an etheric plane before continuing on with their evolution in the astral plane (in Western countries, three days is the average wait time before burying or incinerating a body).

Yet, some human souls remain prisoner in the elementary etheric plane, which is located between the dense material plane and the more subtle etheric plane. Here they are blocked in their evolution—sometimes for long periods of time. This is the case of souls who were very much attached to the material world while they were alive. They had no spiritual openness and thus remain attached to this material world after their death. They have not understood that they are dead and that they have a path to follow in other worlds. They therefore remain in the places where they once lived (often in their houses) or near other human beings they had lived with.

Because the elementary etheric plane is in proximity to the dense material plane, these human souls are able to show themselves in the material plane in the form of light or sounds if they have the required energy.

They can show themselves in the form of glowing lights in the bedroom or through partially dense forms that are visible to certain people with psychic-medium abilities. This generally takes place at night when the house is quiet. They can also appear in a photograph or via security cameras, all the while not being seen by the human eye.

These human souls can also make their presence known through sounds that the living can perceive: doors that creak, knocking on the walls, footsteps, or currents of air.

In all these cases, these souls remain near the places they once lived while they were alive, and they are limited to wandering or "haunting" these areas—sometimes in an attempt to get the attention of the living. This is the true explanation behind sightings of ghosts and other paranormal phenomena occurring in houses.

We need to understand that in all these cases, these wandering human souls are suffering. Their consciousness has left their physical body, but their excessive attachment to the material world keeps them from being aware of it. They have not understood that they are dead. These souls remain blocked in a place or in a house either until their energy dissipates or a medium helps them become aware of their situation so they can continue on with their evolution.

But wandering human souls cannot serve as an explanation for all paranormal phenomena, because they show themselves only near where they were formerly living. Their existence cannot explain UFOs or crop circles, nor can it explain the phenomenon of abductions of human beings into UFOs.

Basic Notions of Cosmogony

According to spiritual science, Earth is a living planet, a celestial body, or sphere, and like all living things, it has gone through alternating phases of growth and rest. It has gradually materialized by passing through four successive stages, or four different spheres, interspersed with phases of spiritualization known also as "cosmic nights."

Phase 1: A celestial body was formed, composed only of heat. This element of heat was put forth by superior or creator spirits. Spiritual science calls this celestial body "Ancient Saturn." Please note there is no direct connection between this name and the planet we call "Saturn."

Phase 2: A beginning of the materialization process brought forth the element of air, along with aerial, gaseous movement. The element of the air thus was added to that of heat. This materialization process is in agreement with Einstein's famous formula, $E = mc^2$, which represents the equivalence between mass and energy. Spiritual science calls this celestial body "Ancient Sun."

Phase 3: The materialization process continued and the element of water appeared and thus was added to the elements of air and heat. This celestial body is called "Ancient Moon."

Phase 4: The element of earth appeared and was added to the other elements of heat, air, and water. This completed the materialization process and culminated in planet Earth.

The Evolution of Human Beings on the Successive Spheres

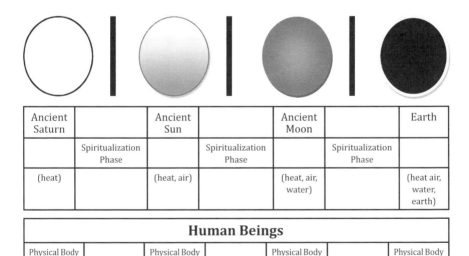

Ancient Saturn		Ancient Sun		Ancient Moon		Earth
	Spiritualization Phase		Spiritualization Phase		Spiritualization Phase	
(heat)		(heat, air)		(heat, air, water)		(heat air, water, earth)

Human Beings						
Physical Body		Physical Body Etheric Body		Physical Body Etheric Body Astral Body		Physical Body Etheric Body Astral Body Mind

Simultaneously, the human being acquired its four components during these four phases.

Phase 1: On Ancient Saturn, the human being appeared, or rather the first precursor to what would later on become a human being. In this ball of heat, the human being was formed only from moving heat fragments that formed what would later become its physical body.

Phase 2: On this second sphere (Ancient Sun), the ancestor of the human being's physical body was completed by a life-giving body. This is the ancestor to the etheric body of today's human being.

Phase 3: For human beings, an astral body was added to the physical body and the etheric body.

Phase 4: The human being received its last component—its mind.

The Appearance of Inferior Evolutive Beings on the Successive Spheres

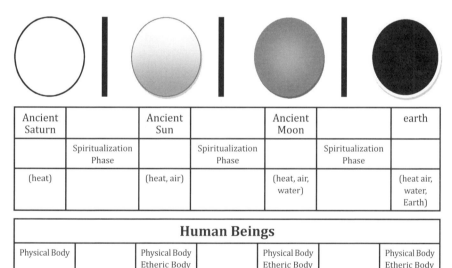

Ancient Saturn		Ancient Sun		Ancient Moon		earth
	Spiritualization Phase		Spiritualization Phase		Spiritualization Phase	
(heat)		(heat, air)		(heat, air, water)		(heat air, water, Earth)

Human Beings						
Physical Body		Physical Body Etheric Body		Physical Body Etheric Body Astral Body		Physical Body Etheric Body Astral Body Mind

Inferior Evolutive Beings						
Physical Body		Physical Body ↓ **Mineral**		Physical Body Etheric Body ↓ **Vegetal**		Physical Body Etheric Body Astral Body ↓ **Animal**

MINERAL, VEGETAL, AND ANIMAL KINGDOMS:
INFERIOR EVOLUTIVE BEINGS

Throughout each phase, the bodies of future human beings were prepared so they could receive another component from the following phase. But a general principle is that during evolution, some beings evolve and progress normally, while others are not sufficiently prepared and cannot continue with their evolution. These beings are called inferior evolutive beings.

Thus, when future human beings found themselves on the second sphere to add an etheric body to their physical body, some of these beings were not ready to receive this life-giving body. They therefore left the process of evolution and remained with only their physical body. Spiritual science teaches that these are the ancestors of today's mineral kingdom.

Later, when the future human beings found themselves on the third sphere (Ancient Moon) to take on an astral body, some of these beings were not ready to receive it. They therefore left the evolutionary process and remained with only their physical body and their etheric body. These are the ancestors of today's vegetal kingdom.

At the following planetary stage (Earth), when human beings received mind or "I," some of them were not ready to receive this. They therefore left the evolutionary process and remained in their physical, etheric, and astral bodies. Spiritual science teaches that these are the beings of the animal kingdom.

According to spiritual science, this is how minerals, vegetation, and animals are inferior evolutive beings; that is, inferior to those who became human beings. *But up to this point we have not yet found intelligent beings with physical bodies that are present on Earth to respond to our initial question: "Who are the abductors?"*

THE HUMAN BEING AND SPIRITUAL HIERARCHIES

According to spiritual science, all beings in our universe include three hierarchies of spiritual beings who are more evolved than human beings and who are invisible to us. Using the names given by Catholic tradition, the third hierarchy, which is located right above humans on the scale of evolution, is made up of angels, archangels, and archai. These entities correspond to the multitude of beings that were called gods in the mythology of pre-Christian and pagan religions.

RANKING OF THE DIFFERENT KINGDOMS ON THE SCALE OF EVOLUTION			
Visible Material World	↑	Invisible World World of Mind/Spirit	
	↑	First Hierarchy	
	↑	Second Hierarchy	
	↑	Third Hierarchy	Archai Kingdom
	↑		Archangel Kingdom
			Angelic Kingdom
Human Kingdom	Direction of Evolution		
Animal Kingdom			
Vegetal Kingdom			
Mineral Kingdom			

Among the beings of the third spiritual hierarchy, angels are those who are located just above human beings on the scale of evolution. They guide and direct each human being in their personal destiny (guardian angels). Meanwhile, groupings of humans—peoples, races, et al.—are guided as a whole by beings who are more advanced or higher on this scale; they are known as archangels. Higher still on the scale are beings called archai.

These spiritual beings have attained a more advanced level of evolution than that of human beings because they were created before them. They belong to the waves of past lives of the wave of human life. But they followed the same path of evolution as human beings throughout the four stages seen above. With each sphere, some of them continued to evolve normally, while others left the process of evolution to become inferior evolutive beings.

HIERARCHICAL BEINGS HAVE NO PHYSICAL BODY

It is thus that on the first sphere (Ancient Saturn), while there were future human beings having only physical bodies, there were also those who were to become beings of the third spiritual hierarchy. On this first sphere:

- The precursors of the human beings of today had a physical body.
- The precursors of the angels of today already had a physical body and an etheric body.

On the second sphere, these future angels acquired an astral body, and on the third sphere, Mind was added. The beings that we now call angels therefore went through a human phase on the third sphere (Ancient Moon). This same general principle continued beyond the level of human beings. With each change of sphere, a superior component was added ("I" spirit, spirit of life, and human spirit). But at the same time, with each stage, angels also lost an inferior component, beginning with their physical body—which was the most ancient.

Because they no longer have a physical body, angels are no longer present in the physical world and can no longer intervene directly in this material plane where human beings live. This is why they cannot be seen; they live in a world that is invisible to human beings. This also goes for archangels and archai; they don't have physical bodies and therefore cannot show themselves in the material plane.

Second Response: Elementals

Let us first take a closer look at angels. We will then be able to apply the same reasoning for archangels and archai. Before moving to the current planetary stage of Earth, the then-future angels of today were composed of two categories. There were those who were ready to attain this level and who evolved normally, and those who did not follow the path of evolution. Spiritual science teaches that these latter, inferior evolutive beings are the elemental beings of today, associated with the element of air.

These elemental beings therefore kept a physical body, but it is a body that is formed from matter that is more subtle than that of the human body, and is generally not visible to us. Furthermore, spiritual science also teaches that elemental beings did not keep the immortal part of the mind/spirit. They did, however, keep the ability to think, the intelligence that allows them to acquire knowledge—but they do not have the immortality associated with mind/spirit.

According to the same reasoning, the future archangels, who belong to a wave of life that preceded that of angels, reached the level of human evolution on the second sphere, Ancient Sun, upon acquiring mind/spirit. Some of them continued their evolution from human to angelical by moving to the third sphere, while others did not evolve. These are the elemental beings who today are associated with the element of water.

The Appearance of Elementals as Inferior Evolutive Beings

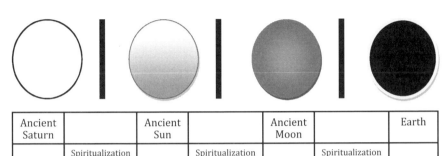

Ancient Saturn		Ancient Sun		Ancient Moon		Earth
	Spiritualization Phase		Spiritualization Phase		Spiritualization Phase	

Angels						
Physical Body Etheric Body		Physical Body Etheric Body Astral Body		Physical Body Etheric Body Astral Body Mind		Etheric Body Astral Body Mind "I" Mind

Inferior Evolutive Beings						
						Physical Body Etheric Body Astral Body Thought ↓ Elementary Beings of Air

Likewise, the archai of today were already at the human level on the first sphere, Ancient Saturn. When they moved to the second sphere, some of them evolved normally and then moved from the human level to the angelic level, while others who were not ready did not continue with their evolution. Spiritual science teaches that these inferior evolutive beings are the elemental beings of today that are associated with the element of Earth. The elementals associated with the element of fire were born of another process.

Beings at the Service of Nature, Formed from Submatter

Although the beings of the third hierarchy, each at their level, are at the service of human beings, the elementals are at the service of nature, each in its element. They reign over the elements of solid, liquid, and gas and act as the architects and artisans of nature's different kingdoms. They are intermediaries between the spiritual and natural worlds because they have kept a bond with the hierarchical beings they were born from.

Elemental beings therefore have a physical body, but it is made up of a matter that is more subtle than the one we know. Spiritual science mentions "submatter," and esoteric knowledge mentions "ethers," which are made up of several degrees of density as shown on the chart that follows. Elemental beings have a physical body that is invisible to us and belongs to the etheric, elementary world—in proximity to our dense material world. They also have an etheric body and an astral body but they do not have mind/spirit (they have kept only the ability to think). These etheric levels can be seen by psychics or young children.

Solid State	**Matter**: These three states of denser matter are well known to us	
Liquid State		
Gaseous State		
Chemical Ether	**Submatter**	Level of Earth Spirits
Vital Ether		Level of Water Spirits
Light Ether		Level of Air Spirits
Reflective Ether		Level of Fire Spirits

The Physical World Comprises Seven Vibratory States

Levels of Evolution That Are Comparable to Those of Human Beings

Another essential point to note is that the elementals of earth, water, and air reached the same level of human evolution as the human beings of today. We can understand then that they have the ability to think, they have intelligence, and they have a knowledge and an understanding of the world that is comparable to that of human beings. But because they did not keep mind/spirit, they do not have an ethic or a moral sense of responsibility.

Now we can better understand Rudolf Steiner's description of them: "They are beings who, in some ways, are not that different from human beings. It is true that they do not have a dense physical body, but they have intelligence. At the same time though, there is a difference between them and human beings in that they have intelligence but are devoid of a sense of responsibility. They therefore do not experience any feelings following an act of injustice, such as when they play tricks on humans."[27] Indeed, they often have a tendency to tease human beings.

Note: We can quote here a comment made by the psychiatrist John Mack: "It seems obvious in Peter's reports as in those of other abduction victims that the "extraterrestrials" come from the same source as we do, but we were separated at a certain point. This long quest to reunite with each other would correspond to this desire to find a lost brotherhood."[28] This comment was based on information that had come out of numerous hypnosis sessions that he had with his patients. He seems to confirm that the kidnappers are elementals.

THE ONLY INTELLIGENT, NONHUMAN EARTH BEINGS WHO HAVE A PHYSICAL BODY

Let us return now to our opening question: Who are the abductors? We have seen that they are certainly intelligent beings who have a physical body or are present in a plane that is in proximity to our material plane, making it possible for them to intervene in our material world. Spiritual science teaches that there are two categories of beings, present on Earth, that meet these conditions:

1. **Wandering human souls.** They can manifest themselves in their former homes and be the explanation for haunting phenomena occurring in houses at night (ghosts, light, or sound manifestations). But they cannot be responsible for all the other numerous, mysterious phenomena that exist, and, in particular, for abductions.
2. **Elementals.** They are the only intelligent, invisible beings that are present on Earth and have a subtle physical body—*the only Earth beings who have a subtle physical body*.

It is therefore important not only to acknowledge the existence of these beings, but to know their abilities, their characteristics, and their behaviors.

Spiritual science teaches that elementals have the ability to show themselves in any form. They can appear as light or as matter, or as objects of any shape or size, or as animals, and therefore can take on human forms as well.

They love to make fun of human beings and play all sorts of tricks on them in order to then poke fun at their reactions.

They have great telepathic abilities.

They are able to see human beings, although the opposite is not true.

From this, we can understand that they have fun pretending to be what they are not. They pretend to be extraterrestrials by manifesting flying vessels, and they pretend to be doctors by making abduction victims lie down on operating tables and showing interest in their physical bodies.

This knowledge is essential and indispensable if we hope to understand the abduction phenomenon and, more generally, all the other mysterious phenomena that occur in the material world, before we resort to the extraterrestrial hypothesis. The difficulty is that these beings, who are invisible due to how humans have evolved, have been forgotten by humans since the onset of the materialist vision of the world in Western society.

Helena Blavatsky, known for developing Theosophy, wrote, "Elemental beings do not have an immortal spirit nor do they have a tangible body. The most solid part of their body is ordinarily just immaterial enough so that it escapes the perception of our physical vision, but they can be seen perfectly using internal, psychic vision. They live in the ether and can condense it in order to make tangible bodies out of it and give them whatever form they please."

Rudolf Steiner, founder of Anthroposophy, wrote, "All of the mysterious phenomena make sense when we take into account the existence of human souls and elemental beings in the elementary, etheric plane."

Selim Aïssel, founder of Psycho-Anthropology, wrote, "The world of nature beings is just as real as animals or flowers, even if it is no longer perceivable by our senses. Modern, rational, and scientific thought, while allowing human beings to do an often marvelous investigation of matter, has also obscured or reduced our field of vision. It has led us to be unaware of an entire part of what is real. This was a necessary step in human evolution, but perhaps the time has come for humanity to open itself to other realities."

Conclusion

The Abductors Are Elementals

As a conclusion to this chapter and in response to the question "Who are the abductors?," we can't help but observe that, no matter what path we took to answer this question, the response has always been the same. All the knowledge we based this study on has brought us to the same response: elemental beings.

Ancient knowledge about fairies, religious knowledge about djinns, traditional knowledge about "these beings from another world," and spiritual knowledge all converge to remind us of the existence of elementals. And even if the abductions of humans as we know them today date back only a few decades, we have shown that elementals have manifested themselves throughout time in slightly different ways, while always being focused on sexual relations. It is only the form of their manifestations that has evolved over time.

The existence of these elemental beings who live in parallel worlds has been forgotten by most people because they no longer have the ability to see them, and yet, elementals have always manifested themselves in the material plane. They have done so in diverse ways and through diverse phenomena considered to be paranormal, and they continue to do so.

Now it is important to realize that these elementals live on the same planet as we do—Earth—and that they are living forces of nature. They are the primary victims of the sometimes irreversible pollution and waste that humans inflict on nature and on this planet. It is understandable that elementals would be quite concerned about this situation because they suffer directly from it, and they have an intelligence and an understanding of the world that is comparable to ours. So they try, in their way, to make human beings aware of ecology in order to get them to change their actions. This preoccupation with ecology has indeed been a common thread in the abductions of human beings and in the UFO appearances around nuclear sites of the past fifty years or so.

Thus, as much as the primary characteristic of abductions—the sexual plan—still seems absurd to us, the second characteristic—information about the earth's ecology—is perfectly justified.

Elementals Are Master Illusionists

Now we must try to understand why the kidnappers tell their victims that they are from such and such a star or constellation, and why they take their victims into a space vessel. Through these two aspects, they show themselves clearly as extraterrestrial beings visiting the earth, and this is why the extraterrestrial hypothesis is almost unanimously used to explain the abduction phenomenon today.

But this interpretation is completely opposite the conclusion we have arrived at in this work. So either the elemental hypothesis is false, and this would mean that all the sources of knowledge used throughout this study are false, or what the abductors say is false, and the way in which they show themselves in a space vessel is a deceitful mise-en-scène.

In order to choose the right answer from these two contradictory proposals, we need to know elemental beings better. We have seen how Islamic knowledge describes djinns:

Dj5: "Incorrigible liars, they take impish pleasure in disorienting and confusing humans in all sorts of absurd ways."

Dj10: "They also possess immense telepathic abilities and the power to easily seduce their human victims."

Spiritual science also describes elementals as intelligent beings having knowledge comparable to that of humans, but who are at the same time mischievous and dishonest. They are capable of playing all sorts of tricks on human beings so they can then poke fun at their reactions. They have no moral conscience, which is what we have indeed observed in the way they treat their victims. Furthermore, spiritual science teaches that elementals have the ability to manifest all sorts of objects.

This knowledge of elemental beings allows us to confirm the coherence among all the analyses that we have done: the kidnappers are indeed elemental beings. But we must also recognize that they are master illusionists. When they kidnap human beings, they give themselves a good image—an image that is serious and modern—by pretending to be extraterrestrials that they are not. Let us remember that this mise-en-scène has been a common theme in kidnappings only since the 1950s and '60s, when human beings started being open to the possibility of life existing elsewhere than on Earth. But these same elementals have always made their presence known to human beings through inflicting unwanted sexual practices on them.

A small, revealing element can be found in the account of the abduction of Ed: "The female entity started to convey information concerning the way in which humans behaved concerning ecology and the way they manage resources. She explained that humans are doing stupid things and are on the wrong path, a path that is leading us to a worldwide disaster that also threatened the planet of humanoids." It is difficult for us to fathom that the widespread pollution of nature here on Earth can have a direct consequence on another planet, but it is another thing altogether if this "planet of humanoids" is our own planet Earth. We can therefore understand the kidnappers' motivation to help humankind become aware of its responsibility.

CONCLUSIONS

Although humankind has been confronted with the UFO phenomenon—appearances of unidentified flying objects—since ancient times, the phenomenon of the abduction of human beings into UFOs is much more recent and dates from the 1950s to 1960s. It is therefore logical to think that there is a link between these two forms of mysterious manifestations.

UFOs and Abductions

CORRELATION BETWEEN THE RESURGENCE OF UFO SIGHTINGS AND ABDUCTIONS

We know that there was a resurgence of the UFO phenomenon starting in the 1940s, when we began to experiment with nuclear fission and started manufacturing our first atomic weapons.[1] From that time on, we have witnessed a large proportion of UFO apparitions near nuclear installations, leading us to believe that the intelligences associated with UFOs were quite preoccupied by nuclear technology and its devastating powers. Furthermore, if the first media-covered abductions were those of the Brazilian Antonio Villas-Boas in 1957, followed by those of the American couple Barney and Betty Hill in 1961, we can easily imagine that there had been others that were not reported. It is also reasonable to assume that perhaps those concerned preferred to remain silent out of fear of being ridiculed for their outlandish, far-out accounts. We can also assume that, for this same reason, the reports were deliberately not made public.

We can thus observe a relationship between the increase of UFO phenomena starting in the 1940s and the subsequent proliferation of cases of abduction into UFOs. (There does exist, however, an eyewitness account from the Middle Ages of an abduction into a flying vessel taking place in the city of Lyon, France. But since this is the only account we have, it would seem that this phenomenon was not widespread at the time.)

Moreover, between these two phenomena, another correlation appears. Often during abductions, a recurring characteristic over the past few decades is that the victims undergo a sort of "awareness raising" about the serious ecological threats weighing on planet Earth. They are shown apocalyptic images of a devastated planet, similar to what it would look like after a nuclear war. These two correlations support the hypothesis that these are indeed the same entities who are manifesting themselves through these different forms.

WARNINGS GIVEN TO HUMANITY BY NONHUMANS

We can therefore see these two phenomena—which leave us baffled and feeling helpless—as warnings to humankind given by nonhumans. They take on, therefore, a considerable significance by their philosophical implications, although still little known by the public. It is true that in all countries, one can see a deliberate attempt on the part of governments to keep this information secret. The result is that both the nature of the UFO phenomenon and the abductions of humans into these vessels are still mysterious today.

Two Different Sources of UFO Phenomena

KIDNAPPERS WHO ARE DEVOID OF ANY SENSE OF MORALITY

The way in which abductions take place is much more violent and a far cry from the luminous unidentified flying objects, which simply seek to titillate the curiosity of their observers. These "beings from another world" intrude upon the lives of humans with no regard for those they kidnap.

The study of different cases of abductions by UFOs has shown that the kidnappers in the majority of cases take on the appearance of humans from distant stars arriving aboard their space vessels, but who lack the moral conscience of humans and treat their victims without any respect for human dignity. They have their victims undergo experiments, which appear to be medical in nature but seem absurd. Above all, they subject their victims to sexual abuse, which most often leaves deep trauma. These practices show a serious lack of respect for human beings, and these entities therefore do not deserve to be considered as "superior," which is contrary to how we tend to characterize anything that is extraterrestrial.

VISITORS WHO ARE RESPECTFUL OF MAN

Thanks to Ardy Sixkiller Clarke's book *Encounters with Star People*, we learn about several cases of American Indians finding themselves faced with this same type of kidnapping experience. Other Amerindians reported having encountered beings with a humanoid appearance who also introduced themselves as coming from faraway stars in their space vessels. But they exhibited radically different behavior, which was based on respect and an attitude of warm, caring detachment. We also learn that these "visitors" abided by a strict rule not to interfere with the affairs of humans and consequently avoided contact with them. These Amerindian testimonies are very informative because in the rare cases where the visitors had to come in contact with humans for some reason or another, we were able to gain some priceless glimpses into their way of life and, above all, their behavior. The analysis of these eyewitness accounts led to a series of revelations about these beings.

Two Categories of UFOs

This is how the idea that there are two types of UFOs coming from two different sources became so apparent. In fact, we can more accurately say that there are two different categories of nonhuman beings who have come to us in space vessels, or that there are two radically different kinds of "close encounters of the third kind," according to the classification provided by J. Allen Hynek. Furthermore, we were able to come up with a simple way to distinguish between these two different species of beings or these two types of "close encounters of the third kind," thanks to Amerindian accounts:

1. In the first type, the beings force their way into the lives of human beings and inflict upon them a pseudomedical protocol followed by a traumatizing rape, without any feelings of regret. They also convey information about the alarming ecological imbalances of the earth, for which man is responsible. We have shown that these abductions into these flying vessels are, in reality, a "staged setting" allowing the abusers to come across as extraterrestrials, and that these abductions are indeed real, truly affecting their victims, but they occur in a parallel dimension.
2. In the second type, the beings avoid contact with humans and, in all cases, show an attitude of respect and kind detachment. As soon as they are surprised by human eyewitnesses, they disappear swiftly into their space vessels and quickly fly away, or they dematerialize in order to disappear out of sight of their human observers. In every case, their rule is to not interfere in the affairs of humans and to act as neutral observers only.

We can distinguish between these two categories by referring to them as "close encounters of the third kind with avoidance," which corresponds to the second kind, and "close encounters of the third kind with abduction," which corresponds to the first category.

In this study, we were able to gather eleven cases of "encounters with avoidance." Others had probably been reported, but it turns out that this number is very limited in comparison to the number of abductions into UFOs, which reaches into the hundreds of thousands. It is important to point out that this number of eleven known cases of "encounters with avoidance" is not the ultimate count of all the instances of extraterrestrials who have paid a visit to Earth. Since the main characteristic of these visitors is to remain discreet, they make it a point to avoid being seen by humans so as not to disturb them. Furthermore, according to the several visitors who have communicated to us, their ancestors were already visiting planet Earth thousands of years ago.

A Series of Revelations

A New Light Shed on the UFO Phenomenon

This distinction between the two types of experiences clarifies in a completely new way the UFO phenomenon in general, and the phenomenon of abductions into UFOs in particular. This should have important implications in the study of UFO phenomena, which can even be extended to the study of the paranormal. Ignorance of the fact that two different categories of nonhuman beings can come into contact with humans can necessarily cause a lot of confusion, which in turn can make it harder to have a correct understanding of these phenomena.

Once we were able to distinguish these two categories, we then had to determine the identity of these beings who have been revealing themselves to us.

Extraterrestrial Human Races

Because it had been generally accepted that human beings had never had any veritable contact with extraterrestrial civilizations, the extraterrestrial hypothesis has been up until now only a rational but unproven one. But this is no longer the case. The testimonies of Amerindians documented by Ardy Sixkiller Clarke and analyzed here have completely changed the data and are extremely valuable to this research.

These eyewitness accounts provide an unexpected, bewildering revelation: several Amerindians were surprised one day to run into beings with a human aspect, but who were not men and women like us. For example, they were able to become invisible or visible at will and had arrived and left again on space vessels. Even more extraordinary was that even though a universal rule of these beings was not to interfere in the affairs of humans—and several among them had reiterated this— it so happened that in several specific cases, they had to come in contact with humans for a limited time. We thus also learned that they are real space travelers who collect mineral and vegetal samples, observing the evolution of life on the planets they visit, and all the while remaining neutral and kind toward all forms of life they encounter. They affirmed that their ancestors had been visiting Earth for thousands of years.

But what is perhaps the most disconcerting for us, with our limited knowledge, is that these beings with humanoid appearances seemingly have been coming from different extrasolar planets and have adapted themselves to the physical conditions of life on Earth, which leads us to think that our conditions of life are similar to the planets they come from. Even though some of these beings are different from us (in size, for example), others are exactly like us. Some of their attributes show that they are superior to us in an evolutionary sense; that is, they can travel in space, make themselves invisible or visible at will, communicate using telepathy, go without eating, get by on very little sleep, etc. But in spite of these differences, we can consider them as human beings in a broader sense; that is, human beings belonging to different extraterrestrial races.

Consequently, these eyewitness accounts incite us to considerably enlarge our perspective and force us to let go of our customary concept of life in the universe, which tends to be too rigid and egocentric.

Extraterrestrial Humans Who Are Living among Us

Even more surprising: several accounts from Amerindians reveal that extraterrestrial human beings are already living among us on Earth. They are doing so incognito, either by choice or because their space vessel crashed and they were unable to get help from their fellows. Among these accounts, the most troubling is perhaps the one where a woman appeared and showed that she had no navel. This means that she belonged to a "human" species that had evolved beyond the stage of "sexual" reproduction, or the union of two individuals of complementary genders, and had attained the level of androgyny. Spiritual science teaches us that humanity will achieve this level of evolution in the distant future.

Something else that is equally extraordinary and unbelievable for those interested in modern biological science: an Amerindian woman explained that she had herself been the offspring of the union of an extraterrestrial man and an earth woman. This means that the genetic characteristics of her father's race were completely compatible with ours. This observation confirms that her parents belonged to two races of the same species: the human species.

Another Extraterrestrial Visitor

All the testimonies and observations that we have been able to gather and analyze in this book come together to support the fact that these extraterrestrial visitors are never aggressive or ill intentioned, but, rather, always neutral and caring. They abide by a strict rule not to interfere in the lives of humans. This information is obviously fundamental for all those who live in fear that one day the earth will be invaded by an extraterrestrial race.

The account that follows is incredible and surprising, but complementary to the preceding ones. Before we explain further, it is important to first understand that in this domain, it is illusory and virtually impossible to research proof in the scientific sense of the term, since this would involve obtaining results through methodical experiments—and we are dealing with nonhuman intelligences, which, by definition, we do not comprehend, Thus, the knowledge that we can hope to obtain must necessarily be based on eyewitness accounts, which can be supported by analyses of soil or vegetation as in the cases of Valensole or Trans-en-Provence.

One day, in 1980s France, a man encountered another "man" who introduced himself as having come from another star system. What makes this account original is that this "visitor," after having shown the Frenchman that he was able to read his mind, proposed that he personally and directly convey to him a teaching. They therefore met five times at the Frenchman's home to complete this mission. All of this seemed so unconceivable that the incredulous host had to wait ten years to seize the significance of what had been communicated to him and to realize that it was up to him to get the message out himself. He did so by publishing a book, whose title is an explicit one: *Réflexions sur le destin de la Terre et de l'Univers—le point de vue d'un extraterrestre*, by Jean de Raigalgue.[2] Unfortunately, this book is out of stock today.

In this account, the visitor came across as being of extraterrestrial origin with a humanoid appearance, and he did so without having to climb into a space vessel. When the time came for a teaching session with his host, he would simply appear on the Frenchman's couch, and when the session was over, he would disappear. He also demonstrated all sorts of wonders with his "magic ball": actions that proved that he possessed a level of mastery over matter completely beyond our understanding. And when he communicated about the history of Earth, he focused greatly on the era of the lost city of Atlantis by expressing facts totally consistent with the information we can find on the subject passed down from spiritual traditions. It is this very quality and coherence that allow us to render a positive verdict on this extraordinary account and accept its authenticity.

It is evident that this account is similar to those of the Amerindians in the sense that it was truly a superior human being who appeared. However, it is set apart by the fact that the visitor in question came not as a neutral observer, but as someone with the intention of being a beneficial, civilizing influence on humankind by conveying a message that was to be passed on. He showed himself to be discreet in his appearances, addressing himself to one chosen person. Here we find the qualities of respect, kindness, and caring mentioned before, but the extraterrestrial visitor also intervened in the destiny of the man to whom he communicated, and through him, in the destiny of those who would read the Frenchman's book. He came to Earth to support the evolution of humankind, all the while respecting its free will. Because it is from a different source, this account reinforces the credibility of those of the Amerindians. Perhaps there are others that are similar.

The True Identity of the Kidnappers

So Who Are Those Committing the Abductions?

Let us remember that even if the phenomenon of human abductions into UFOs has been known only for several decades, we have shown that its main characteristic is no less than sexual abuse inflicted on the victims, without any respect for human dignity. We have also shown that such abuse had already been practiced in ancient times, without flying space vessels, at least as early as the Middle Ages, and most likely long before. This fact is virtually unknown by the public, probably because anything dealing with sex is considered taboo in all human societies. In the Middle Ages, these abusive sexual practices were imposed as much on men as on women by entities known as succubae or incubi, later called demons: entities whose nature was not understood. In Celtic countries, these practices were equally known and ascribed to fairies or elves.

It is interesting to note that in the Muslim religion, abductions of human beings and imposed sexual relations were equally known and attributed to djinns or genies: beings who, according to the Koran, live on Earth among men and angels. Furthermore, these beings were so well known that Islamic jurisprudence acknowledged their existence, and possible relationships between djinns and human beings were seriously examined by jurists in Muslim countries.

The Christian faith, on the other hand, condemned and fought these same sexual practices where men and women were abused. The religious authorities in the Middle Ages were quite preoccupied with this, judging from the numerous texts that have come down to us. These authorities seemed not even to recognize the existence of the entities who were the cause. The bishops were quite alarmed at these practices and pondered how they were to judge the victims. The tragedy of the witch hunts that ravaged Europe for two centuries, where many men and women—particularly women—were sent to the stake, is a consequence of this ignorance about the entities who manifested themselves to men and women in order to impose sexual acts upon them without their consent.

Our study has shown that these supernatural entities called incubi, succubae, demons, fairies, elves, sylphs, and djinns, or other names according to the time and place, are referred to as "elemental beings" or "nature spirits" in our day. These beings are well depicted by spiritual science—indeed, all the ancient traditions clearly recognized their existence, judging from their presence in the innumerable tales and legends throughout the world. But they were forgotten over time by Western civilization. The Christian religion owns some of the responsibility, but it is above all the development of technological, material-based civilizations that distanced humankind from nature, and, subsequently, it gradually lost the ability to perceive nature spirits. It is therefore the evolution of humankind that has caused these elemental beings to become invisible, and as a result, their existence has been forgotten. But they are no less real and manifest themselves from time to time in multiple ways.

Thus, we have arrived at the conclusion that abductions of human beings into UFOs, which belong to the "close encounters of the third kind with abduction" category, are in fact not the work of extraterrestrial beings but, rather, elemental beings: beings who, like us, are earthbound. This phenomenon is therefore of a terrestrial nature according to our analysis, and not extraterrestrial. This conclusion is supported by a large amount of knowledge coming from different sources, all converging in this direction. It is the ignorance of the existence of these nature spirits in our modern materialistic civilization that has led humans to put forward an extraterrestrial theory that has never really been proven.

We can also add that the thesis of the origin of the abductions being connected to the earth is coherent with the large number of incidents taking place at this time in the United States, along with the long-standing, centuries-old occurrences of this phenomenon throughout the world.

ELEMENTAL BEINGS ARE MASTER ILLUSIONISTS

This conclusion contradicts the extraterrestrial interpretation, which in our day is generally accepted by most. Let us remember that numerous testimonies of abduction victims reported that their perpetrators told them that they were from faraway stars. When added to the fact that the victims were taken into space vessels, it appeared logical to think that the kidnappers were extraterrestrial beings.

This contradiction of the extraterrestrial argument is explained by two dominant features of elementals:

They have the reputation of being intelligent but are in fact deceivers and disdainers. We have indeed seen that they are devoid of any moral conscience and are indifferent to the confusion they cause and the wrong that they inflict on humans through their lies. They are capable of deliberately deceiving us, for example, by pretending to be extraterrestrials.

They are able to manifest any form. We have seen how they can modify the decor around the people who are abducted (a forest inside the space vessel, or simply a conference room). We have also learned from two eyewitness accounts that their visitors materialized out of a ball of light. They therefore are able to manifest even a space vessel, if they so desire, in order to mislead us as to their true identity. The knowledge of this ability is equally essential for understanding the reality behind all UFO phenomena.

The consequence is that if we want to determine the truth, it is impossible to trust what they say and what they do, and impossible to take at face value how they reveal themselves to us. Our analysis is supported by diverse sources of knowledge about elementals. It is only with the knowledge of their dominant traits that we can keep elementals from leading us down the path of illusion and confusion.

A GREAT DIVERSITY AMONG ELEMENTALS

Previous studies done to understand the nature and the origin of other phenomena such as crop circles, disappearing objects, mysterious falling rocks, etc. have shown, by using the same knowledge base as in this current study, that all these occurrences can be attributed to elementals. Furthermore, UFO appearances that most often take place to arouse the interest of witnesses have equally been analyzed on the basis of the same information and can also be attributed to elementals. We decided to gather together all these manifestations that have different forms but that come from the same source, and that are nonhuman in origin but stimulate the curiosity of man, under the acronym IDIMM for Interdimensional Manifestations.

We therefore understand that the phenomenon of abduction of human beings into UFOs clearly stands out from other forms of elemental manifestations in that these acts have no moral conscience and are motivated in general by malice toward the victims. This observation confirms that there is a large diversity among these beings, just as there is a large diversity among human beings on Earth. A more in-depth study of these diverse forms of manifestations will soon be disclosed and will show that they seem to come from a large diversity of beings, all of which can be designated as "elemental beings."

The Meaning and Final Aim of the Abductions of Human Beings

This issue was deliberately left out of this current study and will be addressed in a subsequent work that will include updated information concerning the implications these abductions represent for humanity. In this next work we will discover that these actions have completely unexpected and considerable repercussions on the evolution of humanity in our times. It will be explained how the high number of hybrid beings born of the genetic manipulation performed by the kidnappers has allowed them to insidiously interfere in the evolution of human society. We will also see that these hybrid beings even represent one of the most serious causes of the upheavals that our society has been facing for the past several decades, and of the dangers it will have to face in the future.

Paradigm Shifts

Very Different Proportions of Extraterrestrial and Terrestrial Origins

We have been able to gather only eleven known cases of "close encounters of the third kind with avoidance," which are veritable cases of encounters with extraterrestrial human beings. The account cited in this conclusion represents a twelfth case of an encounter with an extraterrestrial human, but without the aspect of avoidance. On the other hand, the "encounters of the third kind with abduction," which we have chosen to attribute to elementals, number in the dozens and perhaps even the hundreds of thousands. Further, the number of authentic manifestations of UFOs is in the millions. It is important to appreciate the significance of this disproportion.

This means that virtually all the accounts of "close encounters of the third kind" and virtually all the observations that have been made of UFOs in general and not involving encounters with entities are manifestations coming from elementals. In France, the cases of Valensole and Trans-en-Provence have fascinated UFO enthusiasts, who don't have to analyze things any further to understand that they are not like the other cases; they can easily conceive that they are of an extraterrestrial origin. But we are still aware that the lack of knowledge we have about elementals and their abilities is a source of much confusion for all the other cases.

If we were to sum up the situation at the end of this study by a "shock" statement, we can say that virtually all the UFO observations generally attributed to extraterrestrials seem to be in reality manifestations of elementals! These results are in opposition to the mainstream opinions on the subject.

A Twofold Paradigm Shift

Thanks to an analysis of the testimonies of the Amerindians who had had "close encounters of the third kind," we were able to reveal two diametrically opposed behaviors that led us to determine two distinct origins of the entities encountered:

In a very small number of cases, witnesses did indeed encounter beings of extraterrestrial origin who were similar to human beings. Thanks to the information available to us, we can consider them as human beings belonging to extraterrestrial races. We have even discovered that some of them are living among us on Earth.

In all the other cases, which represent virtually all the close encounters of the third kind, our analysis has shown that in reality, the witnesses had been confronted with elemental beings who pretended to be extraterrestrials coming from faraway stars. They are entities who are earthbound like humans, have the ability to take on a human appearance, and are normally invisible to us because they live in a parallel dimension.

This dual origin gives us a vision that is clear and coherent, particularly of the abduction of humans into UFOs and of the UFO phenomenon in general. We are thus confronted with a double paradigm shift, which is going to considerably modify our perception of humankind's place in the universe among other forms of life. This new vision will necessarily have huge philosophical and spiritual repercussions for humanity.

APPENDIX

Other Famous Abduction Cases

The following is our analysis of two abductions into UFOs. Not only are they among the first ever reported in our time, but they are also among the most famous. These analyses were made using logical reasoning and a rational approach, both uniquely scientific—but they were also made without being influenced by the limitations of today's science and by the erroneous lines of thinking related to the materialist view we have of the world.

The Abduction of Barney and Betty Hill
(UNITED STATES, 1961)

On September 19, 1961, Barney and Betty Hill were driving back home after a week of vacationing in Canada. At around 10 p.m., they saw a bright light in the sky, making erratic movements. On the back seat of the car, their dog, who had been quiet during the whole trip, began showing signs of uneasiness. The couple decided to pull over so they could take the dog for a walk. Through his binoculars, Barney spotted a large, luminous disc in the sky. It had two pairs of finlike wings with red lights at the ends and rows of round windows, and it seemed to be coming toward him. When it got to within 100 feet of him, Barney was terrified; he rushed back to his car and took off at high speed. This was the last thing the couple remembered.

When the couple came to, they twice heard a "beep-beep noise" without knowing what it was, and found themselves in their car about thirty-five miles farther south from where they had been, with no recollection of how they had gotten there. They were driving in silence, numb, as if sleepwalking. When they got back home at 5 a.m., they realized that this was two hours later than planned. Moreover, Barney discovered numerous scratches on the leather of his shoes, as if someone had dragged him across the ground. He also felt a sharp pain in his back. On his car he noticed several spots where the body paint had disappeared, leaving bare metal.

Sometime after this occurrence, Barney and Betty complained of mysterious ailments as well as nightmares. In the spring of 1962, after several ineffective treatments, their family doctor recommended them to a psychiatrist, who diagnosed both of them with posttraumatic stress disorder. This psychiatrist in turn recommended them to a colleague who specialized in hypnotherapy, in the hopes that a regression session would bring any traumatic memories to the surface. In December 1963, Barney and Betty started a series of hypnosis sessions that would go on for more than seven months.

Under hypnosis, they recounted that after seeing the UFO, Barney had attempted to escape from it and started driving down a forest path, where their car then stalled. The UFO landed at about 200 feet from their car, and a dozen small creatures came down out of it and toward the couple. The creatures made the couple climb up into the UFO, separated them, and had them undergo what looked to them like a sort of medical exam. A device was placed on Barney's genitals, most likely to take a sperm sample. As for Betty, the creature who seemed to be the one in charge showed her a map of space. During the sessions of hypnosis, Betty and Barney were always questioned separately, and their versions always matched up. They even gave the same description of their "kidnappers"; they were very small with enormous heads that were pointed at the chin. They had wide eyes that narrowed on the sides, a line for a mouth, and a barely perceptible nose.

The psychiatrist who conducted the hypnosis sessions concluded that it was a "shared fantasy," while at the same time admitting that "to them, the experience was undeniably real." It is worth noting that at the time, the phenomenon of abductions related to UFOs was not at all known.

ANALYSIS

1. Something significant:

The UFO first appeared as a bright light in the sky before changing into an object that looked material: a luminous disc with wings and small, round windows. This change of appearance is a very significant characteristic of the UFO phenomenon. It is frequently reported that these flying objects seem to change form or color (or both), even though they appear to be solid. It is clear that this is not compatible with the laws of science. A change in form such as what Barney and Betty observed cannot take place in our material world because it does not respect its laws. This object could not have been a real, solid object—in the ordinary sense. The logical conclusion is that the object came from another world and was present in another world, even if it was visible to Barney and Betty. It seemed to belong to a parallel world that is close enough to the material world so that it appeared to Barney and Betty as a solid material object.

2. Extraterrestrial beings:

According to the information that came out of the hypnosis sessions, the kidnappers showed themselves with features that fit the description of "extraterrestrial beings" in popular culture. These beings are sometimes called "gray aliens," which is believed to be the most common type of extraterrestrial observed today. But the extraterrestrial origin of these creatures has never been proven.

3. Proof that the occurrence really happened:

Even if there weren't any witnesses, the trauma that Barney and Betty experienced, along with the fact that their versions were exactly the same, coupled with the marks on Barney's shoes and car, showed clearly that "something had really happened" between the moment when Barney rushed back to his car before starting it and the moment when the couple found themselves on the road thirty-five miles farther south two hours later—even if they had no recollection of what had happened during this period of time.

The hypnosis sessions revealed that during the time when Barney lost all recall, he had first attempted to escape by driving down a forest trail. Marks left on the car and on his shoes confirmed this; they seemed to show that this path was full of brush, explaining the scratches on the car, and the scratches on Barney's shoes confirmed that Barney got out of the car after the motor stalled. This happened in the material plane since there were material traces.

4. A significant time lapse:

The fact that they arrived home two hours behind schedule, without any explanation, confirmed that "something had happened" that held them up, something that they had forgotten.

5. The car engine stalled:

Barney's escape attempt was thwarted when the car stalled. It is frequently noted that when a UFO is nearby, all types of motors stop functioning.

6. Inside the UFO:

The rest of the account obtained under hypnosis reveals that a dozen small creatures came to get Barney and Betty to take them into the UFO and perform what looked like medical exams on them.

We can imagine that what happened inside the UFO was really experienced in a material sense and that Barney and Betty underwent a mise-en-scène against their will, a mise-en scène that included a medical exam.

We can also imagine that this occurrence had been imprinted on their memory without having really existed, meaning it would have been "etched" on their minds through mental manipulation.

But neither of these two hypotheses is compatible with the end of the account, which says that Barney and Betty found themselves driving their car thirty-five miles farther down the road.

7. An interdimensional phenomenon:

When the couple regained consciousness, two hours had elapsed and Barney was at the wheel of the car, driving. He was about thirty-five miles farther down the road from the place where the UFO encounter took place. It is impossible to envision that he had driven such a distance while unconscious. This implies that the car and its two passengers had been "transported" thirty-five miles without them knowing it, during the two-hour time lapse. How could such a move have taken place? Would the car have been driven by one of the creatures? This would not make sense because it was Barney who was driving.

Furthermore, Barney and Betty were in a silent stupor, as if sleepwalking, and felt as if they had just awakened from a deep sleep. Thus it is as if the move had taken place right before they woke up. In fact, they had not slept at all—since it was established that something really did happen. The traces on the car and on the shoes, as well as the relocation of the car, confirmed this.

Knowing that the UFO behaved in the beginning as if it were present in a parallel world (which would explain its change of appearance), the hypothesis that logically comes to mind is that the abduction also took place in the same parallel world. Barney and Betty were transported by the creatures of the UFO into another world, along with their car—before being put back into the material world thirty-five miles farther away. In this hypothesis, the abduction that they described during their hypnosis sessions was not a dream. It was perfectly real, as they had always firmly believed, but real in another dimension. *The abduction was an interdimensional phenomenon.*

8. Oddly, the dog was not there to protect its masters:

The couple's dog had been the first to feel the presence of an abnormal energy, visibly associated with the UFO that was nearby, inciting Barney and Betty to pull over and take the dog for a walk. Yet, there was no mention of the dog during the abduction; it did not try to intervene to protect its masters as would have been expected. We can imagine that the dog had been "neutralized," or numbed, and therefore also manipulated by the kidnappers. Indeed, it has often been reported that, for example, a person lying in bed next to an abduction victim at night did not respond to the victim's desperate pleas, as if the person were neutralized and plunged into a deep sleep.

The Abduction of Travis Walton
(NEAR SNOWFLAKE, ARIZONA, 1975)

The following is a chronological account of reported events. Travis was a young lumberjack working on a team of seven men in the state of Arizona. In the evening of November 5, 1975, while driving home after work in a pickup truck, the men saw a bright light through the trees. As they got closer, they saw a golden, shiny disc about fifteen feet in diameter hovering above a clearing. Since there had already been a lot of sightings of UFOs in the region, Travis, who was fascinated by these accounts, jumped out of the truck and ran toward the luminous object in spite of the protests of his coworkers. His coworkers then saw a beam of light shoot out from the UFO and strike Travis. It was as if he had been electrocuted. With arms and legs spread, he was lifted nine feet from the ground. He then fell back hard on the ground, unconscious. His coworkers, panic stricken, took off at once in the truck. After driving several hundred feet, they noticed that the UFO was not following them, so they went back to the spot where they left Travis, but he had disappeared. They searched the area for a half hour but did not find him.

The police were notified as early as the next morning and started a search to find Travis with the help of several dozen volunteers. For five days they deployed considerable means to find him (helicopters, mounted police, jeeps), but without success. Travis was found five days later on the side of a road after telephoning for help. A medical exam would later confirm that he was disoriented, in a state of shock, and extremely thin and dehydrated.

Travis Walton went on to tell the following story. He lost consciousness after being hit by the light beam. When he came to, he saw that he was surrounded by three small bald creatures with large eyes, who were dressed in a sort of one-piece orange suit. Seized with panic, he violently pushed them away and tried to get out of the room through a door— which led to a circular room that had a chair in it. He sat down on the seat, which was facing a sort of control panel, and he started trying to operate it. A rather tall humanoid then came into the room, smiled at him, and took him to another part of the vessel, which turned out to be much bigger than how Travis had imagined it. Seeing several flying saucers in a large room, he surmised that he was on board a sort of "mother ship." He finally found himself in another, smaller room, where a respiratory mask was placed over his face and he again lost consciousness. He then woke up on the roadside where he was subsequently found.

A local doctor confirmed Travis's extreme state of confusion and severe dehydration when he was found on November 10. During the numerous interrogations of Travis and his coworkers, there was not one single flaw or variance in their testimonies. They agreed to take a lie detector test, and they all passed. According to the expert who administered the test, Travis was telling the truth—or at least he believed he was.

ANALYSIS

Here we see several elements frequently observed in UFO phenomena and in abductions:

1. A flying vessel:

A strange, powerful glow, taken for a UFO, is seen above the trees before the disappearance of Travis. The object is then described as a "disc" hovering over the ground, in other words a "flying vessel" with a material appearance. The apparent transformation of the bright light into a golden disc is already an indication that this object did not belong to our material world.

2. A nonhuman intelligence:

The vessel emits a beam of light directly at Travis Walton, lifting him from the ground. This action cannot be explained using current scientific knowledge, implying that this vessel was not of human origin. It came from "another world" and was controlled by a nonhuman intelligence, even if the witnesses did not see any living creatures.

3. An abduction:

The young man disappeared. This occurred without any eyewitnesses, but Travis's coworkers did not find him upon returning to the area immediately after the light beam incident. The search carried out over the following days—using considerable material and human resources—was unsuccessful. This remains unexplained, yet Travis was found several days later. This is why this occurrence is described as an abduction.

4. A disappearance of five days:

Travis Walton suddenly reappeared five days later—physically very weakened and in a state of shock—several miles from the spot where his coworkers had last seen him.

This temporary material disappearance, which kept Travis's physical body intact, could be explained by saying that his body had been materially transported far away from the spot where he was taken, and then brought back five days later to an area nearby. But how and why?

We can also envision that even if it is difficult for a mind conditioned by a materialist vision to understand, Travis's body had been "dematerialized" for a while and then "rematerialized." This means that for five days he was transported into another dimension, into a parallel plane, before being put back in the material plane. This would mean that his physical body would have only "disappeared" from the sight of his coworkers for five days, but without being destroyed. This would imply that the abduction took place through a change in dimension, or a change in space-time.

5. A large, invisible vessel:

Travis Walton naturally retained a part of the memory of what he experienced during these five days. He had lost consciousness between the moment he fell back onto the ground after the UFO light beam struck him, and when he found himself in a struggle with several creatures, who then took him from room to room. This could have taken place only inside the UFO. This account is therefore consistent with the fact that he really was taken into a vessel, all the more so because he had seen small flying saucers stacked in one of these rooms. This implies that the vessel was very large . . . and yet not one of the dozens of people actively searching for him for five days saw it. This seems to mean that the vessel was not visible and was therefore present in a parallel plane, and that the encounter Travis had with his captors took place in another dimension. In Travis's account, he then "lost consciousness" when a mask was put over his face. This could have been a way to make sure he would not remember what was going to happen next—what he would undergo throughout the whole duration of his disappearance.

6. A caricature of extraterrestrials:

Travis said he was taken inside a "mother ship" by beings he described as small and terrifying, with big heads and large eyes. This consistently fits the way "extraterrestrials" are depicted by media and popular culture. The beings used this appearance when showing themselves to Travis.

7. In front of a control panel:

In one of the rooms, Travis saw a control panel with commands. He tried to operate it but without success. It does not seem likely that a real control panel was there for him to operate without anything happening. This brings to mind, rather, that it was an illusion or a virtual image.

8. An interdimensional phenomenon:

Travis's perception of the space vessel's size changed between the moment he first saw it as a simple disc in the clearing and the moment when he saw several flying saucers in one of the rooms of the "mother ship." This type of observation is relatively common in UFO sightings—such as when witnesses on the ground perceive a UFO as having varying sizes. As in the case of Barney and Betty Hill, this means that the UFO was not a material object in the ordinary sense, even if it looked like one. It was necessarily present in another plane or in another dimension, in proximity to our material world.

This also means that Travis Walton, with his physical body, was transported into this other dimension when he was kidnapped and taken inside the vessel. He was taken back into the material world and was found "completely disoriented"—a state similar to the one Barney and Betty Hill found themselves in when they came to in their car "numbed and if sleepwalking." Thus, the fact that Travis Walton had really disappeared and remained invisible for five days leads us to think that he was no longer present in the material world during this time, and that his body was not damaged, because he returned totally intact. He therefore was alive the whole time, but in another world, another plane of existence. This logical reasoning implies that he had been taken into a parallel world, invisible to human beings. During the five days of his "absence," he was in contact with other creatures and subjected to their will—without food or drink—before being returned to the world of human beings.

This analysis of available information seems to plead in favor of an interdimensional phenomenon.

9. Hypnosis:

It is generally reported that Travis Walton did not undergo hypnosis, which would have allowed him to have a better recall of what he went through during his five days of "absence." Yet, Jacques Vallée wrote in one of his books that "Dr. Jim Harder, professor of civil engineering at Berkeley and a supporter of the extraterrestrial hypothesis, had Travis Walton undergo hypnosis." Travis remembered encountering several entities on board the vessel, three of which were small humanoids with "enormous, luminous, elongated, brown eyes. With them was a tall, gentle man, dressed in blue." These fragments of information do not provide us with any further answers, other than the presence of a being who looked human.

ENDNOTES

Introduction

1. The COMETA Report—*UFOs and Defense* (Paris: J'ai lu, 1999).
2. Robert Hastings, *UFOs and Nukes: Extraordinary Encounters at Nuclear Weapons Sites*, www.ufohastings.com.
3. Jacques Vallée, *Passport to Magonia* (Paris: Ed. Robert Laffont, 1978); and Fabrice Bonvin, *OVNIs: Les agents du changement* (Paris: Ed. Le temps présent, 2005).
4. Jean Sider, *La solution du mystère?* (Paris: Ed. Ramuel, 2001).
5. Marie-Thérèse de Brosses, *Enquête sur les enlèvements extraterrestres* (Paris: Ed. J'ai lu, 1997).
6. John E. Mack, *Abduction: Human Encounters with Aliens* (Paris: Ed. J'ai lu, 2012); and John E. Mack, *Passport to the Cosmos* (Paris: Ed. Dervy, 2016).

Chapter 1

1. Mack, *Abduction: Human Encounters with Aliens*.
2. Mack, *Passport to the Cosmos*.
3. Mack, *Abduction: Human Encounters with Aliens*.
4. Budd Hopkins, *Alien Abductions: Witnesses speak* (Paris: Ed. du Rocher, 1995).
5. David M. Jacobs, *Secret Life: Firsthand Accounts of UFO Abductions* (New York: Simon & Schuster, 1992).
6. Aimé Michel, *A propos des soucoupes volantes* (Paris: Ed. Planète, 1966).
7. Jean Sider, *Ovnis: Les envahisseurs démasqués* (Paris: Ed. Ramuel, 1999); and Jean Sider, *Extraterrestres—Mystère et magie des enlèvements* (Paris: Ed. Le temps présent, 2009).
8. Gildas Bourdais, *Visions célestes, visions cosmiques* (Paris: Ed. Le temps présent, 2007).

9. Brosses, *Enquête sur les enlèvements extraterrestres*.
10. Gildas Bourdais, *Ovnis, vers la fin du secret* (Paris: Ed. Le temps présent, 2010); and Daniel Harran, *Ovnis, Crop Circles & MIDIM: Phénomènes mystérieux élucidés!* (Paris: Ed. EccE, 2016).
11. Ardy Sixkiller Clarke, *Encounters with Star People* (Paris: Ed. Atlantes, 2016).
12. Coral Lorenzen and Jim Lorenzen, *Flying Saucer Occupants* (New York: Signet, 1967).
13. Mack, *Abduction: Human Encounters with Aliens*.
14. Ibid.
15. Ibid.
16. Ibid.
17. Ibid.
18. Brosses, *Enquête sur les enlèvements extraterrestres*.
19. Roger K. Leir, *UFOs and Implants* (Whitley Streiber's preface) (Paris: Ed. Mercure Dauphinois, 2003).
20. Ibid.
21. Ibid.
22. Ibid.
23. Ibid.
24. Ibid.

Chapter 2

1. Daniel Harran, *Les ovnis et le nucléaire—le choc d'une réalité ignorée* (F. Bonvin's preface) (Paris: Ed. Le temps présent, 2017).
2. Ibid.
3. Ibid.
4. Thibault Laurent, Christine Thomas-Agnan, and Michael Vaillant, "Spatial Point Pattern Analysis of the Unidentified Aerial Phenomena in France," https://hal.archives-ouvertes.fr/hal-01187046.

5. Ibid.

6. Harran, *Ovnis, Crop Circles & MIDIM: Phénomènes mystérieux élucidés!*

Chapter 3

1. Vallée, *Passport to Magonia*, 171; and Saint Augustin, *La Cité de Dieu*, book 15, chapter 23 (Paris: Ed. Poche, 2004; original version 413 CE).

2. Sider, *Ovnis: Les envahisseurs démasqués*, 99; and H. Institutoris and J. Sprenger, *Le marteau des sorcières* (Paris: Ed. Plon, 1973; original version 1486), 167.

3. Sider, *Ovnis: Les envahisseurs démasqués*, 100; and J. Görres, *La mystique divine, naturelle et diabolique* (Grenoble, France: J. Million, 1992; original version 1836), 255.

4. Sider, *Ovnis: Les envahisseurs démasqués*, 100.

5. Jacques Vallée, *Autres dimensions, chroniques des contacts avec un autre monde* (Paris: Ed. Robert Laffont, 1989), 319.

6. Sider, *Ovnis: Les envahisseurs démasqués*, 103; and Jules Baissac, *Les grands jours de la sorcellerie* (Marseille, France: Laffitte-Reprints, 1982; original version 1890), 15.

7. Institutoris and Sprenger, *Le marteau des sorcières*, 167.

8. Ulrich Molitor, *Des sorcières et des devineresses* (Paris: Tiquetone, 1981; original version 1489).

9. Sider, *Ovnis: Les envahisseurs démasqués*, 107; and R. H. Robbins, *The Encyclopedia of Witchcraft & Demonology* (New York: Bonanza Books, 1981), 127.

10. Sider, *Ovnis: Les envahisseurs démasqués*, 108; and Robbins, *The Encyclopedia of Witchcraft & Demonology*, 464.

11. Jules Delassus, *Les Incubes et les Succubes* (Paris: Ed. de la Corne d'abondance, 2010; original version 1897).

12. Ibid.

13. Sider, *Ovnis: Les envahisseurs démasqués*, 110.

14. Ludovico Maria Sinistrari, *De Daemonialitate et Incubis et Succubis* (De la démonialité et des animaux incubes et succubes), trans. Isidore Liseux (Paris: Ed. Le Terrain vague, 1956; original version 1680).

15. Vallée, *Passport to Magonia*, 164–76.

16. Francesco Maria Guazzo, *Compendium maleficarum* (English translation) (London: Dover, 1988).

17. Agobard de Lyon, *De la grêle et du tonnerre* (Paris: Hachette, 2017; original version 1841).

18. Vallée, *Passport to Magonia*, 25.

19. Vallée, *Autres dimensions, chroniques des contacts avec un autre monde*, 319.

20. Nicolas P. de Montfaucon de Villars, *Comte de Gabalis, ou Entretiens sur les sciences secrètes* (Kila, MT: Kessinger, 2010; original version 1715).

21. Walter Yeeling Evans-Wentz, *The Fairy Faith in Celtic Countries* (Glastonbury, UK: Lost Library, 2010; original version 1911).

22. Vallée, *Passport to Magonia*; and Vallée, *Autres dimensions, chroniques des contacts avec un autre monde*, 319.

23. Evans-Wentz, *The Fairy Faith in Celtic Countries*.

24. Vallée, *Passport to Magonia*, 161.

25. Ibid., 161.

26. Gordon Creighton, "A Brief Account of the True Nature of the UFO Entities," *Flying Saucer Review* 29, no. 5 (1983).

27. Ibid.

28. Ibid.

29. Geoffrey Hodson, *Fairies at Work and Play* (Paris: Ed. Adyar, 1966).

30. Clarke, *Encounters with Star People*.

31. Ibid.

32. Ibid.

33. Henry Steel Olcott, *A la découverte de l'occulte: Histoire des débuts de la Société théosophique* (Paris: Ed. Adyar, 1976).
34. Ibid.
35. Clarke, *Encounters with Star People*.

Chapter 4

1. Clarke, *Encounters with Star People*.
2. Ibid.
3. Ibid.
4. Ibid.
5. Ibid.
6. Ibid.
7. Ibid.
8. Ibid.
9. Lucy Pringle, *The Greatest Mystery of Modern Times* (London: Thorsons, 1999).

Chapter 5

1. Daniel Harran, *La révélation de Chilbolton* (Paris: Ed. EccE, 2011).
2. Brosses, *Enquête sur les enlèvements extraterrestres*.
3. Clarke, *Encounters with Star People*.
4. Ibid.
5. Ibid.

Chapter 6

1. Evans-Wentz, *The Fairy Faith in Celtic Countries*.
2. Ibid.; and Vallée, *Passport to Magonia*, 86.
3. Harran, *Ovnis, Crop Circles & MIDIM: Phénomènes mystérieux élucidés!*
4. Creighton, "A Brief Account of the True Nature of the UFO Entities."
5. Harran, *Ovnis, Crop Circles & MIDIM: Phénomènes mystérieux élucidés!*.
6. Patrick J. Petri, *Connaissance initiatique 3—Etres élémentaires & entités angéliques* (Barr, France: Spiritual Book France, 2008).

7. Claude Lecouteux, *Les nains et les elfes au Moyen-Age* (Paris: Ed. Imago, 2013).
8. Malidoma Patrice Somé, *The Healing Wisdom of Africa* (New York: J. P. Tarcher, 1999).
9. Maen, *Rencontre avec des êtres d'un autre monde, au cœur de l'Afrique* (Paris: Ed. Les impliqués, 2014).
10. Somé, *The Healing Wisdom of Africa*.
11. Ibid.
12. Ibid.
13. Maen, *Rencontre avec des êtres d'un autre monde, au cœur de l'Afrique*.
14. Edouard Brasey, *Enquête sur l'existence des fées et des esprits de la nature* (Paris: Ed. J'ai lu, 1999).
15. Ibid.
16. Daniel Harran, *Crop Circles: Les clés du mystère* (Paris: Ed. EccE, 2013).
17. Ursula Burkhard, *Karlik: Encounters with Elemental Beings* (Edinburgh: Floris Books, 2017).
18. Alexandre Koyré, *Paracelse* (Paris: Ed. Allia, 1998).
19. Villars, *Comte de Gabalis, ou Entretiens sur les sciences secrètes*.
20. Robert Kirk, *The Secret Commonwealth of Elves, Fauns and Fairies* (New York: Cosimo Classics, 2005).
21. Marko Pogačnik, *À la rencontre des êtres élémentaires* (Donzy le National, France: Ed. Mouvement de culture biodynamique, 2006); Christine Beusch, *Nous existons! Dans l'intimité des êtres élémentaires* (Laboissière-en-Thelle, France: Ed. Triades, 2007); Sylvie Hetzel, *Nature: Au-delà du silence* (Illats, France: Ed. co-créatives, 2006); Christopher Vasey, *Gnomes, Elfes, Dieux de l'antiquité: Mythes ou réalité?* (Montreuil-sous-Bois, France: Ed. Monde du Graal, 2003); Jean-Paul Ronecker, *Encyclopédie illustrée des esprits de la nature* (Paris: Ed. Trajectoire,

2005); Jorge Livraga, *The Elemental Spirits of Nature* (Madrid: New Acropolis Cultural Association, 2000); and Pierre Lassalle, *Natura ou les secrets du livre de la nature* (Geneva, Switzerland: Ed. Terre de lumière, 2013).

22. Peter Caddy, Eileen Caddy, Dorothy Maclean, David Spangler, Roc Watson, and Alan Watson, *The Findhorn Garden* (Findhorn, Scotland: Findhorn Foundation, 2008).

23. Machaelle Small Wright, *Perelandra Garden Workbook: A Complete Guide to Gardening with Nature Intelligences* (Jeffersonton, VA: Perelandra, 1993).

24. Harran, *Ovnis, Crop Circles & MIDIM: Phénomènes mystérieux élucidés!*

25. Harran, *Les ovnis et le nucléaire—le choc d'une réalité ignorée* (Bonvin's preface).

26. Ibid.

27. Rudolf Steiner, *Etres élémentaires* (Geneva, Switzerland: Ed. Anthroposophiques Romandes, 2004), 17.

28. Mack, *Abduction: Human Encounters with Aliens.*

Conclusions

1. Harran, *Les ovnis et le nucléaire—le choc d'une réalité ignorée* (Bonvin's preface).

2. Jean de Raigalgue, *Réflexions sur le destin de la Terre et de l'univers: Le point de vue d'un extraterrestre* (Béning-lès-Saint-Avold, France: Ed. de la lumière, 2000).

ABOUT THE AUTHOR

DR. DANIEL HARRAN holds a PhD in science and was assistant professor and researcher in physics at the University of Pau, France. For the past sixteen years, he has studied mysterious phenomena, which science has yet to explain (crop circles, then UFOs) using a rational approach. He has developed an interpretation different from the classic extraterrestrial hypotheses. Sources of knowledge left behind by science have served as support for his arguments. He shares his findings through his publications (eight books so far) and via his website: https://listentotheearth.net. This site receives an average of 5,000 visits per month. Now retired from his university occupation, Dr. Harran is fully devoted to his research. He regularly gives lectures, and in addition to his website, he maintains an interactive blog on these subjects.